BEYOND THE RESERVATION

Beyond The Reservation

INDIANS, SETTLERS, AND THE LAW
IN WASHINGTON TERRITORY, 1853–1889

Brad Asher

UNIVERSITY OF OKLAHOMA PRESS : NORMAN

970.4
A825b

This book is published with the generous assistance of The McCasland Foundation, Duncan, Oklahoma.

Library of Congress Cataloging-in-Publication Data

Asher, Brad, 1963–
    Beyond the reservation : Indians, settlers, and the law in Washington Territory, 1853–1889 / Brad Asher.
        p.   cm.
    Includes bibliographical references and index.
    ISBN 0-8061-3107-1 (cloth: alk. paper)
    1. Indians of North America—Washington (State)—History—19th century.   2. Indians of North America—Washington (State)—Government relations.   3. Indians of North America—Legal status, laws, etc.—Washington (State).   4. Frontier and pioneer life—Washington (State)—History—19th century.   5. Washington (State)—History—19th century.   6. Washington (State)—Race relations.
    I. Title.
    E78.W3A84   1999
    979.7'00497—dc21   98-42128
                                                                        CIP

The paper in this book meets the guidelines for permanence and durability of the Committee on Production Guidelines for Book Longevity of the Council on Library Resources, Inc.∞

1   2   3   4   5   6   7   8   9   10

AFR-7835

For Dad

CONTENTS

ILLUSTRATIONS

ACKNOWLEDGMENTS

Every graduate student working on a dissertation envisions it as a book and therefore fantasizes about the acknowledgments page, mentally writing and rewriting it until it has just the right balance of good humor and scholarly gravity. Yet in the actual writing, I have found much of this practice wasted; straightforward gratitude has replaced most of my attempts at sophisticated irony.

The idea for this book first took form as a master's thesis for Kathleen Conzen's graduate seminar on the social history of the American West at the University of Chicago. In that form, it dealt with an entirely different group of Indians in an entirely different location: the eastern Sioux of Minnesota. Yet that project got me thinking about the social history of the relationship between American Indians and American law, and from there I proceeded through a mixture of design and accident until I ended up in the Pacific Northwest.

The progression from an idea in a master's thesis to a completed dissertation would not have occurred without the encouragement and guidance of Professor Conzen. Without her intellectual openness, her astonishing command of the historiography, her patience, and her extensive comments on various drafts, this project would not have been possible.

The other members of my dissertation committee also played vital roles in the completion of this project. William Novak's unfailing encouragement and enthusiasm frequently buoyed me up and kept me going.

Raymond Fogelson repeatedly challenged me to learn more about the native cultures of the region, which I did, aided by his good humor and immense personal library.

Others were kind enough to read drafts of chapters in various forms. David Smith and George Guilmet of the University of Puget Sound, Shari Rudavsky of the University of Pennsylvania, and the assorted members of the social history workshop at the University of Chicago all deserve my thanks.

John Drayton, Alice Stanton, and the rest of the staff at the University of Oklahoma Press, as well as copy editor Patricia Heineke, Jr., have given me consistently good advice and assistance in preparing the manuscript. Portions of chapter 7 previously appeared in slightly different form as articles in *Pacific Northwest Quarterly* and *Western Historical Quarterly*. I thank the editors of those publications for permission to reprint and for the help they gave in improving the content of those articles.

Throughout the research for this project, I depended on the patient assistance of various archivists and court clerks. Joyce Justice and the staff at the Seattle branch of the National Archives, Pat Hopkins at the Washington State Archives in Olympia, and Phil Stairs at the Washington State Archives regional branch in Burien all deserve my special thanks for their efforts.

I owe the biggest debt of all to my family. At a time when I was isolated from some critical newspaper sources, my brother Curt provided much-needed research assistance. My father, who did not generally have much patience with academic histories, patiently read the entire manuscript in an earlier form. He died suddenly before this book went to press, and it is dedicated to him. My wife, Sue Coventry, has been my strongest supporter and fiercest critic, sensing accurately when I needed her to play each role. And my daughter Lila gave me the biggest incentive of all to finish—so I could spend more time just being her father.

Despite all the errors, flaws, and omissions detected and corrected by the above-named people, they could not possibly have found them all. Any remaining ones are entirely my responsibility.

BEYOND THE RESERVATION

INTRODUCTION

In January 1874, Edwin Eells attended a meeting of the citizens of New Dungeness, Clallam County, Washington Territory. Eells served as the Indian agent on the Skokomish Reservation, located some eighty miles to the south along Puget Sound. As a representative of the Office of Indian Affairs, he had come to the meeting to investigate settlers' complaints about the Clallam Indians resident in the New Dungeness area. Although the Indians did not "molest the whites in any way," a lively debate ensued over "the pros and cons of their removal." During the discussion, Eells reported, "quite a strong party were in favor of their [the Indians'] remaining provided the civil authorities should extend their jurisdiction over them." This party argued that the Indians "were a great benefit in the way of help in harvesting and potatoe [*sic*] digging time. Their work being had at those times much cheaper than any other help could be had [*sic*]."

Despite the benefits of a cheap and available labor force, the pro-removal forces carried the day. They emphasized the expense of extending civil jurisdiction over the Indians and drew up a petition calling for the Clallams' removal to the Skokomish Reservation. Eells doubted the settlers' demands could be accommodated. The reservation did not have sufficient resources to support the Indians, so they "could not remain long without leaving to get work and would soon be scattered as far from the Reservation as they are now."[1]

This minor episode in the territorial history of Washington highlights two central but neglected themes in American Indian history.[2] First, contact between settlers and Indians continued long after the official establishment of reservations and the supposed abrogation of Indian title to the surrounding land. The Clallam Indians, for example, had signed a treaty with the federal government in 1855, yet twenty years later they were living on the same land they had occupied at the time of the treaty, supporting themselves through a combination of labor for settlers and more traditional subsistence activities. Like the Clallams, many Indian communities across the nation never resided on reservations, and those who did often found the boundaries between reservations and white society quite permeable.[3]

General history texts and traditional histories of the West, however, routinely consign the nation's Indian tribes to reservations during the last half of the nineteenth century, and they routinely describe these reservations as prisons from which escape was impossible without incurring severe chastisement. "The beaten natives," states the classic textbook on the American West, "were crowded onto reservations where they no longer blocked the westward march of settlers." A recent American history textbook states that "the whites took away the tribes' sustenance, decimated their ranks, and shoved the remnants into remote and barren corners of their former domain." The standard history of the nineteenth-century Indian wars declares that by 1881 "only the Apaches had not yet been made to face the truth that the reservation represented their only possible destiny."[4]

The "new" western history and the "new" Indian history challenge most of the conventions of the older scholarship but leave the reservation emphasis firmly, if more subtly, ensconced. Richard White's synthesis of the new scholarship in western history begins by describing the diverse and fragmented implementation of reservation policy, but it loses much of its complexity in the ensuing discussion of federal policy initiatives. Specialized ethnohistories of Indian communities, meanwhile, depict the diverse and culturally grounded responses of Native groups, which altered outcomes of federal Indian policy in unanticipated ways. Most of the action in these studies, however, takes place within reservation boundaries, implicitly highlighting the separation of Indians from settler society. These studies do occasionally acknowledge the permeability of reservation boundaries, but usually give it only passing mention.[5]

Of course, reservations remain the central fixture of contemporary Indian life in the United States, and there is no denying their importance in the general narrative of Indian history. But the openness of reservation boundaries has had immense importance for both whites and Indians. Certainly reservation boundaries helped mark racial boundaries, with Indians on one side and whites on the other. These boundaries gave physical expression to the ideology of white civilization against Indian savagery, an ideology central to the justification of Indian dispossession and white settlement throughout the West. Yet ongoing Indian-white contact blurred the lines between Indian society and white society and complicated issues of racial identity.[6]

Indians who lived off reservations, worked for white employers, or married into white families did not necessarily highlight their membership in an Indian "tribe."[7] Instead, they claimed the status of ordinary citizens or taxpayers or workers. These individuals were not trying to "pass"; only in rare instances did they try to assume a white identity. Nor should these assertions of identity be understood simply as assimilation or "civilization," to use the rhetoric of nineteenth-century Indian policy. Although Indians might employ that rhetoric, they usually did so in order to preserve or extend their freedom to "be" Indians, to engage in behavior that American authorities sought to penalize because the participants were Indians. These individuals challenged the meaning of the term *Indian* and the consequences of that racial designation.[8]

Obviously, the fluidity of reservation boundaries varied across the nation. Indians perceived as particularly troublesome or as obstacles to U.S. economic expansion found reservations quite confining and well-policed. Frederick Hoxie has described the Crow reservation of the 1880s, for example, in these terms: "They [the Crows] could not travel beyond the invisible boundaries of their reserve; they could not resist the power of federal troops; they could not escape the government-subsidized missionaries who now lived among them."[9] But such restriction was not uniform across all reservations or among all Indian communities in the nation. During the territorial period in Washington, for example, Indians routinely traveled beyond the boundaries of their reserves, rarely encountered federal military repression, and frequently ignored the government-subsidized missionaries sent among them. Moreover, recent research suggests that Washington Territory was not unique either in the prevalence of the interactions between Indians and whites or in the porousness of reservation boundaries.

Several scholars have begun to examine the diversity of the local outcomes of Indian policy and to outline the various patterns of inter-action between Indian communities, settlers, and government officials. At different times and places, Indians were the neighbors, customers, sex partners, employees, and occasionally employers of whites. Unless Native communities engaged in some kind of collective violence or blocked important avenues of economic development, they often did not attract enough official attention to warrant the trouble and expense of forcing them onto reservations and keeping them there.

In the light of this scholarship, Washington Territory appears to fit a larger Far West pattern of Indian-white relations. In the Far West, white settlement overwhelmed the national government's efforts to create reservations, leaving Indians in the middle of a flood of white settlers. Later federal efforts to isolate Indians on reservations generally proved too little, too late. In California, for example, the rapid population influx after 1849 swamped the weak federal effort to establish reservations. Albert Hurtado characterizes the federal reservation system in California as a "stopgap measure, ministering to only a fraction of the Indians." In other areas of the Far West, such as Oregon, Washington, and the Great Basin, the failure of the reservation system was equally visible, although the number of white settlers never equaled the magnitude that invaded California.

In California, where interactions between Indians and whites have been most extensively studied, Indians survived by finding niches in the margins of the white-dominated economy. According to Hurtado, who has studied northwestern and central California, Indians worked as household servants, mine laborers and, later, agricultural workers. George Phillips has documented a similar integration of Indians into the settler economy in southern California.[10]

Similar patterns of economic incorporation occurred in the Great Basin. Increased white settlement during the 1850s destroyed the fragile Native subsistence base in central and western Nevada. Many of the western Shoshones in the region began to work for local ranchers or farmers or in the mines of the Comstock Lode. Similarly, Northern Paiutes living in southern Oregon, northern Nevada, and eastern California quickly became integrated into the white mining economy of the region, establishing Indian camps on the edges of mining towns.[11]

The integration of Indians into the white economy was not, however, just a Far West phenomenon. In the East, Indian groups who resisted removal or were the remnants of groups who had been removed faced similar circumstances. Often the government never assigned reservations to these groups, and when it did, the boundaries rarely restricted contact between Indians and whites. James Merrell has studied the incorporation of the Catawbas into the white economy of South Carolina, tracing their strategies for resisting both removal and extermination during the eighteenth and early nineteenth centuries. In a similar fashion, the Ottawas of lower Michigan used their contacts with local traders to resist pressures for removal in the 1830s. In the 1850s they agreed to individual allotment of tribal lands, which thrust them into further contact with settler society but allowed them to remain on their traditional lands.[12]

Remnant bands left behind after removal of a larger tribal group also had to find methods of coexisting with white settlers. Joseph Herring has studied the small community of Indians in Kansas that remained in place after the removal of most of the Kansas tribes to Indian Territory. The Eastern Band of Cherokees, the remnant Seminoles in Florida, and even groups previously thought extinct, such as the Pequots in New England, all needed to find modes of survival in an economy and society now dominated by a hostile majority population.[13]

The list continues, and more research needs to be done on the unique ways in which individual Indian groups coped with such dramatic changes. Nonetheless, the experiences of these particular Native communities from both the Far West and the East have certain factors in common, including the absence of overt and continuing military resistance to the white invasion. All these Indian groups engaged in forms of resistance, but few engaged in sustained campaigns of collective violent struggle.

A second factor was the character of the local economy. Some of these Indian groups occupied less desirable land or land outside the main area of white agricultural settlement. In these areas, off-reservation Indians were able to remain in place while augmenting their traditional subsistence activities by trading with neighboring settler communities. The contact economy in eastern Washington, for example, followed this pattern.

In other cases, a more labor-intensive industry, such as logging or mining, marked the local economy. In these areas, Indians found niches as laborers. In Washington Territory, the nascent timber economy west of the Cascade Mountains, especially in the area around Puget Sound, allowed Indians to fill roles as wage laborers when white settlement disrupted their traditional subsistence patterns. East of the Cascades, this type of contact economy developed mainly in urban areas and in mining regions.[14]

Finally, the nature of the American state augmented these local economic and cultural factors. In 1880, there were 141 reservations scattered across twenty-one states and territories. To believe that all 141 were policed with the same degree of efficiency that Hoxie found on the Crow reservation is to overestimate the powers of the federal government in the nineteenth century. The resources of the national government tended to be concentrated in areas where local interests were influential enough to demand federal action or where acts of collective violence by Indians (often in response to white provocations) triggered military responses. Thus while government policy makers talked of sequestering all Indians on reservations, local reality often fell far short of the rhetoric.[15]

Historians of the American West have long grappled with the role of the national state in the process of white conquest and colonization. For Frederick Jackson Turner's self-reliant frontiersman, the state played virtually no role at all. In Turner's view, western settlement was local, individual, and beyond the reach of national institutions. Critics of this aspect of Turner's thesis have rightly noted the importance of federal land grants, federal contracts, and the U.S. Army in the conquest, development, and settling of the West. This "imperial school" of historiography made the national state the determining factor in the successful colonization of the West and a primary force in shaping the region's economic and political development.[16]

Scholars of the "imperial" cast of mind, however, often attribute a coherence and far-sightedness to federal policy that students of policy making and the legislative process at both the local and national levels have disputed. While not denying the importance of federal programs and, more important, federal money, these scholars note how locals reshaped federal policy and diverted federal largesse to their own ends. In place of the classic statist conception of an autonomous and administratively coherent national state, these studies substitute a vision of a central state manipulated and mobilized by local interests. As Howard Lamar notes in his study of Dakota territorial politics, "It was the settlers' use of government on the spot, and not necessarily a government policy, which was the key factor in settlement."[17]

The resulting fragmentation of the powers of the national state made it possible for numerous Indian communities to avoid or reduce the oppression of reservation confinement. Students of Indian history, of course, have never attributed omnipotence to the national government. Reservation agents never commanded as much authority as they assumed, and historians have documented the varied and creative responses of Indians to the oppression of reservation life. But the focus on "reservation history" tells only a partial history of Indian-white relations in the nineteenth century. A full history of Washington Territory's Native communities must integrate the on-reservation and off-reservation Indian populations into the history of the surrounding area by focusing on the interactions between the Indians, who "belonged" on reservations, and the settler community.[18]

The circumstances under which these interactions took place threatened Indians both physically and culturally, for the shortcomings of federal policy did not free Indians from the oppression and burdens of white settlement. Indeed, in some ways, federal failures moved Indians from the frying pan into the fire. As Sidney Harring recently pointed out, it was the state governments—not the national government—that first developed a coherent and intelligible body of law regarding the governance of Indians in the late nineteenth century, one that stridently denied Indian sovereignty and ignored treaty guarantees.[19]

Harring's observation leads directly to the second theme of this study. Policy makers intended reservations to isolate Indians from white populations, prevent unregulated interaction between Indians and whites, and thus solve the problems of such interaction. These problems included not only conflicts between settlers and Indians but also threats to orderly settlement as a result of conflicts between Indians. Once the shortcomings of the reservation policy are acknowledged, however, the question arises of how continuing contact between Indians and settlers was governed.

One possible alternative was simply not to regulate such interactions at all, allowing settlers and Indians to work out private solutions to disputes. Such a laissez-faire solution appealed to many settlers. Sub-jugated militarily and politically, Indians thus faced a situation ripe with potential for exploitation and abuse. Such potential was realized most tragically, perhaps, in California during the gold rush. Miners brutally exploited Indian labor, shot and killed Indians at will, and expropriated Indian property without any official sanction. Eventually the state govern-ment stepped in, albeit rather weakly, to try and regulate the behavior of the settlers and the recruitment of Indian labor.[20]

An alternative to the chaos and violence of the laissez-faire solution lay in the extension of the Indian agents' administrative powers. These officials had sweeping powers over Indians on the reservation; by extending their powers beyond reservation boundaries, they could exercise control over Indian behavior and supervise interactions between settlers and Indians. Eells's presence at the citizens' meeting in Clallam County suggests that some settlers conceived of his role in this way. Certainly, Indian agents, Eells among them, pushed for such broader powers and sometimes exer-cised them unilaterally, arguing that if Indians could elude their authority by simply leaving the reservation, then they would never follow the dictates of the Indian Office.[21]

One historical analogue to such sweeping powers is the Freedmen's Bureau, established after the Civil War to oversee relations between newly freed slaves and their former masters in the defeated South. Freedmen's Bureau officials vetted contracts, oversaw labor conditions, and investigated complaints of crime and abuse. The Bureau represented a dramatic extension of federal power into relations previously deemed either local or private. As a result, it did not survive long, and such rela-tions were soon returned to local control. It is doubtful that western interests would have tolerated such an administrative intrusion into local affairs.[22]

A third possible regulatory alternative fits better with the traditions of a national state of limited power. This was the option considered, but eventually rejected, by the citizens of Clallam County: the extension of American law over the Indians living in their midst. Indians committed crimes, suffered abuse, signed and broke contracts, demanded freedoms, and generally engaged in behaviors that law is supposed to regulate, punish, or encourage. Extending civil jurisdiction over the Indians would vest power in the local courts and the local legislature, the traditional forums for adjusting difficulties between competing ethnic groups in the United States.[23]

Even this solution presented problems. As the Clallam County citizens noted, it increased the burden on local taxpayers. This burden represented not simply a monetary concern, though that was certainly important. It also symbolized an acceptance of the Indians' place within the community, and it accorded them standing, however unequal, in courts of law. As of 1874, these misgivings prompted the Clallam County petitioners to favor removal rather than the extension of civil jurisdiction over the Indians in their neighborhood.

Indian communities also resisted the imposition of American law, especially in conflicts among their own members. Native leaders continually insisted on the primacy of their own law-ways and norms in intra-Indian disputes. Even in disputes with whites, they frequently demanded acknowledgment of their customs and sanctions, criticizing the weaknesses and biases of territorial legal practice.[24]

Despite these problems, law and the courts did emerge as the primary mechanism for regulating the continuing off-reservation interactions between settlers and Indians during the territorial period in Washington. This outcome resulted not from the injunctions of federal policy but from a series of local political and legal struggles. These struggles pitted settlers against Indians, authorities against citizens, federal officials against local officials, and ultimately some Indians against other Indians.

Several scholars have noted the courts' central role in governance in the nineteenth century. Political scientist Stephen Skowronek, for example, memorably describes the nineteenth-century American state as a "state of courts and parties." For an earlier generation of historians, this decentralization and fragmentation of state power meant that the socio-economic upheavals of the last few decades of the nineteenth century proceeded largely ungoverned until a regulatory and administrative bureaucracy began to grow at the national level toward the close of the century.[25]

Legal historians have recently begun to question this conventional notion. They have examined law as a "modality of rule," a method of governance different in form but not necessarily in function from a centralized administrative state. Through the vehicle of courts and judges, these scholars argue, the power of the state was fully implicated in the regulation of the society and the economy. The nineteenth century, far from being an era of laissez-faire—as a previous generation of scholars characterized it—was in fact an era of regulation through law.[26]

Despite the growing emphasis on local courts and legal actors in the historiography of nineteenth-century America, students of the West and of Indian history still tend to privilege the federal over the local, particularly in the area of Indian affairs. While not denying the importance of the federal role in the conquest of the West, this study emphasizes the limits of that role and the consequent importance of other institutions of governance, particularly the courts.

An analysis of local statutes and legal cases is, therefore, of more than just local interest. These records provide an important window on the neglected world of Indian-settler contact and they reveal the day-to-day workings of Indian-white interaction. But they do much more than that. They also show how these interactions were governed. After all, these records document specifically *legal* instances of social conflict, thus illustrating the role of the law in regulating those conflicts.

A study of legal materials moves the locus of regulatory power from the pronouncements of federal policy to the proceedings of local courts and legislatures, where federal power was only one of many factors. In conjunction with other records, legal materials show how both Indians— facing a dominant and hostile majority population—and whites—confronting a culturally different and militarily subjugated indigenous population—negotiated the terms of Indians' incorporation into the economy and society of Washington Territory.[27]

The core of this book thus consists of an analysis of criminal and civil cases involving Native American defendants and complainants in the territorial district courts. The district courts heard matters arising under both territorial law and federal law.[28] The primary business of the district courts was the adjudication of civil suits. The courts heard a total of 25,093 civil cases during the territorial period, compared to 6,834 criminal cases. In matters regarding Indians, however, criminal cases predominated over civil matters. The district court records contain 182 criminal cases in which Indians were named as defendants and 16 civil cases in which Indians were either plaintiffs or defendants.[29]

The territorial Organic Act created three judicial districts in Washington, and the president appointed the territorial district court judges.

12   Introduction

Judges generally held two terms of court per year in at least three locations within each district. Several counties in their early years were attached judicially to a more established neighboring county, but counties continually lobbied for additional court sessions. By the time Washington acquired statehood in 1889 nearly every county seat hosted a term of district court.[30]

Once a year the district court judges convened to hear cases as the territorial supreme court in the territorial capitol of Olympia. The judges thus held appellate jurisdiction over their own lower court decisions. In 1886, Congress created a fourth judicial district and added a fourth justice to the Supreme Court. After 1886, judges were excluded from acting on appeals from their own court.[31]

Beneath the district courts in the judicial hierarchy sat the various justice courts and later municipal police courts. These courts had original jurisdiction over small civil claims and misdemeanor crimes. John Wunder's study of the territorial justice courts found that nearly 92 percent of the cases were civil complaints. Seattle justice court dockets for the years 1877 to 1887 showed sixty-four Indians named as defendants in criminal proceedings—mostly misdemeanor assault and disorderly conduct offenses—out of a total of 2,900 civil and criminal cases. Besides adjudicating misdemeanors, justice courts also held preliminary examinations of defendants in felony criminal proceedings. Felony proceedings generally began with a citizen's complaint to a local justice of the peace, who issued an arrest warrant to the sheriff or local constable. After preliminary examination, the justice of the peace could bind the defendant over for trial in district court if the evidence warranted it. Justices of the peace very often sat also as United States commissioners, with the power to take evidence and bind over defendants in federal cases. Numerous other officials—including some Indian agents—also sat as United States commissioners.[32]

There has been relatively little research on cases involving individual Indians brought before local courts, particularly in the nineteenth century. Scholars who have examined such cases in other areas have tended to produce individual case studies, emphasizing either the injustice of subjecting Indians to alien legal norms or the consequences of the case for local politics and policy. These "snapshots," however, do little to convey changes over time, either in the function of the law or in attitudes toward the law among settlers and Indians.[33]

Instead of local courts, the standard domain of Indian legal history has been Congress and the appellate courts, tracing the ebbs and flows of tribal sovereignty enunciated in legal doctrine. Formal legal mechanisms like treaties and federal policy, their legitimacy upheld by the courts, justified and enforced the dispossession of Indians, their sequestration on reservations, and bureaucratic intrusions into tribal life in the name of assimilation. These mechanisms "legally" eroded tribal authority over Indian land and people, restricting it to the limited sphere of reservations. One scholar has described the process as "genocide at law."[34]

A study of local court records provides critical detail to this sweeping picture of United States legal imperialism. White settlers and officials in Washington Territory did use law as an imperial tool to subjugate Indians in several instances, but law did not serve merely as an instrument of oppression. Struggles and divisions within the white community often prevented purely instrumental uses of the law. Authority in the territory was vested both in federal appointees—Indian agents, superintendents, governors, and district court judges—and locally elected representatives—territorial legislators and justices of the peace. The latter, more beholden to the will of the settlers, often conflicted with the former group of officials.

In particular, the officials of the Indian Department frequently clashed with settlers' interests. The Indian Department was charged with protecting Indian resources and using them in the way best suited to further the "civilization" of their charges. Appointees who took this charge seriously, and there were some, found themselves fighting infringements of Indian rights and the exploitation of Indian people by settlers. Men who served long tenures in the Indian Service often found themselves in the ambiguous position of defending Indians' rights from white encroachments even as they waged war on Indian culture. These conflicts, as will become clear, affected the law's impact on Indians in Washington.[35]

In addition, Indians themselves rapidly grasped the symbolic and substantive power of American law and mobilized it to resist white encroachments and pursue their individual interests. Such instances clearly complicate any simple and straightforward notion of law serving only as an instrument of white domination. More significantly, they bring to the fore questions about the role of the law in regulating interaction between Indians and whites and about attitudes toward the law among both groups.[36]

In a social context marked by extensive Indian-white contact, law played a crucial role in establishing and attempting to maintain racial boundaries. In determining who could speak in court, who was subject to the courts' jurisdiction, and who came under local and federal laws regarding Indians, the territorial courts continually drew and redrew the line between the presumed savagery of the Indian and the presumed civilization of the settlers.[37]

The courts did not enjoy absolute autonomy when making their determinations of these boundaries. The actions and attitudes of Natives, local settlers, and federal officials set limits on the courts' power. But the shape of the law was not simply the product of these various social inputs; law, in its turn, reshaped the actions and attitudes of these social actors. In other words, law neither absolutely dictated social behavior nor was absolutely conditioned by society.

Over the course of the territorial period, one can distinguish two distinct legal approaches to the governance of Indian-white relations. During the early territorial period, local statutes and court decisions emphasized the exclusion of Indians from the territorial social order. In a social environment marked by ongoing contact between Indians and settlers, this emphasis on exclusion facilitated the exploitation and abuse of Indians by whites. Indeed, the vernacular legal culture of the settlers supported such an emphasis on exclusion and resisted early efforts by officials to bolster legal intervention into "private" transactions between Indians and settlers.

Ongoing contact shifted the law's emphasis from exclusion to control during the later territorial period, as lawmakers and territorial residents acknowledged the necessity of regulating Indian-white interaction more closely. Indians gained standing in territorial courts, and legal authorities were increasingly cognizant of disputes between Indians and whites and even of disputes within Indian communities. This shift in legal emphasis acknowledged the porousness of racial boundaries but still sought to preserve and uphold critical legal distinctions between Indians and whites.

This change from exclusion to control resulted from and contributed to changes in the attitudes toward law among both the settlers and the Indians. It is clear, for example, that the revolution in legal attitudes that followed the Civil War was echoed in legal changes in Washington Territory, as jurists and lawmakers increasingly asserted the primacy of law in regulating interracial relations. Such changes coincided with noticeable alterations in Indian legal consciousness, as well. Having gained access to American law, Indians began mobilizing it for their own purposes. Ongoing contact facilitated this mobilization. Contact familiarized Indians with the workings of the law and fostered alliances with members of the white community who helped Indians pursue their claims. The use of American law in these cases evidenced an adaptive response by Indians to a period of rapid social change.

The mobilization of American law by Indians raises intriguing questions about sovereignty and the ideological power of law. Legal mobilization by Indians increased the "reach" of American law into Native life, and thus signaled an erosion of traditional authority structures. Individual Indians turned to American law to resolve disputes when traditional structures either proved ineffective or were unavailable.[38]

The rule of law, in other words, was becoming an increasingly hegemonic ideology. Recent legal histories have argued that the nineteenth-century American state's reliance on law and the courts had important consequences for the world view of contemporary Americans. It forced those who would challenge the status quo to rely on legal concepts and categories. In this fashion, law became hegemonic—an ideology that limited the range of possible alternative outcomes.[39]

The concept of hegemony, developed by the Italian Marxist Antonio Gramsci, refers to the power of a ruling class to persuade oppressed groups that the existing social order is fair and natural. To be ideologically stable, the hegemonic function of law depends upon the existence of a common legal culture among both the oppressors and the oppressed.[40] Both sides must accept that due process represents "fairness"; both sides must view courts as legitimate arenas for the resolution of disputes where substantive justice is delivered for reasonable claims of injury. Examining law in the colonial context of United States westward expansion helps determine the extent to which a common legal culture developed among Indians and Euro-American settlers following contact and colonization. The data from Washington suggest that while Indians came to view American legal institutions as possible avenues for redressing wrongs, the biases and weaknesses within the legal system limited the degree to which the law became hegemonic.[41]

This study, then, seeks to broaden the understanding of the relationship between Indians and American law. It begins by sketching the general outlines of Native culture and dispute resolution practices existing at the time of initial white settlement. Chapter 2 documents ongoing contact between Indians and whites and the failure of the reservation policy. Chapter 3 details the impact of Indian-settler interactions on territorial lawmaking. Chapters 4 through 6 analyze different types of court cases that reflect both Indian-white contact and the changes in Indian and white legal cultures as American law assumed greater importance in the management of such contact. Chapter 4 examines prosecutions under the federal law prohibiting the sale of liquor to Indians; chapter 5 focuses on the conflict between official and popular legal culture and the effect of that conflict on prosecutions of interracial crime; chapter 6 examines Indian responses both to interracial conflict and to the official efforts to police such conflict through the law. Finally, chapter 7 shows how ongoing Indian-white contact and the growing importance of legal remedies affected dispute resolution among the Indians themselves.

In discussing the Native cultures of the region this study commits at least two ethnohistorical sins that should be acknowledged at the outset. First, this is not the history of a particular people, but rather of several peoples' interaction with a particular U.S. institution—the law. Second, it thus glosses over significant cultural differences between Native groups in the belief that such differences do not invalidate the basic accuracy of the generalizations put forth.[42] Such generalizations are based to a great extent on a culture-area concept, although limited to the cultural continuum within the geographic area of Washington Territory. Native groups within a culture area share general characteristics as a result of their common environment and subsistence base, but typically differ in particular and significant ways from each other.[43]

Geographically, this study deals for the most part with the area contained within the current boundaries of the state of Washington. Congress created Washington Territory in 1853, carving it out of that part of Oregon Territory north of the Columbia river. Initially, the new territory's eastern border extended into present-day Montana. With the creation of Idaho Territory in 1863, Washington Territory assumed the boundaries of the present state of Washington.

Chronologically, the study begins with the creation of the territory and ends with Washington's admission to the union in 1889. These years roughly correspond to the years in which the reservation policy sprouted and flowered. By the time Washington gained statehood, federal Indian policy had entered a new era. The new policy of land allotment decreed the destruction of reservations and the full immersion of Indians into white society. This new departure sought to bring Indians fully under the sway of American law.[44] Although reformers never appreciated the irony, they took the failures of the previous policy—so evident in Washington, California, and other locations—and turned them into a blueprint for future Indian policy.[45]

By focusing on the limitations of the reservation policy and the neglected history of Indian-white contact, this work forces a more inclusive vision of the history of Indian-white relations in the American West and amplifies the concerns of Indian legal studies beyond questions of territorial sovereignty. It thus incorporates Indians into a broader stream of United States legal history by addressing the function of law in interracial relations and the development of legal consciousness among minority groups.

Chapter 1

AN ATTACK ON OLD MAN PULSIFER

NATIVE LANDS, NATIVE LAW

Citizens across Washington Territory complained frequently about the Indians living among them. They perceived Indian society as disorderly, immoral, and chaotic, and many of them resented having to share "their" space with such people, no matter how useful the Indians might be come harvest time. These perceptions lay at the root of the citizens' meeting in Clallam County in 1874; they wanted to know who was going to exercise authority over the Indians living in their midst. For Clallam County's white residents, that authority had to come from outside Indian society; they would have dismissed as absurd the suggestion that the Indians govern themselves. While the impacts of white settlement had disrupted Native societies, the Indians did retain mechanisms for maintaining social order. Notions of order and authority within Native communities differed so sharply from American preconceptions, however, that the settlers largely failed to recognize these mechanisms.

Consider, for example, what a settler might have made of the following tale. Sometime around the year 1850, at the mouth of the Skokomish River (about forty miles southwest of present-day Seattle), an unknown attacker nearly murdered a Twana Indian called Old Man Pulsifer while he was playing a disk game called *slahal*. Just as Pulsifer rolled the disks, the attacker, another Twana man, grabbed him by the hair and plunged a knife into him. Bystanders quickly summoned a shaman—a Native healer—who saved Pulsifer's life by sucking blood from him.

Although Pulsifer did not die, the attempt on his life led Pulsifer's brother to kill a kinswoman of the attacker in retaliation. By a strange coincidence (perhaps not so strange given the complex kinship ties among the Twanas), this woman was also related through marriage to the man who killed her and to Pulsifer himself—in fact she was his "step-mother." In a further turn of the screw, this retaliatory murder resulted in the killing of the avenging brother by his own father. To the settlers' eyes, such familial bloodletting would doubtless have appeared merely as irrational savagery, but a close look at the repercussions that followed the attack on Pulsifer reveals the intricate workings of Native legal culture in Washington.[1]

One must be careful when generalizing about such things as a "Native legal culture," for Washington Territory was home to a remarkably diverse indigenous population. Tens of thousands of Indians, grouped in dozens of distinct communities, resided within the area Congress demarcated as Washington Territory in 1853 (see map 1).[2] Many aspects of culture varied significantly from community to community, and each community had its own law-ways and methods of resolving disputes.

Scholars have used various ways to contain and categorize this Native diversity. They have grouped most of the Native languages into three families. Coast Salish predominated among the Indians west of the Cascade Mountains, with the exception of the Makahs, whose language is Nootkan, and the Quileutes and the Chemakum, whose languages do not fit into any existing language family. East of the mountains, Interior Salish predominated in the northern half of the area, and Sahaptin predominated in the southern.[3]

It paid to be multilingual in such a rich linguistic environment, since even languages within the same family were not necessarily mutually intelligible. Many Washington Indians spoke two or three different Native tongues, as well as the Chinook Jargon, the crude trade language that spread through most of the region following the arrival of European traders in the late eighteenth century.[4]

Like language families, culture areas provide another convenient device for imposing order on the diversity of Native Washington. The land included within the territorial boundaries encompassed parts of two different Native culture areas, the Northwest Coast, which extends along the Pacific Coast from southeastern Alaska to southern Oregon, and the

An Attack on Old Man Pulsifer

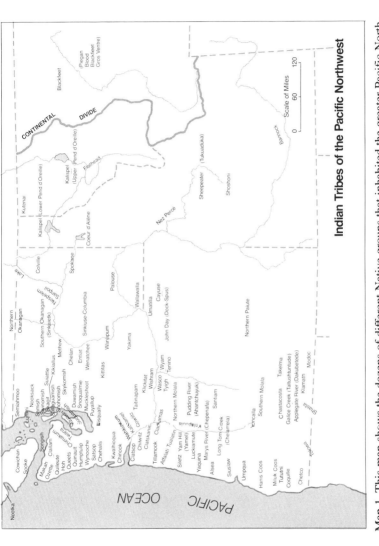

Map 1. This map shows the dozens of different Native groups that inhabited the greater Pacific Northwest prior to the arrival of white settlers. (Ruby and Brown, *Indians of the Pacific Northwest*, 39.)

Plateau, which includes the Columbia and Fraser River drainages east of the Coast Range in Canada and the Cascade Range in the United States. The Cascade Mountains, stretching north to south the entire length of Washington, provide a stark physical border to this cultural division.

No one crosses the Cascades without noticing the dramatic contrasts between the eastern and western slopes. The western side is wet and temperate, marked by the lush growth of large coniferous forests. This is the side of the Pacific Ocean, the side of Seattle, the side of nearly constant winter rains. The eastern side is arid, marked by extremes of temperature, and is dominated by the treeless expanse known as the Columbia Plateau. This is the side of agriculture, the side of Spokane, the side of enormous sky. The Columbia River brings vital force to this region, slicing through the Plateau before turning west at its junction with the Snake River.

Given the environmental differences, it is not surprising that Indian communities dwelling on opposite sides of the mountains diverged culturally. The coastal climate meant that Native communities on the western side of the mountains enjoyed more abundant food resources than those on the Plateau. Western Washington consequently supported higher population densities, and this both permitted and encouraged the development of a more elaborate cultural complex.

This cultural complex shared many of the traditional hallmarks of the larger Northwest Coast culture area. Most of the peoples of western Washington practiced hereditary slavery, taking captives in raids on enemy peoples and consigning them to slave status for life. Within the population of free people, western Washington Indians paid great attention to social status and rank based on wealth and descent. Although anthropologists continue to debate the nature of the class structure, it basically consisted of a relatively small lower class of free persons—so-called "worthless people"—a larger group of upper-class people, and a smaller, changing group of headmen who came out of the upper class. The peoples of western Washington also shared the quintessential Northwest Coast institution, the potlatch. Headmen and other upper-class individuals validated their high status and consolidated their leadership positions through intercommunity give-aways of property.[5]

The emphasis on social rank, the institution of slavery, and the display of wealth inherent in the potlatch all set the western Washington peoples off from the communities on the Plateau. Anthropologist Verne Ray associated the Plateau with an image of egalitarianism and pacifism. Ray contrasted the equality he found among the Plateau groups with the social hierarchy that marked the groups to the west. Similarly, he compared the Plateau groups' cultural emphases on peaceful coexistence with the strong warrior tradition found among their neighbors on the Plains further east.[6]

Like most convenient organizing devices, culture areas risk becoming too rigid, suggesting cultural homogeneity within their borders and overemphasizing cultural differences between areas. In fact, the Cascades did not represent an impassable barrier. Indians on each side of the mountains regularly engaged in trade and visits with Indians on the other side, resulting in the transmission and spread of reciprocal cultural influences. Indians from all over the Pacific Northwest met and traded, for example, at the Dalles, on the Columbia River.[7]

In addition, significant distinctions existed among peoples within each culture area. Among some western Washington groups, village location gave rise to cultural distinctions between "salt-water" Indians, on the one hand, and "stick," "prairie," "inland," or "horse" Indians on the other hand. The former dwelled on the shores of Puget Sound; the latter dwelled upriver. Upriver and downriver peoples frequently viewed each other with suspicion and distrust. Indeed, some upriver peoples had closer ties to Plateau groups than to their neighbors on the western side of the mountains.[8]

To return to the question at hand, in the face of such cultural and linguistic diversity, how can one possibly speak of a "Native legal culture"? Anthropological descriptions make it clear that communities on both sides of the mountains had their own customs and traditions for resolving disputes among their members. These customs and traditions, however, drew upon similar premises regarding insult or injury to another and its consequences. So while the practices and processes of Native law differed from community to community, at an appropriate level of abstraction one can speak of a shared set of legal-cultural concepts.

These legal concepts reflected broader cultural emphases on kinship, autonomy, and supernatural agency. Of these three, kinship is perhaps the most important in understanding the aftermath of the attack on Old Man Pulsifer. In Native legal practice, the kin group of the injured party bore the responsibility for the investigation of an offense and the imposition of sanctions. The sanctions, moreover, might fall not on the attacker but on a relative of the attacker. A kin group thus shared responsibility for the actions of any one of its members.[9]

Old Man Pulsifer came from a respected family in the Twana village of Quilcene; his father Sbithla was a village headman. When news of the attack on Pulsifer reached Quilcene, another of Sbithla's sons, named Yixwuct, decided to avenge the assault. His vengeance fell, however, not upon the man who had attacked Pulsifer, but upon one of Sbithla's wives, who happened to be related to the man who had stabbed Pulsifer. Yixwuct killed her in retribution for the act of her kinsman.[10]

Although kin-group responsibility structured dispute resolution in Native communities on both sides of the mountains, it did not work simply or automatically. Most Native societies within Washington reckoned kinship bilaterally, so a number of persons within a kin group might be recognized as having legitimate rights to retaliate against an aggressor. In addition, as Pulsifer's case shows, kinship could prove to be a tangled web. In order to avenge the attack on Pulsifer, Yixwuct killed one of his own father's wives—his own "stepmother," to use modern American kinship terminology.[11]

Such tangled webs of kinship, of course, also tied Native communities together. Family connections determined village structure on both the Coast and the Plateau. Several related nuclear families dwelled within each of the large cedar-plank houses that made up the permanent winter villages of the peoples of western Washington. Villages on the Plateau also consisted of several nuclear families, but these families did not necessarily share a common ancestor.[12]

Kinship ties also united people in different villages. Among the western groups, upper-class people married outside their home village, linking the extended families of husband and wife into a lengthening chain of kinship. In the summer, when the winter villages broke up and each family went its separate way to hunt and gather foods, they often joined relatives from other villages on food-gathering expeditions. Similarly, Plateau people tended to marry outside their bilateral kin group and, as on the Coast, kinship ties linked people residing in different villages. People on the Plateau moved frequently from village to village, relying on family ties to claim a place in a new village. "Between one's own blood kin and one's in-laws an individual could expect a welcome in villages throughout the Plateau," notes one ethnographer.[13]

These intervillage kinship links helped redistribute food resources and alleviate local food shortages through reciprocal exchanges within kin groups. Native groups in both culture areas preached an ethic of generosity and sharing with one's kin. Among the Sahaptin speakers of the mid-Columbia River, for example, a young boy takes none of the meat from his first successful deer hunt for himself; rather, it is distributed among an extensive set of family relations and fellow villagers.[14]

A wide-ranging net of kinship links and the sense of mutual obligation that they entailed worked to maintain social peace among Washington's Indians. The pressures of family and public opinion generally sufficed to prevent violence within and among Native communities, at least before the coming of whites, and recourse to retaliation was fairly uncommon. Skagit Indian informants, for example, described a "relatively peaceful" life marked by little conflict during precontact times. "Adults who received insults without retaliating were given the highest praise. Those who easily took umbrage and entered quickly into quarrels brought on disapproval from their own family."[15]

When quarrels did occur, they did not necessarily escalate to violence. The payment of compensation by the aggressor's kin group usually smoothed over the sore feelings of the victim or the victim's family. The amount of compensation varied and was the subject of negotiation between the two kin groups. On the Plateau, according to Ray's study of the Sanpoils and Nespelems, the amount generally varied with the attacker's degree of guilt. Among most of the western groups, by contrast, it varied with the victim's social status. Only when it became evident that no compensation was forthcoming did the victim's kin gain a generally understood right to retaliate against the attacker and/or the attacker's family.[16]

Given the traditions of village exogamy among both Coast and Plateau peoples, the basic legal principles of kin-group responsibility and compensation-in-atonement structured relations not just within a village or among a single people but between different villages and different peoples. In 1869, for example, a mixed Snohomish/Snoqualmie group from the Tulalip Reservation journeyed to the Nisqually Reservation to negotiate the settlement of a number of murders. Plateau mechanisms of social control also extended to intervillage conflict. Compensation could smooth over intervillage disputes that might otherwise have led to war.[17]

Negotiations did not always work. At the level of the actual practice of dispute settlement, there were notable differences between groups. These differences meant that negotiations over a settlement could take a very long time when members of different groups were involved, and that the process often went awry, leaving troubles unresolved and tempers uncooled.

The initiation of the settlement process differed among different peoples. Among some western groups, like the Twanas and Clallams, the kin of the victim demanded compensation from the family of the attacker. Among other groups, such as the Puyallups and Nisquallys, the victim's kin waited for an overture from the attacker's kin before demanding payment.[18]

The cultural meaning attached to the payment of compensation also differed among the various Native groups. Little social stigma attached to the payment of compensation among the Twanas, Puyallups, Nisquallys, or Skagits. Indeed, in the case of an accidental killing among the Twanas, the offending party sometimes paid compensation even when the victim's family made no demands, just to avoid any hard feelings. On the other hand, among the Clallams and some other central Coast Salish peoples, "refusal to pay [compensation] is regarded as the most dignified procedure, regardless of any question of right or wrong."[19]

The meaning of a refusal to pay compensation constituted a third area of variation. George Gibbs, who was probably most familiar with the Puyallups, wrote that if a killer or his kin refused to pay atonement, then the victim's kin could kill the perpetrator with no repercussions. Refusal to pay among the Twanas and the Clallams, on the contrary, indicated a denial of guilt. If the victim's kin took revenge, the perpetrator's kin group viewed it as an unprovoked attack, leading it to either demand compensation or retaliate in turn against the rival kin group. Thus an unresolved dispute could result in a prolonged bout of retaliatory feuding.[20]

Adultery and shamanism provided the two principal exceptions to the general rule of kinship responsibility. Most ethnographers write that a man cuckolded by another could kill the adulterer without fear of repercussion from the adulterer's kin group. Among some Native peoples,

An Attack on Old Man Pulsifer

cuckolded men might kill their wives, as well, without fear of retaliation from the wife's family. Among the Clallams, for example, the family of an adulterer killed by a cuckolded husband recognized that "the murderer acted in consonance with public opinion." A similar tolerance existed among the Sanpoils and Nespelems on the Plateau.[21] Similarly, the killing of a shaman who used magic to cause harm did not generally result in retaliation or a demand for compensation from the shaman's family.[22]

The groups west of the Cascades made a third exception to the general rule of kinship responsibility for the killing of slaves by their masters. "The Indians . . . seem to consider the murder of a slave as a matter of course and that a Tyee [chief] has a right to put to death his own slave, just as the fancy takes him," observed one Indian agent in 1857 after a local headman killed a slave. Killing someone else's slave, however, could create a grievance between the killer and the slave's master, who would regard the destruction of property as an affront.[23]

The cultural ideal among most groups was to treat slaves well, but as slaves had no kinship links with their masters or with others in the village, the killing of a slave triggered few sanctions. Families did not kill their slaves as part of ceremonies, as often occurred among other Northwest Coast peoples, but Myron Eells, missionary at the Skokomish Reservation, wrote that when a master died, the family killed some of his slaves.[24]

Despite protracted negotiations and occasional outbreaks of feuding, goods flowed fairly regularly between kin groups to assuage perceived strains in relationships and thus preempt efforts at retaliation. Although not as important for subsistence as reciprocal exchanges within kin groups, these transactions formed a significant part of the overall networks of exchange among the Natives of Washington Territory and contributed to the maintenance of cordial social and political relations.[25]

Among Old Man Pulsifer's people, the Twanas, the negotiation and payment of compensation provided a reasonable and honorable solution to kin-group quarrels. The Twanas paid close attention to possible slights given to and received by people. As a result, the Twana community widely condemned Yixwuct's rash killing of Sbithla's wife, especially because it took place before any effort to negotiate a settlement for the attack on Pulsifer. "People said that was no way for him to have done," said Henry Allen, the Twana informant who recounted the incident.[26]

Yet within Twana society, almost no sources of authority or power existed that could have restrained Yixwuct. The kinship-mediated dispute settlement procedures outlined above did not function as a set of rules; they were not referred to and applied like a legal code. They are better understood as expressions of cultural norms, of the way people should act to resolve disputes. Actual behavior could differ, and frequently did.

Among the Twanas, for example, a man whose wife committed adultery had the theoretical privilege under Native law of killing his wife and her lover without incurring reprisals. But in actual practice, cuckolds rarely killed either the adulterer or the wife for fear of angering their relatives. In a similar vein, while adulterous men among the Puyallups and Nisquallys were often killed, their families frequently harbored secret longings for revenge, rather than simply accepting the killings as legitimate reprisals. Such dark thoughts often culminated in a covert killing of the cuckold.[27]

Within the broad parameters established by social convention and the relative power of other families, in other words, Native law enforcers acted autonomously. In this aspect, Native law reflected a cultural emphasis on personal and familial autonomy found among Native groups on both sides of the mountains. Among the western Washington Indians, village headmen had little coercive power over their fellow villagers and depended on their upper-class status, generosity, and overall reputation to persuade their followers. Likewise, the villages themselves enjoyed political autonomy; no overarching structure united the villages into anything approaching a "tribe," although stronger leaders with wider followings did emerge after contact with whites.[28]

Plateau culture also prized autonomy. Individual families enjoyed political and economic autonomy within politically autonomous villages. Village headmen held authority only if they maintained the respect of their fellow villagers and demonstrated the qualities of generosity and wisdom expected of leaders. As on the Coast, a widely respected leader might attract a following among several different villages, and large intervillage confederacies developed following white contact.[29]

One important limit pertained to the Plateau with regard to the autonomy of the family in law enforcement matters. Among some peoples on the Plateau, there existed what anthropologists have labeled the "Plateau

An Attack on Old Man Pulsifer

whipping complex." In some villages, an official "lasher" administered corporal punishment to wrongdoers after judgment by a village headman. The whipping complex augmented the kinship-mediated system of sanctions with a system of public judgment and punishment. It thus reduced the risk of feuding between rival kin groups, since a headman could settle the dispute if the families themselves could not agree.[30]

According to Ray's work on the Sanpoils and Nespelems, when a crime occurred, the village chief held an open hearing, in which all who knew anything about the offense could speak. The accused then made a statement, and those who wished to plead for the accused made their case. The headman then determined the punishment, which could consist of either compensation paid to the injured party or whipping. The offenses for which whipping might be meted out included murder, stealing, perjury as a witness, improper sexual relations, and abortion.[31]

The headman's powers of investigation also extended to retaliatory killings in cases of adultery or shamanism. If all agreed that the person killed had been guilty of the offense charged, that ended the matter. If the headman determined that the killer had acted inappropriately, then he might order the payment of compensation to the family of the dead person.[32]

Although ethnographers disagree on its history, the whipping complex, or something akin to it, has been reported for various Plateau groups. In the most recent Plateau ethnography, Eugene Hunn states that "many villages had a 'whipper' who administered discipline." Hunn focuses particularly on the Sahaptin-speaking groups of the mid-Columbia River, but Thomas Garth also found whipping among the Sahaptin-speaking Cayuses, Nez Perces, and Wallawallas. Other scholars have described a similar system among the Interior Salish speaking Southern Okanagans and the Spokanes.[33]

Ray treated the whipping complex as an indigenous phenomenon, yet made no effort to explain the apparent divergence between the ability of a village headman to determine corporal punishment and the Plateau cultural emphases on pacifism and individual equality. Hunn explained the institution of the lasher as a diffusion of the headman's power through an intermediary, thus deflecting "the resentment that is engendered by the exercise of authority." Other anthropologists have suggested that the whipping complex emerged out of Catholic missionary efforts, from

Plateau exposure to corporal discipline in the Southwest, or from experiences at the Hudson's Bay settlement at Red River.[34]

The whipping complex appears to be related to the dramatic set of cultural changes and adaptations that occurred on the Plateau following the advent of the horse and the onslaught of epidemic diseases. A number of ethnographers have noted the increasing influence of Plains culture on Plateau groups as the Plateau Indians became more mobile and began to cross the Rockies to hunt buffalo. These social changes led to the development of a stronger political structure within villages and more inter-village contact. In addition, social change and the trauma of epidemics touched off a burst of religious ferment, which persisted well into the territorial period in Washington. This religious fervor found its expression most notably in the Prophet Dance. Although there is, again, sharp disagreement on the origins of the Plateau Prophet Dance, the confession and punishment of wrongs formed an important part of the ritual.[35]

Like these other cultural influences, the whipping complex spread unevenly among the various groups on the Plateau. Mourning Dove, a Colvile writer and activist, relates that in her village the Colville chief Kinkanawah introduced the practice of whipping, but not until the 1890s, and that the practice died out with him. She also wrote that her grandmother moved away from her village at Kettle Falls in the early nineteenth century because she objected to the whipping of criminals.[36] Despite its uneven spread, by the beginning of the territorial period numerous Plateau groups had a tradition of social control of wrongdoing administered through a recognized authority. This tradition existed in tandem with a tradition of dispute settlement carried out by autonomous kin groups.[37]

No whipping complex existed among the Twanas, and so the cycle of violence that began with the attack on Old Man Pulsifer and continued through Yixwuct's assassination of Sbithla's wife took a further turn a few months later. During a potlatch hosted by the Squaxin Indians, a neighboring Coast Salish group, the Twana guests challenged the Duwamish, who were also guests, to a war game. In this game, a type of tug-of-war in reverse, the two sides pushed on opposite ends of a long pole. Whichever side was pushed back the farthest lost.

In issuing their challenge, the Twana guests, who included Sbithla and Yixwuct, began a war dance. They leapt into the air, each man

An Attack on Old Man Pulsifer

brandishing two knives made of cedar. For some reason, however, Sbithla carried a real knife. At the climax of the song, the men all stabbed downward in unison. Sbithla jumped high and brought his knife down directly into Yixwuct's neck, severing a major vein. Although the Native doctors present worked on Yixwuct, he died soon thereafter.

As Yixwuct lay dying, a Twana woman from the village of Skokomish approached him. "So a knife *can* be sharp," she told him. The woman was related to Sbithla's wife, whom Yixwuct had killed, and she had used hate magic against Yixwuct because he had murdered her kinswoman. Such magic, carried by a messenger spirit and invoked through ritual songs, attacked a person's or family's "foundations," namely, "your life, luck, prosperity, or your power," according to Elmendorf's informant. She, and not Sbithla, had caused Yixwuct's death. More accurately, it had been the force of hate magic, which she had unleashed. Under Native legal theory, supernatural forces could play a primary role in causing harm to an individual.[38]

With this concept, too, Native law echoed broader cultural notions about personal agency. The Natives on both sides of the mountains shared a general set of beliefs in guardian spirits. People obtained special skills, or "power," from these spirit helpers. Young people obtained power primarily through vision quests, but among the western groups individuals could also inherit power. An individual's guardian spirit accounted for a person's prowess in particular endeavors. Personal achievement was not generally recognized as the result of individual effort, but rather as a reflection of the power of one's guardian spirit.[39]

Shamans obtained a particular type of power during their vision quests, power that allowed them to both help and harm people. While Yixwuct was felled by magic deployed by a layperson, shamans were the most frequent purveyors of malignant magic. Shamans therefore occupied ambiguous social positions as both curers and potential sources of harm. Although the mechanisms of shaman-induced sickness varied within each Native group, an ill-intentioned shaman could use his power to bring sickness, misfortune, and death to a person, a family, or an entire village. Often people with scores to settle contracted with a shaman to wage a covert supernatural attack on an enemy.[40]

Shaman-induced sickness could be cured by another shaman, who used his power (shamans were usually men) to counter the magic or extract the spirit causing the sickness. Among many Native groups, the shaman that effected a cure could also identify the shaman who caused the illness. Among other groups, the spirit of the offending shaman revealed itself upon the death of its victim to flaunt its power. ("Every deathbed scene," comments one ethnographer, "might be turned into an orgy of accusal.") Shamans so identified were liable to be killed by the kin group of the victim.[41]

The identification and liabilities of maleficent shamans, however, differed among the various Native groups. Among the Twanas and the Clallams, for example, a shaman called in to cure a sick person might be killed if the relatives of the victim did not think he had exerted sufficient effort to cure the afflicted person, again with no recourse by the shaman's family. Among the Puyallups and Nisquallys, a shaman might be killed as a remedy for shaman-induced sickness. If the patient recovered following the killing, then the shaman's family took no reprisals. If the patient died in spite of the killing, then the family of the dead shaman might legitimately seek compensation or revenge.[42]

The hate magic that killed Yixwuct ended the saga that began with the attack on Pulsifer. The Twana community widely viewed Yixwuct as a bad man and did not mourn his passing. According to Henry Allen's version of the tale, neither Sbithla nor Pulsifer undertook to avenge his death, either directly or with magic.[43]

The story of Old Man Pulsifer and his family forms part of a specifically Twana history, but in its depiction of a violent assault and its consequences it also reveals the central concepts of the region's Native legal traditions. These traditions differed sharply from the procedures and assumptions of American law. While Native law allowed that supernatural forces could cause harm, American law confined itself largely to the visible world. While Native law placed much of the enforcement burden upon kin groups and thus made enforcement, in American parlance, a "private" matter, American law represented the exercise of "public" authority.[44] While Native law envisioned sanctions that might fall upon a relative of the offender, American law sought to identify and punish a unique guilty party. And finally, while Native law gave a great deal of autonomy to enforcers and offenders, American law followed a specific set of established guidelines and rules of procedure.

These differences help explain why many of the settlers who came to Washington Territory did not see a diverse group of Native societies with their own traditions for preserving peace and order. In the eyes of the settlers, the Indians' tendency to rely on "private" acts of enforcement, their "superstitious" belief in harm caused by nonhuman agency, and the lack of formal rules regarding judgment and punishment all marked Native societies as lawless. There is "no punishment for crimes or misdemeanors by the chiefs," commented E. A. Starling, the first Indian agent for Puget Sound. "If an Indian kill another of the same tribe, there is no punishment awarded him by the tribe; but the relatives or friends of the deceased are bound, in honor, to retaliate."[45] Although American officials might speak of such a system as Native "law," most believed law was the very opposite of this. Law sought not revenge, but justice.[46]

American policy sought to restrict the sphere of such Native "lawlessness" and eventually eliminate it by confining Indians to reservations, while imposing American law within the rest of Washington Territory. Indians' refusal either to move to reservations or to reside there permanently, however, meant that Native law continually spilled over reservation boundaries. Native law-ways met and contested with American law over and over again in disputes between settlers and Indians and even in disputes between Indians. It is in the context of these repeated contests that the development of the territorial legal system and the place of Indians within it must be understood.

Chapter 2

IN RE JOHN HEO

INDIAN-WHITE CONTACT AND THE FAILURE OF
THE RESERVATION POLICY

The tragic events that beset Old Man Pulsifer's family took place in a geography still largely Indian-defined. Although in 1850 the land was technically part of Oregon Territory and economically under the sway of the Hudson's Bay Company, the drawing of boundaries and the control of resources still remained mostly in Indian hands. Just a few years later, American officials began to impose a new geography on the land, drawing new boundaries, reallocating resources, and seeking to confine Indians to a few small reservations. In 1880, some twenty-five years after this effort began, an Indian man called John Heo questioned the power and meaning of this new geography in a court of law. Heo was neither the first nor the last to do so, but his effort left behind a paper trail for the modern historian to follow, a trail that leads from Heo's individual story to broader conclusions about the nature of Indian-white relations in Washington Territory.

Despite the Americans' efforts, the reservation policy largely failed. The social reality of Indian-white relations in the territory never matched the situation depicted on the American-imposed map. Many Indians simply never moved to the reservations created for them. For example, Heo lived much of his adult life off the reservation, and this social context shaped his life and fueled his challenge to the reservation regime and the agent's power.

The son of a Chehalis father and a Squaxin mother, Heo did spend some portion of his childhood on the Chehalis Reservation, located in southwestern Washington along the Chehalis River. But Heo was not born into the American-defined geography of Indian reservations and private property. The Chehalis Reservation did not formally exist until 1864, so Heo witnessed firsthand the American effort to impose a new set of boundaries on the land.

Like many of their Native neighbors in the southwestern portion of the territory, the Chehalis people never negotiated a treaty with the federal government. The southwestern groups had attended a treaty conference in February 1855 but rejected the American proposal that they abandon their homelands and move to a coastal reservation. The president created the Chehalis Reservation by executive order in 1864 at a time when white settlers had appropriated much of the Chehalis Indians' traditional territory.[1]

The failed 1855 treaty conference had come at the end of a whirlwind series of negotiations conducted with the Indians of western Washington by the first territorial governor, Isaac Ingalls Stevens. When it created Washington Territory in 1853, Congress authorized Stevens, an energetic and ambitious young military man, to negotiate treaties of cession with all the Indians in the territory. Stevens was the principal draftsman of the new geography of Washington Territory.[2]

He began in December 1854 with several groups from the southern Puget Sound region, including the Squaxin, Heo's maternal relatives. With these groups he successfully concluded the Treaty of Medicine Creek, which created the Puyallup, the Nisqually, and the Squaxin Island Reservations.[3]

A month later, on January 26, 1855, Stevens successfully concluded the Point Elliott Treaty with eighty-two headmen from various northern Puget Sound Indian groups. This treaty established the Tulalip Reservation—intended to serve eventually as a permanent central reservation for all the signatory groups—and the smaller Lummi, Swinomish, and Port Madison Reservations.[4]

Just four days after the Point Elliott negotiations, Stevens concluded the Treaty of Point No Point with the Twanas, Clallams, and Chemakums, who lived on the west side of Puget Sound. This treaty created a single reservation—the Skokomish—at the head of Hood Canal. In all these negotiations, Stevens grouped together Indians that had not previously occupied the same lands or acknowledged any common leader.[5]

Stevens then turned his attention to the Indians on the ocean coast. On January 31, he negotiated the Treaty of Neah Bay with the Makahs, which created a single Makah Reservation within their traditional homelands. He then moved south to the failed February conference with the southwestern groups. After this string of successes, Stevens had been in no mood to listen to the Indians' entreaties to create a second, inland reservation. Either the Indians would accept the treaty he offered—with its single reservation somewhere on the coast south of Neah Bay—or he would walk away from the talks. When the Indians rebuffed him, Stevens held to his word, turning east to negotiate with the Plateau tribes.[6]

In July 1855, four of the southern coastal groups from the failed February talks—the Quinaults, Queets, Hohs, and Quileutes—agreed to a separate treaty negotiated by Michael Simmons, Indian agent for the Puget Sound District. This Treaty of Olympia created a single Quinault Reservation for all these groups. But the other southwestern groups—the Upper and Lower Chehalis, Chinooks, and Cowlitz—never got another chance. The fact that they never signed a treaty did not deter incoming settlers from taking their lands, however, and this land pressure eventually led to the administrative creation of the Chehalis Reservation.[7]

The idea of creating reservations—whether by treaty or executive order—and confining Indians to them had been long discussed by national officials but only recently implemented. In 1858, the federal commissioner of Indian affairs still referred to the reservation system as "only experimental." One of the central premises of the reservation policy was that Indians and whites should inhabit separate territories and have little contact with each other. "Great care should be taken in the selection of the reservations," stated the commissioner, "so as to isolate the Indians for a time from contact and interference from the whites." A nearby military presence, he continued, was desirable "to prevent the intrusion of improper persons upon them, to afford protection to the agents, and to aid in controlling the Indians and keeping them within the limits assigned to them."[8]

In Washington, the assignment of separate territory to Indians and whites was intended, at least in part, to remedy the unintended consequences of the Donation Act of 1850, which granted American settlers free land for moving to the Oregon country. By enticing American settlers to move to the Northwest, Congress hoped to create a bulwark of

In Re John Heo

American residents as a defense against any British claims to the land south of the 49th parallel. The Donation Act was blatantly illegal, for it granted land to settlers despite the Indians' acknowledged rights of occupancy, and it led to several small clashes between whites and Indians in the early 1850s as settlers occupied Indian lands and resource sites.[9]

Congress wanted Stevens's treaty-making trip to straighten this mess out by clearing Indian title to the land and establishing boundaries between Indians and whites. War derailed the immediate implementation of these plans. After his failure on the coast, Stevens had traveled east of the mountains to a large treaty conference at Walla Walla in June 1855. There, he negotiated treaties with the Yakimas, the Nez Perces, the Cayuses, the Wallawallas, the Umatillas, and various other groups living on the Columbia River. This set of three treaties created the Yakima Reservation, the Nez Perce Reservation in what is now Idaho, and the Umatilla Reservation in Oregon. Stevens then moved on to treaty negotiations with the Flatheads and the Blackfeet, planning to return to negotiate with the Colvilles, Spokanes, Okanagans and other Salishan peoples of northeastern Washington.[10]

While Stevens traveled in Blackfeet country, Indians on both sides of the Cascades took up arms against the settlers. Stevens was congratulating himself on his success, but his high-handed manner had angered the Indians. Many of those who had signed treaties were dissatisfied with the provisions. On Puget Sound, the Nisqually leader Leschi emerged as a vocal opponent of the treaties and attempted to bring the other western groups into an alliance. For the most part, though, his efforts failed, and the Puget Sound War consisted of a series of sporadic engagements with little intertribal coordination. At most, a few hundred Indian men participated in the hostilities.

Stevens and his agents moved quickly to separate hostiles from peaceful Indians, creating temporary reservations on the western side of Puget Sound to house and feed the "friendly Indians." Most of the Chehalis people fell into this latter category, and the weeks of war probably introduced Heo's family to reservation confinement. The war-induced confinement proved short-lived, however, as the Puget Sound War ended in late spring 1856.[11]

On the Plateau, trespasses by white miners heading for gold discoveries near Colville and on the Fraser River in Canada exacerbated

Indian dissatisfaction with the treaties. Some portion of almost every Plateau group, with the important exception of the Nez Perce, participated in the hostilities. Combined Indian forces dealt serious defeats to regular army and volunteer troops in 1855 and 1856, eventually leading the military to close the area to white settlement for nearly two years. After a disastrous defeat suffered by Colonel Edward Steptoe in 1858, the regular army sent in a reinforced punitive expedition that finally forced peace on the Indians in September and October 1858.[12]

The wars prevented Stevens from negotiating land cessions with the groups of the northeastern Plateau, who never signed a treaty. The war also delayed ratification of the existing treaties; only the Medicine Creek treaty, ratified on March 3, 1855, had been immediately accepted by Congress. The others stood signed but unratified, their status thrown into doubt by the Indians' obvious displeasure with them.[13]

As the wars drew to a close, officials in the territory embarked on a campaign to win the peace by securing the ratification of the existing Stevens treaties. The arguments for ratification stressed the importance of racial separation as a prerequisite of orderly settlement. In his annual report for 1858, the superintendent of Indian affairs for Oregon and Washington urged that "the whites should be relieved of their [the Indians'] annoying presence by their location upon reservations, and the constant feuds and alarms terminated by a separation of the two races. Until this is done there can be no permanent peace or prosperity in the country."[14]

Puget Sound District Agent Michael Simmons voiced the same concerns. "Humanity, as well as justice, makes it an imperative duty of government to adopt some plan by which the Indians can be separated from the whites," he reported to the commissioner. Congress should ratify the treaties with the Puget Sound groups and implement the reservation policy, Simmons concluded. In a letter to an Olympia newspaper, Simmons touched on the same themes: The Indians should be "allotted to their reservations, and provided for as contemplated in the treaties with them."[15]

Local editorialists joined in the calls for ratification and implementation of the treaty provisions, which meant primarily the removal of Indians from the settlements. "All, we think, that is now required to give permanency and lasting quiet to Indian Affairs . . . is, that the treaties

In Re John Heo

with them be confirmed—that they be placed upon their reservations, *and compelled to remain there*," the *Olympia Pioneer and Democrat* stated. In March 1859, the *Puget Sound Herald* reported that three "vagabonds" who had committed some local thefts had been run out of town. "Would it not be well . . . to disposed [*sic*] of the Indian vagrants in our midst in a similar manner?" the *Herald* asked. "Their proper place is on reservations, where we hope they will speedily be sent."[16]

Officials hoped that removal of the Indians to the reservations would end the indiscriminate contact between whites and Indians that had marked the years of willy-nilly American settlement under the Donation Act. As he argued for ratification in 1858, the superintendent noted that the white population of the territory inhabited the land "almost in common" with the Indians. The situation, he believed, was an "anomaly . . . nowhere else presented within the limits of the United States."[17]

As white settlement increased, the superintendent noted, such indiscriminate contact caused frequent conflicts between whites and Indians. Whites appropriated the best lands, which meant usurping the Indians' potato fields and root grounds. Whites complained that Indians stole their goods and their food. In addition to all of this, there was liquor. The Indians obtained liquor in prodigious quantities from the whites. Without ratification of the treaties, the creation of separate reservations for the Indians, and their removal to those reservations, it was impossible to enforce the Federal Indian Intercourse Act prohibiting the sale or distribution of liquor to the Indians. "In all that vast region thrown open to settlement by the acts of Congress, the intercourse laws are a dead letter and nullity, which the Indian department has long since given up all hope of enforcing," the superintendent stated.[18]

The Federal Indian Intercourse Act gave a clear meaning to the boundary between "Indian country"—those lands not ceded by the Indians or reserved exclusively for their use—and the rest of society. The act provided for the removal of unauthorized intruders on Indian lands, ordained punishments for white trespassers, and forbade liquor within Indian country. In Washington Territory, however, the Donation Act had muddied the distinction between Indian country and white society. Because the Donation Act did not clear Indian title prior to white settlement, essentially all of the territory remained Indian country until the Indians made a formal cession through treaty. The Stevens treaties were meant to resolve that situation, but they had not been ratified. If the boundary between Indian country and white society was to mean anything at all—and the Intercourse Act clearly intended it to mean a great deal—then the treaties needed to be ratified.[19]

The Indians' access to liquor provided the Indian agents with a strong rationale for separating the Indians from white society. "They are constantly drunk," wrote local Agent E. C. Fitzhugh in describing the Lummi, Nooksack, and Samish Indians under his charge in 1858. "Unless the treaties are confirmed, and these Indians placed on a reservation, the government will have no use for an agent here. There will not be an Indian left to tell the tale that they had ever existed." In forwarding Fitzhugh's report to his superiors, District Agent Simmons commented that "the suppression of the liquor trade, as the case stands now, is full of difficulties. This is an Indian country and it is not. Towns now stand upon ground where the Indian title is not extinct; the settlers have a right to bring their goods into the country, yet the intercourse law says that liquor shall not be taken into an Indian country."[20]

After some debate, Congress ratified the seven remaining Stevens treaties on March 8, 1859. The system of reservations planned by Stevens thus achieved full legal existence. In later years, some of the gaps in that system came to be filled by executive order. In addition to the Chehalis Reservation, the coastal Shoalwater Bay Reservation, created in 1866, covered some of the nontreaty groups in the southwestern portion of the territory. In 1872, President Ulysses Grant created the Colville Reservation in northeastern Washington for the nontreaty groups in that region. The Spokane Reservation just to the south of the Colville Reservation was created in 1881 (see map 2).[21]

American authorities thus imposed a new map on Washington Territory, with boundaries that starkly limited the Indian domain. But the lives of Indians like Heo disregarded these boundaries. Heo had relatives on the reservations but spent much of his own life outside their confines, working and residing in the white settlements. For Heo, the division between Indian country and white society meant very little.

The observations of Indian agents and white settlers indicate that Heo's experience was not exceptional. Reviewing the status of the Point Elliott treaty in 1877, the agent reported that fewer than one-half of the

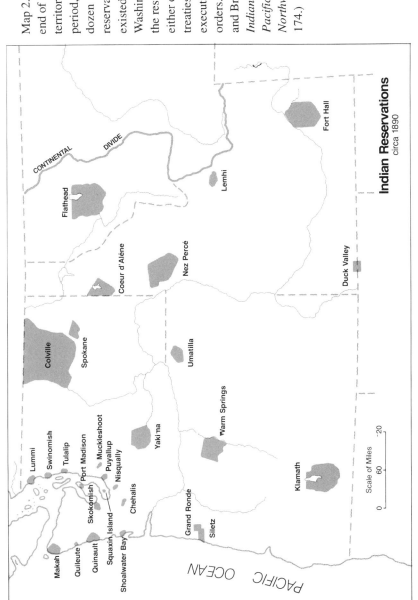

Map 2. At the end of the territorial period, over a dozen reservations existed in Washington, the result either of treaties or executive orders. (Ruby and Brown, *Indians of the Pacific Northwest*, 174.)

Indian Reservations
circa 1890

CONTINENTAL DIVIDE

Flathead

Coeur d'Aléne

Nez Percé

Lemhi

Fort Hall

Colville

Spokane

Umatilla

Duck Valley

Lummi
Swinomish
Tulalip
Port Madison
Muckleshoot
Puyallup
Nisqually
Skokomish
Squaxin Island
Chehalis

Makah
Quileute
Quinault
Shoalwater Bay

Grand Ronde
Siletz

Yakima

Warm Springs

Klamath

Scale of Miles

0   60   -20

PACIFIC OCEAN

Indians covered by the treaty resided on the reservations. "Whole tribes have persistently refused to remove to the reservations assigned them," he wrote.[22]

This was a common lament among the agents appointed to oversee the reservations in Washington. These men were often on the receiving end of nationwide policy directives from the Office of Indian Affairs (OIA), ordering that all Indians be confined to reservations. The agents in Washington Territory inevitably answered with labored explanations for their failure to comply with the directives.[23]

It is difficult to establish precisely how many off-reservation Indians there were in the entire territory. Agents provided population counts in their annual reports, but it was often unclear whether these numbers referred to all Indians nominally under the agent's charge or only those on the reservations. In addition, agents usually excluded nontreaty groups from these population counts. And finally, the wide variability in the numbers makes their reliability suspect. In 1870, for example, the agent estimated the population of the Puyallup, Nisqually, and Squaxin Island groups, all included under the Treaty of Medicine Creek, at 828. But just one year later, the agent reported this population as 1,210. The agent for the Makahs, far out on the west coast, wrote in 1876 that his population counts fluctuated because many of the Makahs intermarried with the Nootkan Indians on Vancouver's Island, across the international boundary. These Indians changed residency from one year to the next. When they lived on the U.S. side of the line, the agent included them in the count. Transience, the timing of the census, and the agents' varying notions of who should be counted all contributed to variations in reported population.[24]

Despite these problems, the figures sometimes state clearly the proportion of Indians living off the reservations. Table 1 shows selected population figures for the groups under the principal Stevens treaties. In the years shown, the agents provided explicit figures on the number of Indians included under the treaty and the number living on the reservations. The table shows that in some areas the reservation population constituted only a fraction of the total number of Indians included under the treaty. It is worth noting, however, that some groups—particularly the Makahs, who signed the Neah Bay treaty—resided, for the most part, within the boundaries of their reservation.

TABLE 1
Populations of Stevens Treaty Reservations

| | Treaty | | | |
| Year | Medicine Creek | | Point No Point | |
	Total	On reserve	Total	On reserve
1858	1357	435		
1860			1500	250
1862	1350	600		
1868			2000	1000
1878	1731	1033	800	250

| | Treaty | | | |
| Year | Point Elliott | | Neah Bay | |
	Total	On reserve	Total	On reserve
1862	3718	"few"	700	700*
1875	2850	1900	560	560
1878	2900	1013	713	713

| | Treaty | | | |
| Year | Olympia | | Yakima | |
	Total	On reserve	Total	On reserve
1862			4000	400
1870	532	130		
1871			3500	2000
1875	479	226	3650	3350
1878	618	227		
1881			3400	2176

* During summer

Sources: *ARCIA*, 1858, 242; *ARCIA*, 1859, 394; *ARCIA*, 1860, 179; *ARCIA*, 1862, 300, 306, 407, 418; *ARCIA*, 1868, 94; *ARCIA*, 1870, 46; *ARCIA*, 1871, 119; *ARCIA*, 1875, 67, 85, 94, 101; *ARCIA*, 1878, 132, 176; *ARCIA*, 1881, 174.

Several factors lay behind the failure of the reservation policy in Washington. First and foremost, the Indians resisted removal from their homelands. The reservations in Washington were often located within the home territory of a single Indian group; communities with neutral or negative feelings toward that group preferred to remain within their own historic territories. When Heo resided on the Chehalis Reservation, for example, his neighbors were mostly other Upper Chehalis people, despite the fact that people from some half a dozen other groups "belonged" there.[25]

When Superintendent Robert Milroy held a council with some of these groups in 1872 to persuade them to move to the Chehalis Reservation, most refused to meet with him. The one group that did attend, the Humptulips, refused to accept any gifts of food or blankets from Milroy so they could not be accused of accepting goods for their land. When Milroy urged them to come on reservation,

> They replied that that was not their home; that they had always lived at the mouth of the Humtolop [sic] and Chinoose Rivers, where their fathers had lived and died from time immemorial, and they wished to live and die there; that they did not know how to live away from salt water, where they could always get plenty of fish and clams.

The Humptulips suggested that Milroy give them "a paper" certifying their possession of their own homeland, in order to protect their homes from land-hungry settlers and speculators.[26]

Like the Humptulips, the Clallam Indians, who lived along the Strait of Juan de Fuca and the northwestern shores of Puget Sound, resisted official efforts to relocate them to their assigned reservation. Clallam headmen had signed Stevens' Treaty of Point No Point in 1855 and been assigned to the Skokomish Reservation. The reservation lay south of their homelands, in the historic territory of their neighbors, the Twanas.[27] They "only make . . . annual visits [to the reservation] to receive their proportion of annuity goods, or to catch fish at their old fishing-grounds on the [Hood] canal," the superintendent wrote of the Clallams in 1862. "All . . . are averse to making the present located reserve a home."[28]

When Edwin Eells assumed control of the Skokomish Reservation in 1871, he set out to persuade the Clallams to move there. In his 1872 annual report, he stated that with some considerable expense and effort, he had moved some chiefs and leading men onto the reservation "by force . . . hoping by this means to draw the whole tribe." The effort, he continued, "has not proved successful." A year later, he set aside the stick and tried a carrot to convince the Clallams to cooperate. He offered them individual allotments on the reservation, but reported that "they are very

In Re John Heo

slow to take in such an idea, because . . . it removes them so far from their old homes. Then there is not a cordial good-feeling between them and the Twanas, who are in the majority on the reservation."[29]

In 1874, in their efforts to stay put, a group of Clallams collected sufficient funds to purchase over two hundred acres of land near the town of Dungeness upon which to site their permanent village. Other families and bands leased lands from whites in order to stay in their traditional homes. In 1879, Eells conceded defeat. The Clallams' "love of home is so strong that, rather than leave their own country and have the use of land free on the reservation, they have in many instances bought land near home; rather than have lumber and tools furnished them on the reservation they have earned and bought them themselves." His own futile efforts with the Clallams had persuaded him, he wrote, that the long-held dream of the Indian Department to consolidate all the Puget Sound Indians onto a single reservation was doomed.[30]

Although whites interpreted the treaties as agreements by the Indians to move to reservations, many Indians saw them differently. The Quileute Indians, for example, signed the Treaty of Olympia and resided on the Pacific coast of the Olympic Peninsula. They consistently refused to move to the Quinault Reservation, which was located in the historic home of the Quinault people. Later, when the OIA transferred the Quileutes to the jurisdiction of the Makah agent, they similarly refused to leave their homes to move to the reservation at Neah Bay. The Quileutes argued that the treaty had simply given the Americans rights to trade and take furs, much like the arrangement with the Hudson's Bay Company. In 1877 they told the Quinault agent that they had not understood the treaty as requiring them to leave their homes.[31]

The Indians east of the Cascades were no more anxious to remove to the reservations than those in western Washington. The government intended the Colville Reservation, created by executive order in 1872, for several of the Interior Salish groups of northeastern Washington, including the Kalispels, Colvilles, Sanpoils, Nespelems, Lakes, Methows, Spokanes, Columbians, and Okanagans, but few of them moved there. William P. Winans, the OIA farmer for the Colville agency, reported in 1872 that each tribe expressed a willingness to reside on a reservation, but they wanted to be consulted as to its boundaries and wanted it located in their own homeland.[32]

Three years later, Colville Agent John Simms reported that only the Okanagans, Sanpoils, and Nespelems resided on the reservation, mainly because the reservation encompassed their traditional lands. The latter two groups, he wrote, made no pretense of obeisance to the U.S. government, refusing to acknowledge the authority of the agent over them. The other groups included in the agency resided off the reservation along the upper Columbia River or in the valleys of its tributaries.[33]

South of the Colville Reservation lay the Yakima Reservation, often held up as a "model" agency because of its success in getting the Indians to adopt agricultural pursuits. But even it failed to gather all its Indians onto a single reservation. In 1881, James Wilbur, the strong-willed Methodist minister who served as agent on the Yakima Reservation for many years, estimated that only about one-third of the Indians who were assigned to the reservation resided there permanently, another third resided there seasonally, and a final third resided permanently off the reservation.[34]

Despite the Indians' various objections to the locations of the reservations, the reservation policy might have been more effective in Washington if the reservation economies had proved viable. But with the exception of the Yakima Reservation, and perhaps the Lummi Reservation, the lands assigned to the Indians were not sufficiently productive to allow the Indians to feed themselves through agriculture. On-reservation logging provided a living for some Indians on the western reservations, but the reserved tracts were not large enough to support whole communities through logging. Appropriations under the treaties came nowhere near the amounts necessary to allow the government to support the reservation populations through the issuance of rations. "Many of the reservations are very small and the land exceedingly poor to confine them entirely," wrote the superintendent in 1867. "To them it would be imprisonment and starvation, as the appropriations are entirely inadequate to their support."[35]

In 1873–74 a controversy over on-reservation Indian logging illustrated the linkage between the reservation economy and Indian residence. Indians on the Tulalip and the Skokomish Reservations had logged since at least the mid-1860s. But on December 1, 1873, the secretary of the interior ordered lumbering operations on all reservations suspended because of a legal challenge to the power of Indians or Indian agents "to

In Re John Heo

make contracts for the sale of timber or other valuable material upon Indian reservations."[36]

The order provoked consternation among the Indians and their agents, who protested to Washington, D.C. that the result would be an efflux of Indians from the reservations as they sought their livelihood elsewhere. A number of headmen from the Tulalip Reservation petitioned the president directly for a modification of the order. "You always tell us to be good and industrious and how can you permit our children to be disturbed and stopped, when following your advices, they try to help themselves and make their living on the reservation?," asked a Snoqualmie headman. Another added, "We cannot stay on the Reservation if we are not allowed to continue our logging"; and a third asked, "How can we stay on the reservation, if we cannot work in the wood, where there is nothing but wood?"[37]

The secretary of the interior revoked the order several weeks later specifically for the Skokomish and Tulalip Reservations, but the controversy clearly showed the Indians' astute perception of the dilemma created by the federal reservation policy. The Indian agents demanded that they stay on the reservations, yet the reservations could not provide a reasonable living.[38]

The need to eat therefore compelled many Indians to leave the reservations during at least part of the year. While some families chose to reside permanently either off or on the reservations, a great number lived on the reservation in the winter and then moved off the reservation for the rest of the year.

The Indians took full advantage of treaty provisions guaranteeing their rights to hunt, fish, and gather food at their traditional sites "in common" with the citizens of the territory. All the Stevens treaties included such a stipulation, as the Indians had insisted upon continued access to their fisheries. "This clause in the treaty virtually allows them to be absent from the reservation all the time," complained Eells, the agent on the Skokomish Reservation, in 1873. He told the commissioner that he could not enforce an OIA circular declaring that all Indians should be confined to their reservations. "As it is impossible for them all comfortably to subsist upon the reservation which has been selected by the government for them, there arises a necessity as well as a right for them to be away most all of the time," Eells wrote. He reminded the commissioner that only about one-third of the Indians under his charge currently resided on the Skokomish Reservation.[39]

Throughout the territorial period, agency employees reported that they had very little to do from spring to early fall, during the Indians' excursions off the reservations. The Yakima agency physician explained the brevity of his July 1865 report, for example, by noting that "the Indians have been absent a large portion of this month at their fishing and root grounds." The following year's reports followed a similar pattern. And in the summer of 1870, the physician lamented the difficulty of administering vaccinations required by the OIA "owing to the absence of most of the Indians from their homes on the Reservation." The same tone can be found in reports filed by agency employees on the western side of the mountains.[40]

These seasonal patterns meant that a significant number of Washington Indians did spend some portion of their lives on reservations, but many, like Heo, drifted away over time. Reservations were not, after all, just holding pens for Indians. They were meant to be schools as well, with federal Indian agents and missionaries teaching Indians the modes of "civilized" life. Like their counterparts across the country, Indian agents and superintendents in Washington Territory tried to get Indians to give up traditional modes of subsistence in favor of more "civilized" occupations, especially agriculture, and they discouraged "uncivilized" behavior among their charges. They attacked Native religious practices, fought polygamy and the easy dissolution of marriage, and enforced the treaties' ban on slavery. They also discouraged head-flattening, a widespread practice among the western groups to mark nonslave children.[41]

Many Indians found reservation discipline intolerable. Smohalla, a Plateau religious leader, rejected reservations and white culture and urged Indians to revitalize traditional ways of life. His message attracted a large number of followers. In his annual report for 1875, the commissioner of Indian affairs drew attention to the existence of some two thousand "renegades" under Smohalla, "roaming" along the Columbia River. "Superstition is fostered, unbridled license is granted to passion, civilization is despised, and reservation Indians are looked upon with contempt and disdain," the commissioner railed.[42]

Heo also found reservation life intolerable. He left the Chehalis Reservation for good sometime in the mid-1870s when the agent there

In Re John Heo

punished him severely for an infraction of the rules. Ultimately, it was another agent's attempt to enforce the rules of "civilization" that led to Heo's challenge to the system in 1880.[43]

In 1879 Heo abandoned his wife, who was then living on the Nisqually Reservation. Traditionally, divorce had been a fairly straightforward matter among the Native peoples of western Washington. Lower-class people broke marriage bonds easily; indeed, the upper classes tended to view with disdain the promiscuity of their social inferiors. Given the role of marriage in cementing cross-kin alliances, upper-class families worked to preserve marriages and discouraged husbands and wives from breaking up. But in the end a bad match could be severed by either party. Heo's class status cannot be known with certainty, but his actions clearly show that he wanted to end the relationship with his wife.[44]

Agents tried to discourage divorce among the Indians, viewing the easy dissolution of marriage as one of those "uncivilized" cultural practices. If they wanted to end a marriage, Indians had to seek the agents' approval. If the agent found good cause for a breakup, then he would grant a formal divorce. In Heo's case, the agent for the Nisqually Reservation was Robert Milroy, the former superintendent of Indian affairs. Milroy wanted Heo to move to the reservation and patch up the marriage. In Milroy's view, Heo "had no just cause for leaving his wife. He did not accuse her of whoring, drinking, or any neglect of . . . household duties." According to Milroy, Heo said only that "he was tired of her and would never live with her again."[45]

Heo's action particularly galled Milroy because of an official favor Milroy had done for Heo in the past. In 1876, Heo had killed another Indian during a drunken quarrel in Lewis County. Convicted of murder in the territorial courts, Heo was sentenced to two years in the territorial penitentiary. After a year in prison, Heo appealed to Milroy to work for his release so that he could support his wife and children, and Milroy successfully lobbied for a pardon by the governor. Heo brought his wife and children up from the Chehalis Reservation to live with him at Olympia, supporting them by his labor among the white settlers. But when his wife chose to move in with her relatives on the Nisqually Reservation, Heo refused to join her.[46]

When Milroy tried to force a reconciliation, Heo protested that the agent wanted him "to cohabit with an Indian woman." When Milroy ordered him to remove to the reservation and live with and support his family, Heo refused. After several months of such defiance, Milroy sent the Indian police from the agency to arrest Heo and imprison him. On May 26, 1880, Heo filed a writ of habeas corpus against Milroy in district court, denying Milroy's authority over him and asking the court to compel the agent to justify Heo's imprisonment.[47]

The district judge granted Heo's writ. At the hearing, Milroy claimed jurisdiction over the entire area of southwest Washington by virtue of his appointment as agent, and stated that his authority extended over every Indian in that area. "The entire control and supervision of said Indian John Heo and other Indians within affiant's [Milroy's] said agency belongs to affiant subject only to the approval of the . . . President [of the United States], Secretary [of the Interior], and Commissioner of Indian Affairs," Milroy stated to the court. He justified Heo's imprisonment on the grounds that Heo had refused to obey the agent's lawfully given directions, with "great injury of the Indian service within said agency."[48]

In his response, Heo admitted he was an Indian, but denied Milroy had "any right to restrain him of his liberty by virtue of his authority as an Indian Agent." Heo based this denial upon both cultural and legal arguments. Legally, he argued that the agent had no authority over him since the Chehalis had never signed a treaty with the United States. Even if the court found that Milroy had authority over the Chehalis, Heo continued, the agent still had no authority over Heo as an individual. He had severed his tribal relations, he stated, and had been "constantly living with the whites, engaged in the pursuits of civilized life." He tilled the soil for a living, he said, and if released from the agent's custody, he intended to labor until he could accumulate enough funds to file a homestead entry under the provisions of the Indian Homestead Act.[49]

Heo thus challenged the meaning of the racial category of Indian. To subvert Milroy's authority over him, he offered up evidence of a cultural transformation—from uncivilized tribal Indian to assimilated, autonomous individual. But the concept of assimilation masks the complexity of what Heo tried to accomplish. He put forward this particular identity in this particular context—an American courtroom—seeking ultimately to validate the traditional Native practice of divorce. He thus pursued a particularly "Indian" end by disputing the legal meaning of *Indian*.

In Re John Heo

Heo's ability to claim this identity stemmed from the failure of the reservation policy in Washington and from the Indian-white contact that grew out of that failure. Heo could make the case that he was not subject to Milroy's authority because, in fact, he had not been directly subject to such authority in the past. Living and working off the reservation allowed Heo to present himself as an Indian without tribal ties who, therefore, should not be forced onto a reservation.

Contact played an especially important role in Heo's case because it allowed him to form an alliance with John Judson, a white settler and lawyer in Olympia who not only employed Heo on his farm but argued his case before the court. "I am disposed to question your authority in the premises," Judson told Milroy in a letter. "Heo has been in my employ for over a year and . . . I am interested in his welfare." The employer-employee relationship between Heo and Judson facilitated the Indian's mobilization of American law.[50]

Their relationship highlights a second factor behind the failure of the policy of reservation confinement. Having obtained Indian lands through warfare, treaties, and statutes of dubious legality, many settlers in Washington found that they could not dispense with the Indians. To wrest a profit from the land, the settlers needed Indian labor—to cut the trees, harvest the fish, clear the land, and provide transportation—and they needed Indian goods—horses, foodstuffs, furs, and other items. Like Heo, many Indians in Washington were active participants in the white economy.

The Indians, of course, had contributed to that economy prior to the establishment of the territory by way of their participation in the fur trade. For roughly two generations prior to American settlement, Indians in the region had direct contact with Euro-Americans through this trade. The Hudson's Bay Company established three fur posts on the Plateau, and the Plateau Indians had access to several other posts in what is now Canada and Montana. West of the mountains, the Indians traded with both British and American ships in the sea otter trade. Other communities traded with the company at Forts Vancouver (opened 1825) and Langley (founded 1827). In 1833 the company established Fort Nisqually, a post on Puget Sound. Fort Victoria, very accessible to the northern Puget Sound groups, opened in 1843.[51]

Some of Washington's Indian groups provided more food than furs to the company posts, which depended on the Indian trade for some of their provisions. As American settlers gained a foothold in the region, Indians continued this pattern, gathering and marketing surplus foodstuffs to their white neighbors. Skagit, Snohomish, and Snoqualmie Indians all gathered in the settlement of Bellingham in 1858 for "the ready market that they find for their game and fish," reported one agent, annoyed at the presence of so many Indians who did not "belong to the place." This type of trade persisted well into the territorial period. Yakima Agent Wilbur reported in July 1872 that hundreds of the Indians under his charge were currently off the reservation at the fisheries. "They put up emense [sic] quantities of salmon for food and sell to the whites."[52]

Indians also provided needed transportation in the young territorial economy. On the Plateau, for example, Indians traded horses to settlers. Agent Wilbur specified in 1881 that the gains from horse trading allowed many of the Indians to remain off the reservation. On the western side of the mountains, Indian canoes often proved to be the only viable means of transportation in many areas. The subagent for the Columbia River district wrote to Governor Stevens in 1854 that the rapid and shallow Cowlitz River would be useless to the whites if it were not for the ferryage maintained by the Indians.[53]

An 1874 petition from a group of Whatcom County citizens indicated the importance of the carrying trade to the settlers. Alarmed by rumors that the Nooksack Indians in the area were to be removed to the Lummi Reservation, the petitioners protested that the county was still new, with few passable roads and trails, and that the Indian canoes were the only means of transportation. Indian removal, they argued, would damage the prospects of the fledgling settlement.[54]

As settlement increased and the white economy diversified, so did Native economic contributions. As logging expanded in the western part of the territory, Indians found they could sell fish oil to white loggers, who used it to grease their log skids. In 1871, the farmer on the Lummi Reservation reported that the Indians were catching an increasing number of dogfish for rendering into oil. Dogfish had not been an important food fish traditionally, but commercialization prompted modifications in traditional food-gathering activities.[55]

The development of a local industry could have a dramatic impact on the Indian economy. In 1870, the Bellingham Bay Coal Company, for example, paid the neighboring Lummi Indians $336.77 for timber, $300 for 1,800 gallons of cranberries; $200 for 1,000 pounds of feathers; and $400 for 800 gallons of oil. Wages, however, made up by far the largest Indian item on the company's cost account, at $3,502.75.[56]

The expansion of wage labor signified the deepening involvement of the Indians in the white economy. A number of Indians had begun working for wages as early as the 1850s. During the 1855–56 Puget Sound War, Seattle pioneer Henry Yesler objected to the proposed removal of the local "friendly" Indians to a temporary reservation because of the disruption it would cause his sawmill operations. Yesler encouraged the Indians to stay around Seattle, so that he would have a readily available labor force. Indians along the lower Columbia River near Vancouver, where whites had resided for many years before the territory was established, depended almost entirely on wages as early as 1857. The local Indian agent reported that they "have heretofore spent their lives in the immediate vicinity of the whites . . . and they could always procure an easy subsistence by working for the farmers and others."[57]

In some cases, the market transformed traditional subsistence activities into paid labor. For the Indians around Shoalwater Bay, for example, harvesting oysters for white employers became an important source of income. Among some of the other coast tribes, particularly the Makahs, who had always gone to sea to hunt ocean mammals, sealing became an important activity in the late 1870s. Sealing schooners contracted for Makah crews and canoes based on a division of the catch. The typical contract gave one-third to the schooner and two-thirds to the Indians. In good years, the business proved so remunerative that the agent complained he could not keep the men at their farms. The Makah men earned so much money from sealing that they hired white men to cut their winter's supply of cordwood, the agent reported in 1882. Eventually, some Makahs purchased their own schooners.[58]

Indians became involved in the wage economy partly because white employers needed bodies. The white population grew only slowly in the early years of the territorial period, so Indians were the most plentiful source of labor. According to the federal census, the non-Native population increased relatively slowly compared to later years, from 1,201 in 1850 to only 22,636 in 1870. Census enumerators estimated the Indian population at 14,796 in 1870. While not all these Indians were in the labor force, they still constituted a significant pool of potential workers.[59]

Even when white population growth accelerated after 1870, Indian labor remained important to the economy. During the 1870s, the white population more than tripled to 70,711, while the estimated Indian population stabilized at 14,189. During the next decade, the white population nearly quintupled to 345,735 as settlers flocked to Washington anticipating the arrival of the Northern Pacific and Great Northern Railroads.[60] The Native population, meanwhile, declined by a fifth to 11,181. Still, employers needed Indian workers to fill low-wage, seasonally available jobs in agriculture, fishing, and lumber. In Milroy's view, this need for an exploitable, low-wage worker motivated Judson to take up Heo's cause. "The secret of said Judson's interest in said Heo," wrote Milroy, "is the fact that he manages to get a large amount of valuable labor out of this simple Indian for very small pay."[61]

The hops boom of the 1870s and 1880s demonstrated the continuing need for Indian labor. The labor needs of hops growers peaked at harvest time, when they needed a large influx of workers to bring in the crop quickly. Indians dominated the hop-picking labor force in the territory from the industry's inception, and the annual hop harvests became grand reunions for Indians from all regions of the Northwest.[62]

The type of labor performed by the Indians depended on the character of the economy in the immediate area. Some of the Indians living west of Puget Sound, on the Olympic Peninsula, harvested potatoes for white farmers. The Clallams, living along the west side of the sound and on the Strait of Juan de Fuca, worked both at harvesting and in the lumber mills, as did the Twanas. Indians closer to white population centers also worked as house servants and farm laborers. The heavy timber of western Washington made clearing land for farming a very labor-intensive task, for which white farmers often hired Indians. In 1878, the agent for the Puyallup, Nisqually, and Squaxin Island Reservations estimated that Indian laborers had cleared two-thirds of the land west of the Cascades.[63]

More Indians were engaged in wage labor more frequently west of the mountains than east. White settlement developed more slowly in the east, so whites had less need for Indian labor. In many areas, agriculture did not require the heavy timber-clearing activities that it demanded in the west. Finally, many Indian groups on the Plateau simply chose to retreat into the open expanses when white settlers penetrated the area. As

In Re John Heo

a result, horse-trading and the sale of fish and other produce constituted the bulk of Indian-white commercial interaction on the Plateau.

In some Plateau areas, however, more complicated relationships developed. In 1857, for example, the local agent reported that the Pend Oreille Indians of the far northeast corner of the territory were friendly to the miners coming into their country after the gold discoveries on the Pend Oreille River. Many of the Indians, the agent stated, engaged in mining. In the Colville Valley, many Indians worked on white farms as laborers, as well as farming their own tracts. The agent at Colville reported in 1878 that demand for the Indians' labor had increased in recent years. "So necessary have they become to the settlers that it is a matter of common remark, 'If the Indians leave the valley, we will have to leave, as we cannot get along without their labor.' They are found behind nearly every plow, and in every harvest-field, and it would seem impossible to put in or take off a crop without their assistance."[64]

For the most part, Indian labor remained seasonal, integrated into a round of activities that included traditional subsistence activities, commodity production for the white economy, and some wage labor. In 1880, the agent for the Puyallup, Nisqually, and Squaxin Island Reservations wrote that the Indians under his charge were "compelled to spend much of their time off the [reservations] working around among the neighboring whites, and in fishing, hunting, gathering berries, etc. upon which they are chiefly dependent for subsistence." The Duwamish on the Port Madison Reservation "are not agriculturists," wrote their agent in 1867, "but make their living by working at the mills, cutting and selling logs from their reservation to the mills, and by fishing for dog and salmon fish, selling the oil from the dog fish and supplying the mills with the salmon."[65]

Involvement in the settler economy exposed the Indians of Washington Territory to the vagaries of the larger national economy. When the demand for lumber slumped, fewer Indians found work in the mills, the mills bought fewer logs, and the logging camps needed fewer supplies. "It may seem strange to speak of the Indians as at all affected by the financial condition of the country," remarked Agent Eells in 1878, "but it is a fact that they are so far advanced in the arts of civilized life that they earn their living as whites do by their labor, and when that is scarce or wages are low, their condition is affected as really as any other class of people."[66]

Indians' labor and trade with whites was not simply the outcome of assimilative pressures on the Indians or a mark of their ascent up the ladder of "civilization," as Eells implied. Rather, it was a necessary part of the Indians' strategy for survival. As whites appropriated traditional hunting and gathering sites and blocked full access to fisheries, Indians could not secure a living by purely traditional means. Wage work and commodity production for the white economy gave them additional means to secure the necessaries of life. These activities fatally undermined the federal objective of confining all Indians to reservations. The American-drawn map dividing Washington Territory into areas of Indian and white habitation remained a fiction throughout the territorial period.

In other areas of the United States, of course, Indians were no more anxious to remove to reservations than those in Washington. As in Washington, many Indians elsewhere found the reservations to be impoverished and incapable of providing a decent living. Yet in several of these other areas, Indians could not leave the reservations at will to procure other means of making a living or to escape the agents' discipline. These Indians found reservation confinement an oppressive reality. What accounts for the permeability of reservation boundaries in some areas, like Washington, and their relative rigidity in other areas?

In addition to the nature of the local economy and the resistance of the Indians, a third factor lay behind the failure of the reservation policy in Washington. The federal agencies assigned to carry out this policy were disorganized and ineffective, particularly in the early years of the period. As political appointees, superintendents rarely enjoyed long tenures. Once Stevens left the post in 1857, ten different men filled the position over the next seventeen years. Thomas McKenny served the longest single term of office, from September 1866 to June 1869, when he was replaced in a short-lived experiment to turn over Indian affairs to the military. Reinstated in October 1870, McKenny served until June 1872. Congress abolished the position of superintendent in 1874.[67]

The administrators below the superintendent enjoyed even less job security. The local Indian agents handled the day-to-day implementation of policy, but their resources were stretched thin. Several western Washington reservations, for example, had no resident officer from the

In Re John Heo

OIA for years at a time. Stronger agents who served relatively long tenures did emerge in the later territorial period, but they could do little to force their charges to move to the reservations.[68]

Like the superintendents, Indian agents were political appointees, and thus embroiled in local party rivalries. Once appointed, agents were continually charged with corruption and incompetence by their political enemies, who in turn were charged with deceit and a desire to swindle the Indians.[69]

These factors played a key role in Heo's case. Judson and Milroy stood on opposite sides of the political and religious fences that divided nineteenth-century Americans. The Protestant Republican Milroy labeled Judson "a bitter Democrat and a Papist-bigoted intolerant, [with] an immense opinion of his own abilities." Milroy had come to Washington Territory after serving in the Civil War; Judson came from one of the first white families to settle on Puget Sound. Judson claimed that his only impulse was to protect Heo against the tyranny of the agent, but given their political differences, he may have challenged Milroy's authority simply in order to embarrass the agent.[70]

The army, the other principal arm of the national state in its exercise of Indian policy, was a relatively weak presence in Washington after the Indian wars ended. The Indians did not mount a serious military challenge to American dominance after the 1850s, nor did they constitute an obstacle to the economic development of the region. Indeed, in some areas Indian trade and Indian labor contributed vitally to economic development. The army in Washington therefore never carried out the kind of continual harassment of Indians that eventually forced Native groups in other areas to relocate to reservations. Like most of the rest of the Indian-fighting army, the military in Washington Territory was dispersed in small detachments at local forts, and its activities were largely limited to minor police actions.[71]

The creation of Indian police forces beginning in the late 1870s furnished the agents with a coercive instrument to fill some of the gaps left by the army. These forces allowed agents to project their power off the reservations. The Yakima agency police, for example, not only patrolled the reservation but also the off-reservation fisheries on the Columbia River and other off-reservation Indian communities. It was a squad of Milroy's police from the Puyallup Reservation that arrested Heo. But the off-reservation use of Indian police forces raised troubling jurisdictional issues, since it extended the agent's authority beyond Indian country, and in 1885 the OIA forbade use of the Indian police beyond the boundaries of the reservations.[72]

In the end, most of the burden of dealing with off-reservation Indian communities and Indian-white contact fell to local lawmakers and local courts. Thus Milroy found himself in a district court in 1880 defending his authority against Heo's challenge. The prospect of losing disturbed Milroy, and he wrote to the commissioner of Indian affairs for advice. Agents on the Pacific coast had always claimed "absolute and unlimited authority over Indians both on and off reservations, the same as fathers over their children," he wrote. "Until the advent of said Judson as the Don Quixote 'to protect' Indians from violence' and oppression, I have never heard of said authority being disputed by any white man." Should the decision go against him, Milroy said, his authority over the numerous off-reservation Indians in the area would come to an end. "There are many vicious Indians who would rejoice in the termination of the authority of U.S. Ind [sic] Agents over them."[73]

Milroy never exercised as much authority over those "vicious" Indians as he claimed, but in Heo's case he need not have worried. On May 27, 1880, the judge denied Heo's petition for freedom. He stated that Heo could not unilaterally dissolve the bonds of authority exercised over him by an Indian agent. Since he had never received the agent's permission to sever his connection with his tribe and reside off reservation, Heo remained under Milroy's authority. The judge remanded Heo into the agent's custody.[74]

Heo's effort to use American law to dissolve the bonds of OIA authority thus ended in failure; the courts rejected his attempt to reconfigure the meaning of Indian identity and refused to disturb the formal power relationship between agents and Indians. In the judge's eyes, Heo remained a tribal Indian, not an independent, "civilized" individual.

Heo's failure, however, should not obscure the larger meaning of his effort. Heo's life typified that of many Washington Indians, who never resided permanently on reservations and fell under both the administrative authority of Indian agents and the legal authority of territorial courts. Heo realized the potential to play these sources of authority against each

In Re John Heo

other to maximize his own autonomy. To do so, he had to contest the meaning of Indian identity and to provide evidence of his own cultural transformation into a "civilized" citizen.

The failure of the reservation policy, which blurred the fundamental legal distinction between Indian country and white society, enabled him to make such a claim and to find support within the white community. That does not mean that Washington's reservations were not "oppressive . . . instruments of imperial control," in Frederick Hoxie's words, or that off-reservation Indians dwelled in a worldly paradise of interracial harmony. The reservations and Indian agents played a large role in the changes occurring in Native life, but the ability of Indians to reside and survive outside the realm of their authority diffused and weakened their influence. Ongoing Indian-white contact gave Heo and other Indian people access to a new set of weapons to defend their autonomy in the face of encroachments by white settlers and impositions by white officials.[75]

Chapter 3

JACK GHO V. CHARLEY JULLES
CONTACT AND TERRITORIAL LAW

In 1870, the justices of Washington's territorial supreme court sat in judgment on a peculiar case. The case involved a Snohomish Indian man called Charley Julles, one of the first Snohomish to begin logging on his own account, and a Chinese man named Jack Gho. Gho had worked as a cook in a logging camp run by Julles on the Tulalip Reservation. Gho claimed that Julles owed him $64.50 in back wages. Gho had won the case in the lower courts, but Julles had appealed the decision to the territory's highest court. He wanted the case thrown out because he was an Indian. He could not, he argued, make a legally binding contract so long as he maintained tribal relations and was under the charge of an Indian agent.[1]

The case is peculiar for a number of reasons. First, it pits members of two minority groups, both of which suffered discrimination at the hands of whites, against each other. Second, it involves an Indian claiming Indian identity as a way to wiggle out of a commitment to a worker he had hired. While Heo had used his participation in the white economy to present himself as a civilized and assimilated Indian who should be freed from the oversight of the Indian Department, Julles wanted to use the oversight of the Indian Department to present himself as a tribalized and dependent Indian who should be freed from the consequences of his participation in the white economy. Finally, the timing of the case adds to its peculiarity. The case occurred in the midst of a dramatic shift in the status of Indians under territorial law.

Ironically, Indians in Washington Territory found themselves more often in situations like Gho's than in positions like Julles's. Indians who worked for white employers frequently were unpaid or underpaid for their labor. Unlike Gho, however, Indians could not force the issue in the courts, at least during the first two decades of the territorial period. The territory's Civil Practice Act, passed for the first time in 1854, denied the competency of "Indians, or persons having more than one-half Indian blood" to testify as witnesses in civil cases to which a white person was a party. This restriction was included in the various reenactments of the Civil Practice Act between 1854 and 1873. Had Gho been white and not Chinese, Julles would not even have been able to confront him in a court of law.[2]

As a logger who was also a full-blooded Indian, Julles existed in a type of legal limbo. His business required him to make contracts for employment and for the sale of timber, but the law severely limited his ability to enforce performance of those contracts. If his transactions with whites went sour, he had to rely on other, nonlegal sanctions.

For most Indians, that meant turning to the officers of the Indian Department. Generally, the agents investigated the contract disputes and then tried to negotiate some kind of settlement. Gho's claim against Julles had, for example, been initially investigated by the agent for the Tulalip Reservation and rejected. When Gho went to court, the agent had recruited a lawyer to help Julles defend himself. The agent also testified in Julles's favor at the proceedings in district court.[3]

Most of the time, however, agents were trying to get money from defaulting white employers, not protecting Indians against disgruntled employees. Agent E. A. Starling commented on whites' disrespect for contracts made with Indians as early as 1853. During Thomas J. McKenny's tenure as superintendent of Indian affairs in the territory (1866–69 and 1870–72), he recorded a number of cases of defaulting white employers in his correspondence.[4]

On March 25, 1867, for example, McKenny wrote to Isaac Pincus, a settler residing at the town of Steilacoom, regarding a complaint lodged against Pincus by "Indian John." John stated that he had worked for Pincus in exchange for a cow and a calf worth about fifty dollars. Immediately after finishing the work, John got sick and went to Seattle. When he later demanded payment from Pincus, the settler offered him forty dollars in goods, which John refused. Prohibited from testifying against a white man in court, the Indian turned to McKenny. "I cannot believe that you wish to act otherwise than justly with 'John,'" McKenny wrote to Pincus. "I am sent here together with the Indian Agents to see that justice is done the Indians and therefore must insist on his rights." McKenny told Pincus that John would accept fifty dollars as a final settlement. He also warned of possible legal action, despite John's lack of standing in court. "John can substantiate his claim by white men if we are compelled to resort to the law," McKenny told Pincus.[5]

More dangerous to Indians than the law excluding them from civil proceedings was the accompanying criminal exclusion. Since the criteria for the competency of witnesses in civil proceedings also generally applied to criminal cases, the law barred Indians from testifying against whites in criminal cases as well. This exclusion allowed whites to beat and otherwise abuse Indians with little fear of punishment. In 1853, the Indian agent on Puget Sound commented that whites "easily avoid prosecution" for beating Indians "by doing it in the presence only of Indians, whose testimony in such cases is not admissible against a white."[6]

In 1858, when a grand jury investigated a soldier named John Crawley on suspicion of having killed an Indian named Goliah, Crawley escaped indictment because none of the white witnesses had seen the victim and the suspect together. A local newspaper interviewed several Indian acquaintances of the deceased, who stated that the two had gone up a hill together with a bottle of whiskey and that Goliah had in his possession several half dollars later found in the soldier's possession. "Of course," noted the newspaper, "Indian testimony could not be taken by the grand jury."[7]

Needless to say, Indians had no voice in the political process by which such laws might be changed. Indians could not vote, and since jury service generally followed the suffrage, they could not sit in judgment on cases involving other Indians, much less whites.

Taken together, the laws denying legal standing to Indians created an image of Indians as dishonest and unreliable. In addition, the laws expressed the idea that Indians were outside of and foreign to white society. As such, the law offered them little protection.

This idea, of course, completely ignored the social reality of Washington Territory. Indians were not outside of white society. They were integrated into white society by the porousness of reservation boundaries and their need to make a living. Julles presented a living refutation of the idea of separate societies.

The significant number of intermarriages between white men and Indian women offered a similar refutation. Historians most frequently associate cohabitation and marriage "in the Indian custom" between Indian women and white men with the Hudson's Bay Company traders, but it continued throughout the territorial period. As the creation of reservations had failed to end commercial contact between Indians and whites, it also failed to end personal contact.[8]

The territorial legislature quickly showed its disapproval of Indian-white intermarriage. In its second session, in 1855, the legislature passed the Color Act. The Color Act declared void all marriages "heretofore solemnized" between a white person and a person of "more than one-half Indian blood." It also decreed penalties for any clergyman or territorial official who solemnized such marriages after the passage of the act. In 1858, legislators amended the Color Act, replacing the word "heretofore" with the word "hereafter," thus voiding all future interracial marriages.[9]

Measures prohibiting the solemnization of marriage did not necessarily disturb interracial marriages "in the Indian custom"—those that had not been solemnized according to American legal requirements in the first place. There were also alternative avenues to legal marriage. Under the common law, "informal" marriage arrangements—such as those that characterized many Indian-white unions—had a long tradition of legality. Indeed, the territorial legislature itself had recognized this common-law tradition in its 1854 Act to Regulate Marriages. This act provided that "no marriage shall be void or voidable for the want of any formality required by law."[10]

By preventing the solemnization of interracial marriages, lawmakers probably had in mind the strategies of some Donation Act claimants to obtain larger parcels of land. When Congress enacted the Donation Law in 1850, it allowed single men 320 acres and married men 640 acres, with half of the latter acreage to be in the name of the wife. Anthropologist Marian Smith has asserted that, with few white women in the territory at the time, some donation claimants legally married Indian women to take advantage of the Donation Act's provisions. The Color Act made it extremely difficult for donation claimants to use this tactic successfully. The lack of solemnization also made it difficult for an Indian wife to inherit her husband's property or to sustain any claim on her white husband in the event of his future or past solemnized marriage to a white woman.[11]

Legislators followed up the Color Act with an even harsher measure. On January 20, 1866, the territorial legislature passed a new Marriage Act, replacing the Marriage Act of 1854. Rather than simply forbidding the solemnization of interracial marriages, the new act prohibited such marriages outright, denying them even the avenue of common-law legitimacy. It grouped marriage between whites and Indians (or those with one-half or more "Indian blood") and whites and blacks (or those with one-half or more "negro blood") with polygamy and consanguineous marriages.[12]

Such laws made race a central ordering principle of territorial society. Like the Stevens treaties, these laws set out to correct the blurring of racial lines that had occurred during the period of white settlement under the Donation Act. The separation of Indians and whites became a key part of the creation of a "civilized" society.

Legislative proscription, however, did not end Indian-white intermarriage. Several conflicts that grew out of these relationships during the 1860s and 1870s testified to the continuing existence of interracial unions. These conflicts serve as warnings against the romanticization of intermarriage. The parties often brought starkly different expectations to the relationship. A white man who paid money to a Native woman's family perceived that he was "buying" her, and that therefore he had a permanent proprietary right to her until he left her. For the Indians, the money was a gift exchange that formalized the marriage bond. If the marriage proved unsatisfactory, either party could dissolve it.[13]

In fact, several conflicts over such marriages resulted when Indian women left their white husbands and returned to their families. In 1864, for example, J. M. Smith, a white resident of Snohomish County, went to a neighboring Indian camp to retrieve "his" Indian woman. "Boys I want you to go and help get my *kloochman* [*woman*, in Chinook Jargon]," Smith told the two men who accompanied him. When he arrived at the camp, Smith apparently negotiated with the woman's father to secure her return to his household. This negotiation must have fallen through, for when Smith afterward tried to take the woman, he claimed that one of the other Indians present stabbed at him with "a knife or a stick." Smith then pulled his revolver and shot at the person who struck at him. This touched off a general gunfight between the whites who had accompanied Smith and several of the Indians, leaving one Indian dead.[14]

The threat of such violence prompted some Indian women who left their white husbands to seek the protection of the reservations and the Indian agents. In April 1868, for example, the physician at the Skokomish Reservation wrote to Superintendent McKenny for advice on such a case. A white man named Francis Roberts came to the reservation and filed a sworn statement that "he lived and cohabited with one Mary (an Indian woman) for a long time; that he loves her well enough to marry her," but that she recently "left his bed and board without cause or provocation." He accused her of stealing thirty dollars worth of blankets from him when she left, but said he would forgive the debt if she returned to live with him.

In his letter to the superintendent, the physician included Mary's answer to this statement. She admitted living with Roberts for two and a half years, during which time she cooked for him and four other men. He provided for her, but "at times he was jealous of her and beat her unmercifully so that five times she left him, . . . but each time returned . . . upon his promising to never repeat such conduct." Roberts never lived up to his promises, Mary stated. Life with him became "unbearable." He beat her with sticks and threatened her life. She denied taking the blankets and vowed never to return to Roberts.[15]

The superintendent responded swiftly. "It is my object to discourage Indian women living with white men," he wrote the physician. "In this case it seems that she has been cruelly beaten by him a number of times and she therefore refuses to return to him. You will therefore give him to understand that she is under our protection and that he cannot take her." As for the blankets, the superintendent ruled that even if Mary had taken them, they should be considered as payment owed for her years of service to Roberts.[16]

Agents in western Washington often noted complaints by Indian men that white men "stole" their women. Thus an official of the Puyallup Reservation stated in 1863 that a white man named Williams had "taken an Indians [sic] wife from him." Williams had lived with her off the reservation, but now she had returned to the reservation and Williams persisted in paying her visits, much to the annoyance of the other Indians. "I have twice notified him to keep off of the reserve," the official noted, "and not create a disturbance among the Indians, but I learn he continues to come here."[17]

How such "stealing" took place is not clear. Most probably, "stealing" meant that the white man had not offered an appropriate gift to the woman's family and instead made offers directly to the woman in question. Alternatively, if the woman was a slave, "stealing" might have been meant literally—the taking of property without compensation.

The mixed-race children of Indian-white unions could also cause friction if those unions turned sour. Skokomish Agent Eells faced charges of assault with a deadly weapon in 1873 for threatening to shoot one Jack Wilson, a white man who came upon the reservation to take his two-year-old child from his former wife, who was Indian. The woman had moved onto the reservation under Eells's promise of protection after she had complained to him that Wilson beat her. The district judge acquitted Eells of the charge, but Eells reported in his autobiography that the woman eventually went back to live with Wilson.[18]

While the laws targeting intermarriage did not end the practice, they did have some effect. Specifically, they made the cohabitation of Indians and whites vulnerable to criminal prosecution under the laws prohibiting adultery and fornication. Since such cohabitation could not be solemnized as legal marriage, the burden of proof was shifted from the prosecutors to the defendants, who now had to show that they intended to live as husband and wife under the common law.

During the entire territorial period, the district courts heard eighty-five adultery and fornication cases; at least thirty-seven of these, or 44 percent, involved the cohabitation of white men and Indian women. Generally, the indictment specified that the female in question was an Indian woman not legally married to the defendant. These prosecutions, which occurred in batches throughout the territorial period and on both sides of the mountains, appeared to be legal harassments more than any serious effort to enforce the sexual morality statutes. They almost uniformly ended in dismissals, and it appears that none of the defendants went to jail. Table 2 indicates the number of cases prosecuted at different times during the period, the counties in which the cases arose, and whether those counties are east or west of the Cascades.[19]

Jack Gho v. Charley Julles

TABLE 2

Adultery and Fornication Prosecutions

Involving White Men and Indian Women

Indictment Date	County	East or West of Cascades	No. of defts
4 Feb. 1854	Thurston	West	7
16 Nov. 1854	Thurston	West	1
29 Oct. 1856	King	West	2
12 Sept. 1861	Thurston	West	3
21 Oct. 1867	Walla Walla	East	2
11 June 1874	Stevens	East	7
14 Sept. -1877	Clallam	West	3
12 Nov. 1878	Snohomish	West	3
5 Dec. 1878	Whatcom	West	9

The fastest way for a man to get a charge of adultery or fornication dropped was either to marry the woman or to stop cohabiting with her. Under territorial law, the first option was closed, so these prosecutions doubtless forced some white men to "put away" their Indian wives.

Even after invalidating or prohibiting white-Indian intermarriage, the legislature still had to deal with the legacy of such marriages: a large population having mixed parentage. This population raised a number of ticklish legal issues. For instance, did they have inheritance rights, given the strictures against Indian-white marriage in the Color Act and the Marriage Act of 1866?

The 1854 Marriage Act had declared legitimate children whose parents were "cohabiting together, as man and wife." Thus, despite the passage of the Color Act the next year, mixed-race children could claim inheritance rights under this law, even though their parents' union had never been solemnized. In 1894, five years after Washington achieved statehood, the federal circuit court endorsed this same position when reviewing the claim of a mixed-race child to the estate of her white father. Although rejecting evidence that the claimant's parents had ever entered into a legal marriage, the judge in the case found that they did cohabit together, and thus ruled in favor of the claimant.[20]

The passage of the 1866 prohibition against interracial marriage clearly jeopardized the standing of mixed-race children because it denied the common-law legitimacy of cohabitation. The legislature tried to avert this consequence of the 1866 Marriage Act by passing at the same time a provision declaring legitimate all the children of Indian-white marriages "heretofore entered into or solemnized . . . in accordance with the forms of law." Given the legal restrictions on solemnization, the generosity of this act is highly questionable, but it appears to represent an effort to guarantee the inheritance rights of mixed-race children before the prohibition on interracial unions went into effect.[21]

The second clause of the Legitimacy Act of 1866 watered down whatever generous intent the first clause contained. The second clause barred mixed-race children from inheritance if children from a previous marriage existed. The concern of the legislature was quite clear; numerous settlers had left wives and families in the states when they moved out to Washington Territory. Some of these men had then taken Indian women as wives and fathered children. The legislature clearly intended to privilege the children of a first marriage—to a white woman, most likely—over the mixed-race children from a second, barely legitimate marriage to an Indian woman.[22]

The mixed-race population thus occupied an ambiguous legal position. They were often spared the full impact of the exclusionary legislation aimed at Indians, but they rarely escaped it completely. Indeed, almost immediately, lawmakers subjected mixed-race people to cultural "tests" to determine their appropriate place within a racialized social system that emphasized the differences between Indians and whites. The Donation Act, for example, allowed "American half-breed Indians," who were either American citizens or declared their intention to become American citizens, to take advantage of its provisions.[23]

A territorial election law passed during the 1865–66 legislative session granted suffrage to "all American half-breeds" over twenty-one who "hold land under the donation law and who can read and write and have adopted the habits of the whites." Over time, the legislature dropped the land-holding requirement and the literacy requirement, requiring only the adoption of "the habits of the whites." By 1887, the election law specified that both male and female "half-breeds," as with whites of both genders, had the right to vote. Women, however, again lost the suffrage in Washington just prior to statehood. Since jury service generally followed

Jack Gho v. Charley Julles

from the right of suffrage, mixed-race electors who followed "civilized habits" probably served on juries.[24]

The case of *Jack Gho v. Charley Julles*, occurring within a legal context marked by severe restrictions on Indians' rights, threw into relief the contradiction between these race-based exclusions and Indians' involvement in the wider territorial economy and society. Julles's legal strategy attempted to use both the segregationism of territorial law and the image created by the territorial statutes to escape from the obligations he had incurred as a result of that involvement.

In response to the legislators' intent to keep Indians separated from white society, Julles challenged the authority of white courts over his actions. At both the justice court and district court levels, Julles demurred to Gho's complaint on jurisdictional grounds. The demurrer alleged that the court had no legal capacity to enforce contracts made by Indians. "Unless it affirmatively appears from the complaint that he [Julles] has separated from his tribal relations the Court has no jurisdiction of his person either civilly or criminally except when criminal offences are committed against citizens," the demurrer stated. Both the justice of the peace and the district judge overruled the demurrer, however, allowing the case to proceed to the jury.[25]

Unlike the lower courts, the territorial supreme court left behind a written decision that revealed its reasoning for rejecting Julles's argument. The court accepted that Julles, as an Indian, was an alien. But as an alien, the court said, Julles had the same rights to contract as "an Englishman, or a Spaniard, or a Dane. . . . The right to contract draws after it, necessarily, the right and liability to be sued." The court conveniently ignored the legal prohibition on Indian testimony, a prohibition to which other aliens were not subject.[26]

Julles's second line of defense played upon the image of Indians imprinted in white law. How could a member of such a dependent and irresponsible race be expected to live up to contractual obligations? Julles argued that he could not, an argument that relied not on the territorial statutes but on an 1847 federal law. This law declared null and void all executory contracts made with Indians for the delivery of money or goods. Congress had passed it to protect Indians from the sharp practices of white traders, who had frequently gotten Indians to sign away large quantities of money or goods received as treaty payments.[27]

The territorial supreme court, however, construed the law very narrowly. It stated that an examination of the entire statute in question showed that Congress had intended to limit contracts made by Indians only for money or goods delivered pursuant to treaty with the United States. It thus aimed to control Indians' disposal of annuity payments. "The whole purview of the section is, to promote the happiness and prosperity of the Indians, by preventing the diversion of the money or goods from proper usefulness, in frivolous or anticipatory expenditure," the court stated.

The statute did not exempt Indians from making contracts respecting individually held money or goods, the court continued, although the justices failed to explain why Indians could be trusted with their own funds but not with treaty monies. "This law, intended to fill a specific, plain, and beneficent purpose, is not to be perverted to work the Indian disadvantage. Engagements of future performance and of future payment, every business man finds an every day necessity. Does this law intend that the Indian, the moment he attempts to enter upon the pursuits that occupy the attention of our race, shall be stopped on the threshold, the door shut in his face?" To interpret the statute in that fashion, the court stated, would leave the Indian "walled up in barbarism."[28]

Jack Gho v. Charley Julles caught the territorial supreme court in the contradictions inherent in trying to keep Indians legally segregated. Julles's "civilized behavior," in the form of his participation in the territory's growing lumber economy, required him to have standing in court, like any other "alien." At the same time, according to several statutes, his racial status denied him such standing. The court refused to confront that contradiction head on, for to do so would have challenged the racial order constructed by the territorial legislature. Instead, the court contented itself with ordering Julles to pay Gho the wages owed him.

Ironically, even as the court presided over *Jack Gho v. Charley Julles*, that same racial order was crumbling. It crumbled partly because of events like the Julles case, which starkly revealed the differences between the social reality of ongoing Indian-white contact and the prescriptive picture of territorial society painted in the law books. But the final blow came from the dramatic upheaval in national legal culture caused by the Civil

War. During the last two decades of the territorial period, in the wake of the postwar laws and amendments passed to protect the civil rights of the freed slaves, territorial lawmakers abolished many of the race-based denials of civil rights affecting Indians. Federal officials continued to lament the porousness of reservation boundaries, but territorial legislators had begun to acknowledge this and to regulate its consequences.

The 1866 act outlawing intermarriage, for example, survived only two years. An 1868 amendment struck the racial exclusion clause from the legislation. In the years after 1868, no legal restrictions existed on the race of the parties to a marriage.[29]

In fact, there appeared a growing tolerance of Indian-white marriages in the later territorial period. The emphasis shifted from trying to combat such unions to making sure they met standards of respectability, which included encouraging "squaw men" to solemnize their marriages to their Indian wives. "I could approve of a man marrying one [an Indian woman]," wrote Superintendent Thomas McKenny in 1867, after receiving a complaint about an agency employee living with an Indian woman, "but not living in an open state of adultery." Similarly, when asked in 1871 whether it was permissible to hire an employee with an Indian wife, McKenny wrote that he had no objection "provided that he [the employee] is lawfully married and is trying to live as a christian."[30]

According to the diary of a settler on Orcas Island, one of the San Juan islands, in the 1870s District Court Judge Joseph R. Lewis ordered whites living with Indian women to marry the women and assign them one-third of their property or face legal sanctions. Indeed, the adultery and fornication prosecutions in Clallam, Snohomish, and Whatcom Counties in the late 1870s may have resulted from Lewis's threat.[31]

In 1879, District Court Judge Roger Greene ruled on a batch of adultery indictments in Whatcom County charging a group of white men with cohabitation with Indian women. One of the defendants challenged the indictment on common-law grounds. He had been cohabiting with an Indian woman (unnamed in the indictment) since 1857 and argued that they lived together "as man and wife." In ruling on the motion, Judge Greene took the opportunity to review the legislation regarding Indian-white unions. Greene concluded that, with the exception of the 1866–68 interlude, Indian-white marriages had never been legally invalid. Greene argued that a marriage contract preceded and trumped recognition of the contract by the state. He thus maintained that the Color Act of 1855 had never meant to disturb interracial marriages; it only proscribed particular forms of solemnization. "The solemnization of marriage is one thing, the contract of marriage is another," he wrote. To read the statutes any other way constituted "an overthrow of the common law," Greene said, and "a change of such sweeping consequence" should "not be judged effected without it is made obvious in the body of the law."[32]

Greene's rather benign reading of the intent of the 1855 law reflected more the new tolerance for Indian-white unions than the true motivations of the lawmakers, but his ruling had very visible results on the case before him. Under Greene's reading of the marriage statutes, the defendants in the case were all legally married under the common law, despite the lack of ceremony and despite the Color Act's strictures. Immediately after the judge's ruling, the prosecutor dropped the cases against the defendants.[33]

The growing tolerance of intermarriage represented an admission that the practice had continued despite the legislature's designs. Federal census manuscripts document the continuing existence of interracial households. The 1880 federal census for Clallam County, for example, listed fifteen households headed by a white man living with an Indian or mixed-race woman. These households contained a total population of sixty-five people. The enumerator also listed four other households containing at least one mixed-race inhabitant. The total population of the county in 1880 was 638.[34]

Territorial censuses also provided evidence of intermarriage. Territorial enumerators counted "taxable Indian half-breeds," including in this category Indian women living with white men and any households with mixed-race children or adults. For example, the 1871 census for Stevens County, in the northeast corner of the territory, showed 36 mixed-race households out of a total of 182 households.[35]

The table below provides 1883 and 1887 census data for Island County—made up of Whidbey and Camano Islands in Puget Sound—showing the three types of mixed-race households found in the census (table 3). The 1887 census also enumerated separately seventy-eight individuals listed as "taxable half-breeds." These individuals, listed separately from the households, indicate the presence of an off-reservation Indian camp, where both full-blooded and mixed-race Indians probably resided.

Jack Gho v. Charley Julles

TABLE 3
Mixed-Race Households, Island County

Type of Household	1883	1887
White man living with Indian or mixed-race woman	19	14
White man or Indian/mixed-race woman living with Indian/mixed-race children	7	2
Mixed-race man living with white or mixed-race woman	2	1

Source: *Washington Territorial Census Rolls*, 1883 and 1887 manuscript censuses.

Ongoing contact between whites and Indians in the economic sphere explains some of the motivations behind intermarriage. Historians have viewed intermarriage during the fur trade era as a way for traders to gain access to Indian kinship networks necessary for trading success. Indian women provided a necessary linkage between the traders and the larger Indian community. This commercial linkage may have also proved valuable to those whites who engaged in the Indian trade during the territorial period. The liquor trade—one prevalent form of commercial contact between whites and Indians—provides one way to trace those linkages. Of the thirty-seven whites indicted for adultery or fornication with Indian women, five at some point also faced charges of selling liquor to Indians. Kinship linkages provided by their Indian wives may have given them valuable access to their customers.[36]

A narrow commercial view of interracial unions, however, does not give full play to the range of human emotions and motivations in these relationships. Many of these unions proved relatively long-lasting; inheritance cases dating from the early statehood period showed that some interracial unions lasted for several years. The desire for companionship, intimacy, and affection had as much to do with interracial marriage as did perceptions of commercial opportunity. These elements explain why William Butler, a resident of Centerville in Snohomish County, left his entire estate upon his death to his "Indian woman Ann Peish."[37]

The prohibitions on Indian testimony in civil and criminal cases also fell away in the aftermath of the Civil War. In 1869, territorial lawmakers had allowed Indians to testify against whites accused of selling liquor to Indians. But in 1873 lawmakers went further, stripping the Indian exclusion out of the Civil Practice Act when they reenacted it that year. Because the Criminal Practice Act retained its provision that witnesses competent in civil cases were competent in criminal cases, and given the liberalized provisions of the Civil Practice Act, Indians could now testify in criminal cases.[38]

The 1875 murder prosecution of John Keefe, John Lewis, Thomas Knight, and John Matthews gave these liberalized provisions a dramatic test. A Port Townsend justice of the peace bound over the four men to district court when they failed to come up with $1,000 bail on a charge of second-degree murder for the killing of an unnamed Haida Indian man in May 1875.[39] On June 2, 1875, the four men petitioned for a writ of habeas corpus to Territorial District Court Judge Joseph R. Lewis. They contested the legality of their imprisonment, they stated, because "the petitioners are white men, and no evidence was given . . . implicating these petitioners as the guilty persons, except by witnesses who are North American Indians."[40]

At the hearing on the petition, the defendants' lawyer argued that the Criminal Practice Act explicitly authorized Indian testimony only in cases involving other Indians or in liquor prosecutions. By explicitly allowing Indian testimony only in these cases, the law implied that Indian testimony was invalid in nonliquor cases with white defendants. The judge insisted, to the contrary, that the statute had to be read in a wider context. "It is a part of the fundamental law of the land as now declared by the Courts 'that all men are equal before the law,'" Lewis stated. That insight had not "been discovered" in previous enactments of the criminal and civil practice acts, which barred "Indians, Negroes, and Chinamen" from testifying.

But, Lewis stated, territorial lawmakers had rectified the exclusion of the latter two groups in 1869, and following the enactment of the federal civil rights law in 1870, had stricken all racial exclusions from the Civil Practice Act in 1873. The elimination of the exclusion in the Civil Practice Act meant a similar elimination in criminal practice. "The modern tendency of Legislation is to permit every person to testify, leaving to the jury to determine as to the credibility of the witnesses," the judge said. "Looking at the whole Statute there is no doubt that our Legislature intended to remedy the mischievous provisions of our Statute making distinctions on account of race and color, and make our laws accord with

Jack Gho v. Charley Julles

the laws of the United States, and with the civilization of the age in which we live."[41] Lewis denied the habeas corpus petition and remanded the defendants into custody. Ultimately, however, the case followed the pattern of other prosecutions of white men charged with killing Indians. On September 16, 1875, the grand jury did not return an indictment against the defendants and they went free.[42]

From his position on the bench, Judge Lewis was instrumental in promulgating the changes brought forth by the Fourteenth Amendment and related legislation. Lewis was one of a number of Republican appointees who served relatively long terms as territorial judges. Appointed in 1872 to the First District, Lewis served seven years. His colleague, Roger Greene, appointed two years before Lewis to the Second District, served an extraordinary seventeen years. Both men brought the legal ideology of the post–Civil War Republican Party to the territorial district courts.

Lewis continually admonished jurors that all men were now equal before the law, but the very frequency of those warnings suggests that popular bias against Indian testimony remained high. Indeed, in an 1874 prosecution of a mixed-race man for murder, the court excused several jurors who refused to accept Indian testimony.[43]

The legal upheaval caused by the Fourteenth Amendment also raised broader questions of Indians' participation in white society. The legal capacities of Indians to own land, to vote, and to become citizens were all open questions in the aftermath of the Civil War, not just in Washington but across the nation.

Within Washington, Julles had presented the territorial supreme court with the logical consequences of viewing Indians as separate from and inferior to white society —they could not be held liable for freely contracted obligations. The court ultimately rejected this logic but not before it hinted at a way around it. In its decision, the court suggested that perhaps Julles was not what he claimed to be. Did Julles really live under "tribal relations"? He did not behave like a tribal Indian "should" behave. His participation in the white economy led the court to question whether he should truly be counted as an Indian. "There might be a question," the court said, "whether the fact of the political condition of the appellant, relied on by him to show lack of jurisdiction, so appears in the record before us."[44]

The court had to let the matter go, as both parties to the case agreed that Julles was an Indian belonging to the Snohomish Tribe. But in the years to come, the distinction suggested by the court between tribal and nontribal Indians came to have increasing importance. Federal officials made a similar distinction when they categorized Indians as "civilized" or "uncivilized," which they began to do more often during the 1870s. Civilized Indians were deemed to have "severed their tribal ties," living off reservation and earning their living in accordance with "white ways." Uncivilized Indians, by contrast, maintained their tribal relations and lived on reservations under the tutelage of a federal agent.[45]

Like other attempts to define Indian identity, these new categories were also largely fictions. Indians like Julles demonstrated that an individual could be a member of a tribe while engaging in behavior that appeared civilized and therefore nontribal, according to these standards. Only within the context of white law did there necessarily exist a distinction between integration into the white economy and Indian identity, conceived as tribal and therefore uncivilized.

After the passage of the Fourteenth Amendment, questions quickly arose over whether civilized Indians should be accorded the rights of citizens. The large number of Indians living and working off the reservations made these questions especially germane in Washington. For his part, Washington's superintendent of Indian affairs, Robert Milroy, interpreted the Fourteenth Amendment in a very broad manner. Milroy took his cue from a ruling of the secretary of the interior in 1870 that the Fourteenth Amendment allowed civilized Indians—that is, those who had severed their tribal ties and renounced all treaty benefits—to make land entries under the homestead and preemption laws. Acting under the terms of this declaration, Milroy began encouraging Indians to take out the necessary papers forswearing allegiance to their tribes and to apply for homestead claims.[46]

Milroy also began conferring citizenship certificates—of Milroy's own design—on the Indians under his charge who severed their tribal relations and took out homestead entries. In a letter to the commissioner of Indian affairs, he wrote that a number of Indians had come to him asking to obtain such citizenship certificates without filing a homestead claim. Milroy stated that he thought the Indians should have this right, but could not locate the relevant legislation. "I had supposed that as a matter of course when an Indian dissolved his tribal relations, and solemnly renounced all treaty rights and benefits, in the manner prescribed by law, that being a native born, he at once became fully 'enfranchised with all the rights, privileges and responsibilities of a citizen,'" Milroy explained.[47]

Territorial law also began to draw distinctions between civilized (or nontribal) and uncivilized (or tribal) Indians. In an 1869 tax law, the territorial legislature implicitly recognized the existence of a group of civilized Indians. Five years earlier, legislators had exempted from tax "the property of all Indians." In the 1869 reenactment of the revenue provisions, however, lawmakers replaced this simple declaration with a provision exempting "the property of all Indians who are not citizens, except land held by them by purchase." The law thus acknowledged the existence both of "citizen Indians" and of noncitizen Indians who had purchased property.[48]

Territorial laws regarding suffrage also showed the impact of the civil rights revolution touched off by the Civil War. The territorial Organic Act had granted the suffrage only to white male inhabitants. By 1866, the provisions had been liberalized to include the civilized portion of the mixed-race population, but still excluded "full-blooded" Indians. In 1873, the legislators passed a curious amendment to the Criminal Practice Act, making it an "offense against public policy" to "induce, or attempt to induce, any Indian to vote." The act provided, however, "that this section shall not be so construed, as to include Indians, who are citizens and entitled to vote under the amendments to the constitution of the United States and the laws of Congress." The provision thus recognized that some Indians were entitled to vote, which prevented legislators from passing a straightforward racial prohibition against Indian voting.[49]

The 1873 law grew out of concerns that white politicians padded their vote counts by recruiting "unqualified" Indians to come to the polls. As officials began distinguishing between civilized and uncivilized Indians, it became easier for politicians to utilize such tactics. Evidence clearly indicates that in the immediate aftermath of the Civil War, some Indians in Washington Territory voted in local elections. In 1871, for example, the *Olympia Transcript* criticized certain "lamentable instances of political imbecility, as the attempts to bring in Indian votes, which was done at our last election at Neah Bay, and several other points." The

Transcript cited a recent federal court decision in Oregon that ruled that "Indians are not citizens, are not included in the 14th amendment, and have no right to vote." Two years later, however, another instance of such "political imbecility" occurred in the election for Clark County auditor. The loser in this election contested the result because of the presence of Indian voters.[50]

If voting rights, citizenship, homesteading privileges and the various other freedoms attending full membership in American society hinged on the adoption of "civilized habits," then substantial numbers of Indians in Washington met those criteria. But a series of judicial and administrative rulings soon closed down this reading of the Fourteenth Amendment and the postwar civil rights laws. The contested election in Clark County, for example, came before Washington Territorial District Court Judge Greene in 1873. Greene ruled that an Indian who severed his tribal ties did not automatically become a citizen of the United States. Citizenship required a positive act of naturalization by the United States, Greene stated, not solely a forswearing of tribal allegiance by an individual Indian. In addition, Greene ruled that no tribal Indians were included under the Fourteenth Amendment, nor could a tribal Indian become a naturalized citizen. "The great point reached by this decision is the closing of the ballot box to the unwashed Indian," the *Puget Sound Daily Courier* reported.[51]

Greene's decision perturbed Superintendent Milroy. If Greene was correct in his view of the law, Milroy stated, "I have misunderstood my duty, and the rights of the Indians in the premises." He would have to recall the certificates of citizenship heretofore issued, he told the commissioner of Indian affairs, "and remand the poor Indians back to barbarism." The commissioner instructed Milroy that he could not confer citizenship upon Indians, but he could certify the dissolution of their tribal relations, thus allowing them to take advantage of the homestead and preemption laws.[52]

But the Interior Department's reading of the Fourteenth Amendment was soon overturned as well. In 1874, Interior Secretary Columbus Delano overruled his predecessor's view that the amendment gave civilized Indians any rights under the land laws. Delano ruled that only a separate act of Congress could confer the benefits of the land laws on the Indians, as they had not been deemed citizens when the laws were passed, and

Jack Gho v. Charley Julles

Congress had not intended the Fourteenth Amendment to confer such benefits on them.[53]

This put Milroy in a ticklish position. On March 23, 1874, Milroy wrote that Delano's decision rendered the land claims taken out by Indians under his encouragement vulnerable to white claim jumpers, and he urged that existing Indian claims be grandfathered. On March 3, 1875, Congress did extend homestead benefits to Indians who severed their tribal relations and confirmed any prior homestead entries that conformed to the rules of the General Land Office.[54]

These rulings made it difficult, but not impossible, for individual Indians to secure their civil rights under American law. More significantly, the debates and decisions regarding the exercise of those rights by so-called civilized or nontribal Indians amounted to a tacit recognition of Indians' continuing presence in territorial society. Legislative objectives shifted from excluding Indians from white society to regulating and controlling that Indian presence. To this end, Indians gained legal standing and some recognition of their individual property rights, but they were still denied full equality as citizens. Of course, gaining such rights required them to abjure their tribal allegiances. The postwar decades thus saw the simultaneous incorporation and marginalization of Indians in white society.

Nowhere is this marginalization more visible than in the area of police powers. The territorial legislature passed several laws in the last decades of the period that targeted Indians as a particular social problem. So at the same time that territorial legislators acknowledged that some Indians could be taxed, could vote, and could be citizens, they passed new legislation aimed at more strictly controlling Indian behavior.

In 1881, for example, the legislature made it illegal for any person to sell or furnish an Indian with "any poisonous drug, or compound, destructive of human or animal life." Besides Indians, the legislature included minors, intoxicated persons, and those of unsound mind in the list of prohibited buyers. The same year saw passage of a provision forbidding "every white man, negro, half-breed Indian, Kanaka or Chinaman" to play any "game of chance" with an Indian or to "run horses on a wager" with any Indian.[55]

These laws reflected whites' perceptions that Indians presented a public-order problem. They sought not to punish Indians directly, but rather those who facilitated Indians' disorderly activities, either by gambling with them or furnishing them with the means (poison) to achieve malevolent ends. In this, these laws followed the pattern set by the most enduring of the police power regulations affecting Indians—the liquor laws.

Laws prohibiting the sale or trading of liquor to Indians have been part of Euro-American legal codes since the colonial period. The Washington territorial legislature passed its own prohibition in 1855. The law forbade any person, white or Indian, from selling, giving, bartering, or otherwise distributing liquor to any Indian within the territory. The territorial statute shared jurisdiction with the existing prohibition under federal law. Congress had prohibited sales of liquor to Indians under the Indian Intercourse Act of 1834, which was extended over Washington with the creation of the territory.[56]

The territorial and federal laws partook of the same set of assumptions, however: Indians were assumed to be dangerous when drunk, so they had to be denied access to alcohol in the interest of public safety. Moreover, it was thought that Indians had no control over their appetites for alcohol. Like minors and habitual drunkards, to whom territorial law also prohibited sales of alcohol, Indians were protected from their presumably insatiable desires for liquor.[57]

The later passage of statutes forbidding the sale of poison to Indians and forbidding gambling with Indians manifested similar concerns about public order. All these laws helped to maintain racial boundaries within the territory following the demise of the absolute legal exclusion of Indians. Adult whites were not subject to such restrictions because they could be trusted to master their appetites. Moreover, as these public-order laws made no reference to "civilized" or "uncivilized" Indians, they made clear that Indians could not acculturate their way out of such restrictions.

Race thus remained an important social category for territorial lawmakers, although in the last decades of the period it began to take on increasingly complex shadings. Indians were no longer viewed as absolutely foreign to and outside white society—they could initiate lawsuits and testify against whites in court; they could legally marry whites; they could own property and pay taxes. But no matter how "civilized" they became, they could not escape lawmakers' perception of them as a disorderly and regrettable presence in white society.

Chapter 4

UNITED STATES V. CHARLES VOGELSONG

FEDERAL LIQUOR LAWS AND RACIAL IDENTITY

When Congress created Washington Territory, it extended over it the federal Indian Intercourse Act, a key provision of which barred the sale of liquor to Indians. As one of the first exercises of its police power, the territorial legislature passed a similar prohibition. These laws drew a sharp racial line between those who could "hold their liquor" and those who could not. The very definition of the crime depended on the racial identity of the liquor buyer, as it was not illegal to sell or dispose of liquor to whites or to other non-Indians. Like reservation boundaries that confined Indians and territorial statutes that denied them standing in court, these laws made clear distinctions between Indians and the rest of territorial society.

Like these other enactments, the liquor laws ran headlong into the social reality of territorial Washington, where these clear distinctions dissolved into blurry smears. Owing to the porousness of reservation boundaries, the integration of Indians into the territorial economy, and intermarriage, exactly who was an Indian and what Indian identity meant was often not at all clear. Heo and Julles had tried to shape the legal meaning of Indian to suit their own purposes. Charles Vogelsong, a white man indicted under the Intercourse Act, flirted with an even more fundamental challenge to the territorial racial order, denying the notion that any reasonable distinction could be made between a white man and an Indian.

In many ways, Vogelsong's case resembled many others that came before the United States District Court in Seattle during its February

1889 term. The indictment charged Vogelsong with selling liquor to an Indian named George Henry in the town of Slaughter on September 9, 1888, in violation of Section 20 of the federal Indian Intercourse Act. Twenty similar cases appeared on the docket for the February term. Vogelsong pleaded not guilty.[1]

As initially passed by Congress in 1834, Section 20 had made it a crime to "sell, exchange, or give, barter, or dispose of, any spirituous liquor or wine to an Indian, (in the Indian country)," or to introduce liquor into Indian country. Federal policy sought to make the boundary between Indian country and the rest of the nation impermeable, and Section 20 penalized the whiskey seller's violation of that boundary.[2]

In 1862, Congress had amended the Intercourse Act, vastly expanding its scope. The amended statute prohibited the sale or trading of intoxicants to any Indian under the charge of an appointed agent or superintendent, whether the transaction took place inside or outside Indian country. This "radical change," as Oregon jurist Matthew Deady described it, extended federal jurisdiction beyond the boundaries of the reservations, and the federal liquor law followed Indians—and the whites who might sell them intoxicants—wherever they might go. The town of Slaughter, where the transaction took place between Vogelsong and Henry, lay some twenty-five miles south of Seattle, between the Puyallup and Muckleshoot Reservations, but outside the boundaries of both.[3]

In amending the act, Congress had taken heed of the complaints of the Indian Department that restricting the act to Indian country allowed whiskey sellers to set up shop just outside reservation boundaries and ply their wares. The amendment constituted one of the first acknowledgments by Congress that the supposedly enforceable boundaries between Indian country and the rest of the nation were in fact quite weak, and it sanctioned a sharp departure from existing federal Indian policy. In the area of criminal law, for example, Congress had never extended federal jurisdiction outside of Indian country.[4]

Given the porousness of reservation boundaries in Washington, the 1862 amendment had a direct effect on enforcement patterns in the territory. By the early 1860s, the agents' reports stated that the on-reservation liquor traffic had been largely stamped out, but that the "liquor problem" remained as troublesome as ever. In 1859, for example, the subagent in charge of the Puyallup Reservation reported that "although we have been

United States v. Charles Vogelsong

successful in stopping the whisky traffic, so far as to prevent its being brought on to the reservations, still those of the Indians who are so inclined, obtain liquor at a distance from the reservation." In fact, most of the infractions in the district court case files occurred, like Vogelsong's, off the reservations.[5]

Most of the cases also occurred, like Vogelsong's, in counties west of the Cascades. Some 83 percent of prosecutions originated in this area, primarily in Jefferson, King, Pierce, and Thurston Counties. Offenses occurring in these four counties accounted for 60 percent of all liquor offenses during the territorial period. This high proportion indicates more than enforcement bias. The liquor traffic was probably heaviest here. The bulk of the white population lived in this area; population densities exceeded those in the sprawling eastern portion of the territory; and off-reservation contact between whites and Indians was more regular and intense in the west.

Vogelsong's case was also typical in other ways. Nearly half the total number of prosecutions occurred, like his, during the 1880s. That is hardly surprising, given the explosive growth in population during the final decade before statehood; the total population went from 75,116 in 1880 to 357,252 in 1890. The 1870s accounted for nearly a quarter of all cases, with the remainder spread among the first two decades of the territory's existence.

Vogelsong could have been prosecuted under the territorial statute forbidding the sale of alcohol to Indians. Since territorial law punished the offense only as a misdemeanor, no doubt Vogelsong would have preferred trial under territorial law. Indeed, territorial jurisdiction typically picked up—and federal jurisdiction left off—at the reservation borders. But the 1862 amendment of the Intercourse Act had subjected liquor transactions with Indians outside of Indian country to overlapping federal and territorial jurisdiction.[6]

The Indian agents' reports make clear that prosecution in the federal side of the territorial courts was the most common avenue of legal action. Vogelsong, like most liquor defendants, therefore faced federal prosecution. From a survey of the records of two justice court precincts in Seattle, it appears that the territorial law was not rigorously enforced. Out of 2,393 total cases heard by justices of the peace in one Seattle precinct between 1877 and 1887, for example, there were just 34 prosecutions for violating the territorial liquor law. In a second Seattle precinct, justices heard a total of 505 cases between 1885 and 1887. Twenty-four of these cases involved violations of the liquor ordinance. John Wunder's study of justice courts in Washington Territory does not even mention enforcement of the territorial liquor ordinance.[7]

By contrast, people devoted substantial amounts of time and money to the enforcement of the federal law. Although these efforts did not put a stop to the liquor traffic, that the law did not simply lie idle on the books is indicated by the sheer volume of cases that came before the district courts. In the thirty-seven-year history of the territory, the district courts heard 708 liquor cases, and the large majority of these (97 percent) were prosecutions under the federal Intercourse Act. Liquor-law prosecutions made up just over 10 percent of the total criminal caseload of the district courts during the territorial period. They constituted the third most common of all types of felony prosecution, behind violent assault and larceny/fraud cases.[8]

Vogelsong's case, then, was hardly unique. District court judges dispensed with a large number of liquor cases at almost every term of court. But the differences between territorial and federal enforcement suggest that perhaps not all territorial residents shared the official concern about Indian drinking manifested in the laws. Indeed, over the course of the territorial period, one even sees a substantial change in the pattern of enforcement of the federal act. Enforcement, as measured by conviction rates, showed a substantial improvement over time. If Vogelsong had been tried in the 1860s instead of the 1880s, his chances for acquittal would have improved dramatically.

Table 4 summarizes the outcomes of liquor cases over the entire period.[9] These general trends in enforcement, however, hide significant differences between the early and late territorial periods. In the years between 1850 and 1865 nonconviction rates in liquor cases hovered around 80 percent. Conflicts between settlers and law enforcement officials, similar to conflicts that historians have noted in other parts of the United States, hampered prosecutions during these years. Among "a certain class of settlers" in the territory, wrote Henry Webster, the agent for the Makah Indians in 1862, "a morbid sympathy with the whiskey seller" prevailed. These settlers "think it no harm to sell an Indian anything he can pay for."[10]

TABLE 4
Washington Territory Liquor Cases in Which Final Disposition Is Known

Initial Disposition	No. of cases		% of total	
Total dismissed	13		2.3	
Dismissed by magistrate		4		0.7
Dismissed by prosecutor		9		1.6
Total brought to district court	560		97.7	
Presented via information		18		3.1
Presented to grand jury		542		94.6
TOTAL	573		100	
Final Disposition of Grand Jury Cases	No. of cases		% of total (573)	
Total true bills	462		80.7	
Convictions		174		30.4
Guilty pleas		135		23.6
Acquitted by jury		66		11.5
Other discharge		87		15.2

This "morbid sympathy" allowed liquor dealers to operate largely unimpeded. Just as early territorial statutes had placed Indians outside the protection of the law, so did lax enforcement of the liquor statutes. One accused liquor seller, listed simply as Fogerty, boasted in 1862 "that he has no fear of the soldiers or of the authorities . . . [that] there is no government, that he is habitually intemperate; also . . . that he will sell liquor when and where he pleases to the Indians or any one else."[11]

Settlers' sympathy with whiskey sellers expressed itself most clearly in jury nullification. Through their verdicts, jurors protected the whiskey traffic from official efforts at prohibition. James Kavanaugh, the sheriff of Whatcom County, wrote to the superintendent of Indian affairs that "there is always a goodly proportion of our juries made up of whiskey sellers and of those who hate the Indians and feel kindly to whiskey sellers. The greatest evil and stumbling block to justice lies in the jury box in this country."[12]

An Indian Department employee echoed Kavanaugh's sentiments in 1865. "I find it a *moral impossibility* to find a bill before a grand jury or *to convict* before a court for selling whiskey to Indians or even murder cases," complained C. C. Finkboner, the officer in charge of the Lummi

Reservation. "The Legislature had better pass an act this winter to license men to sell whiskey and murder Indians. Thereby, it will create revenue to the territory and men wont brake [*sic*] the law, only the law of God, which is nothing in the eyes of those who make a living by stealing and selling whiskey to Indians."[13]

Jurors' deep bias against Indian testimony, frequently the only evidence available in liquor cases, presented a formidable obstacle to obtaining convictions. Although federal law granted competency to Indian witnesses in liquor prosecutions, their exclusion from other cases involving whites reinforced the prejudices of the settlers when it came to Indian testimony. At a term of court at Port Townsend, Kavanaugh reported, he saw every jury member swear that they would accept Indian testimony only in cases against other Indians. Agent Nathaniel Hill wrote in 1856 that "Indian testimony in liquor cases is admitted but juries cannot be found to convict upon that alone; the trader is aware of this fact and is smart enough to hide his actions from the eyes of a white man—they thus can carry on their trade with impunity."[14]

Makah Agent Webster lamented that evidence sufficient to convict a man for murder in other communities "is totally rejected by . . . jurors in cases of whiskey selling." Jurors required white testimony before convicting even "the most notorious offender," and they refused to convict even then, Webster went on, unless the white witness "actually tasted the same to prove that it was spirituous liquor or wine."[15]

The problem of bias extended beyond the jury box, as well. Kavanaugh wrote, for example, that he did not think any committing magistrate would issue a warrant for a liquor dealer on Indian testimony. A group of Duwamish Indians seized two liquor dealers in 1862 and attempted to bring them before a justice of the peace, who nonetheless refused to issue a writ and set the men free.[16]

Despite the continuous reports of bias against Indian witnesses, prosecutors relied on Indian testimony with surprising frequency. Out of 708 cases, 392 included Indians as witnesses before the grand jury. In 129 cases, prosecutors presented only Indian witnesses. More surprising still, grand jurors acquitted only slightly more often in cases without corroborating white witnesses. Of the 316 cases without Indian testimony, the grand jury acquitted the defendant in 10.4 percent of the cases. Of the 263 cases that included both Indian and white witnesses, grand jurors acquitted 12.5 percent of the time. In the 129 cases with only Indian testimony, the grand jury acquitted in 13.1 percent of them.[17]

These figures mask a significant shift over time. The rate of acquittal in cases with only Indian witnesses fell dramatically after 1870. There were thirty-seven cases featuring only Indian witnesses before 1870; grand juries acquitted the defendants in eleven of them (29.7 percent). After 1870, prosecutors brought ninety-two cases featuring only Indian witnesses, but the grand jury acquitted only 6.5 percent of these defendants. In cases where white witnesses testified, the indictment rate stayed roughly the same before and after 1870. This indicates that the bias against Indian testimony shown by grand juries decreased over time.

Petit jurors showed more anti-Indian bias than grand jurors. The law required grand jurors to be qualified electors and householders; trial jurors merely had to be qualified electors. These status differences made grand jurors more likely to be concerned with the public-order problems of drunken Indians, and petit jurors more likely to sympathize with the liquor dealers. As Kavanaugh noted, petit juries often included whiskey sellers. At one term of court, the sheriff complained, jurymen had sold liquor to local Indians while sitting on a prosecution under the Intercourse Act. Superintendent of Indian Affairs McKenny wrote in 1867 that "it is the next thing to impossibility to obtain convictions before juries of this country as every jury perhaps will contain from one to four jurors who have at some time or other been engaged in the same traffic."[18]

The liquor trade exercised a particularly strong influence in the peripheral counties. In 1861, for example, the commanding officer at Fort Colville reported that he had arrested two men on liquor charges. "Nothing will be done," he glumly reported, "as all the civil officers are themselves whiskey sellers." In his book *The Dry Years*, Norman Clark argues that the failure of the first general Prohibition referendum in Washington, in 1855, reflected the fact that "some significant part of the economy was involved in the liquor traffic" with the Indians. The referendum principally targeted the liquor traffic with the Indians. Analyzing the 1855 vote, Clark finds that the most support for the law came from the Puget Sound counties of Jefferson, Pierce, and King, where the white population was most concerned with the problem of drunken Indians. Settlers in the more peripheral counties, Clark concludes, "were probably engaged in the liquor traffic and thus opposed to the law."[19]

Economic self-interest thus reinforced the bias against Indian testimony, frustrating official efforts to enforce the liquor laws during the early territorial years. Indeed, the conflicts between whiskey sellers and the settlers who sympathized with them, on the one hand, and federal and territorial officials on the other reflected a broader social conflict between the "respectable" and the "not-so-respectable" citizens. Thus, when a local physician in Port Townsend was repeatedly accused and eventually convicted of selling liquor to the Indians, a local resident wrote that "such crimes" put him "beyond the pale of honesty, and therefore no companion for a gentleman." Similarly, Superintendent of Indian Affairs McKenny noted that in pursuing prosecutions of liquor dealers he aspired not so much to convict as to harass. Put to the bother and expense of furnishing bail, liquor dealers might be persuaded to adopt some "more honorable" occupation.[20]

Clark notes the elitist rhetoric of those who supported the 1855 Prohibition referendum. One letter to the editor, for example, labeled the liquor sellers "mean-spirited and filthy white scoundrels." One finds similar examples of such rhetoric in the correspondence of the Indian agents and others involved in the suppression of the liquor traffic. Missionary E. C. Chirouse attacked the liquor sellers as "emissaries of Hell" and "destroyers" of the Indians. Agent John Knox referred to them as a "gang of thieves." One letter writer drew the superintendent's attention to a man named Wood, "a drunken worthless person earning a miserable living by hunting and supplying them [the Indians] with liquor."[21]

Officials in counties east of the Cascades employed the same language. In 1861, the army officer in charge of Fort Colville blamed most of his troubles with the Indians on the "miserable squatters" who sold them liquor. Agent George Paige, assigned to the nontreaty tribes in northeastern Washington, expelled from the territory a liquor seller named Fox in 1868, who he labeled "an unprincipled vagabond and thief." Agent William Barnhart of the Nez Perce Reservation described the whiskey sellers as "a depraved class of the genus white man, who seem infatuated with the idea of elevating themselves to the condition of the Indian—in his lowest phase."[22]

Chronic underfunding and the structural weakness of Washington's legal institutions further complicated enforcement. Makah Agent Webster told Superintendent of Indian Affairs C. H. Hale in 1862 that he was happy to do his duty regarding the liquor laws, but he needed money to carry on the fight. Any attempt at enforcement was, Webster wrote, "attended with an expense in paying fees and travelling expenses for white witnesses, for the payment of which I have no instructions as to what fund to draw upon."[23]

In his 1862 annual report, Hale outlined the spectrum of enforcement problems faced by the Indian Department in the territory. The time lag between the preliminary hearing and the term of court when the case was tried, Hale wrote, meant that even when officers obtained "testimony of the most clear and convincing character," the witnesses often could not be located by the time the case came to trial. Hale recommended giving power to the United States commissioner who heard the initial complaint to dispose of the case by levying a fine and seizing the liquor and the vehicle in which it was transported. Summary procedures would spare the interdiction efforts "the slow process of the courts and the technicalities of the law, which only operate to clear the guilty and involve the United States in a bill of costs."[24]

Hale further noted that the territory as yet had "but few jails and no penitentiary." A prisoner who failed to post bond remained in the custody of the U.S. marshall, who bore the costs of the prisoner's board. Yet Congress typically did not reimburse these costs. Hale thus justified his budget requests to cover the cost of holding these prisoners and transporting them to court.[25]

All of these problems generated reservoirs of bitterness among the Indian agents, who vented their frustrations in their official correspondence. In 1854, Agent Simmons arrested four men in the town of Olympia in Thurston County for selling liquor to Indians. Indian witnesses positively identified the culprits, and two white witnesses confirmed the identity of the house where the Indians obtained the liquor. Despite "these damning evidences of guilt," Simmons complained, District Judge Edward Lander "to my consternation & mortification & that of all the citizens with whom I have conversed, dismissed the complaints & refused even to bind them over for trial." Similarly, in 1865, the officer in charge of the Lummi Reservation wrote, "I have been doing all in my power to put a stop to this hellish practice of selling whiskey to Indians, but unless we can get protection from the courts we may as well give up the struggle in despair."[26]

The obstacles to enforcement so frustrated the agents that they meted out summary justice themselves. In an 1858 report, Simmons wrote that the liquor trade had assumed "frightful" dimensions, motivating him to employ an extra man to exercise surveillance. Even so, he had only made two arrests. "In both of these cases, I administered justice myself by tying the offenders up and lashing them well, and then allowing them fifteen minutes to leave the town," he told his superior. "I have tried the courts in such cases until I am completely disgusted with them, and find my measures much more effective."[27]

Simmons's subordinates took similar actions. In June 1858, R. C. Fay, the local agent stationed on Whidbey Island in Puget Sound, accosted an "old Negro" whom he suspected of supplying whiskey to the Indians. When the man protested that the "demijohn" of liquor on his property was for his personal consumption, Fay seized it and emptied it out. Fay then warned the man that the neighbors were watching, and if he were caught trafficking in liquor, they would not hesitate to apply the lynch law. "You are aware of the difficulty of fastening the guilt for an offence of this kind against a party," Fay explained in his report. "[T]he proofs are hard to get at; therefore have deemed it prudent not to hazard the institution of any civil actions in these instances."[28]

The agents viewed such summary actions as necessary adjuncts to a legal system made ineffective by the settlers' resistance to aggressive prosecution. By the late 1860s, however, the agents began to report a greater number of convictions. In 1867, Superintendent McKenny noted that "the time has now arrived when it is no longer impossible to get convictions against such characters [the liquor dealers]." In his annual report for that year, he cited three convictions, out of a total of thirteen cases, as an indication that legal action was proving more effective.[29]

Enforcement statistics support this anecdotal evidence. By the late 1860s, the percentage of liquor cases that ended in conviction or a guilty plea began to climb. Graph 1 shows the dramatic changes in conviction rates by five-year period. In the period from 1860 to 1864, only 18 percent of defendants in liquor cases either pleaded guilty or were found guilty by a jury. From 1865 to 1869 this rate climbed to almost one-third, and by the end of the territorial period over three-fourths of defendants faced punishment.

GRAPH 1
Conviction Rates for Liquor Cases, Washington Territory

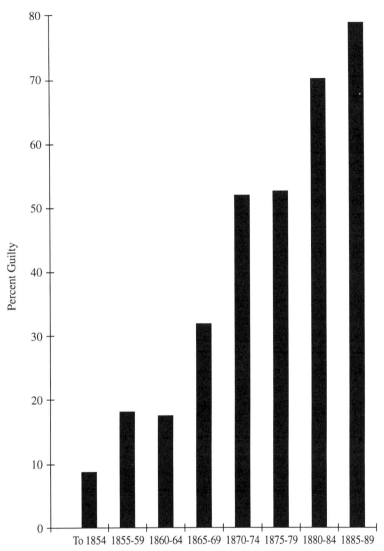

Note: Conviction rate includes total found guilty and pleading guilty.

The effect of this improvement is more difficult to measure. The increasing number of convictions presumably served as a deterrent to at least some potential whiskey sellers, but without knowledge of the total amount of liquor actually flowing to the Indians, an interdiction rate cannot be derived. Given the surge in population during the later years of the territorial period, it seems likely that whiskey was at least as widely available to Indians as it was in the earlier years, despite the improvements in law enforcement.

The increased number of convictions reflected more than just better evidence and better case selection by prosecutors. Judges, jurors, and the population at large took a tougher stance against liquor dealers, and a greater proportion of residents became more concerned with the perceived public-order problems caused by the liquor traffic than with the profits generated by implicitly sanctioning the traffic.

This tougher stance stemmed both from the lessened dependence of the territorial economy on the liquor trade and from the more secure dominance of the "respectable" elements of territorial society. When a merchants' group alerted him to a neighborhood liquor dealer in 1867, Superintendent McKenny wrote that he was "gratified to see the better portion of the community as opposed to this nefarious practice, and I hope soon to be able by the assistance of people who love law and order to be able to put a stop to the same." As the territory became more settled and the timber economy became more established, territorial society grew increasingly concerned with law and order.[30]

By the late 1860s, jurors' anti-Indian biases became less frequently indulged and more firmly combated. With the passage of the Fourteenth Amendment in 1868, judges took an increasingly active role in fighting the bias against Indian testimony. First District Court Judge Lewis, for example, repeatedly instructed jurors that "you must weigh the evidence of the Indian in the same scale as that of a whiteman. If his testimony is reasonable and probable . . . it is worthy of belief."[31]

Although Lewis helped translate the guarantees of the Fourteenth Amendment into practice in Washington, his jury instructions made it plain that the competency of Indian witnesses did not stem from a recognition of the equality of Indians and whites, but from an improved assessment of whites' reasoning skills. In a case from 1876, Lewis told the jurors that America's centennial found "humanity . . . upon a higher plane than ever

United States v. Charles Vogelsong

before and we have reached the sensible conclusion that the American people, especially as educated and unprejudiced men, now deem themselves competent and able to weigh the evidence of all men, white, black, or red, in the same balances and judge of it by the same rules." In a similar vein, Lewis had earlier told a Clallam County jury that allowing Indian witnesses on the stand was "evidence of material progress in the history of civilization in America . . . we have reached that high plane in the scale of humanity wherein that all men are equal before the law."[32]

Prosecutors also grew less indulgent of bias and strived to keep it out of the jury box. In an 1867 liquor case in Jefferson County, for example, United States District Attorney Leander Holmes put to prospective jurors the following question: "Have you any feelings or prejudices against Indians that would prevent you from finding a verdict of guilty against a white man charged with selling spirituous liquor to Indians—on Indian testimony alone?" When the jurors selected brought in a verdict of guilty against the defendant William Parsons, he challenged Holmes's jury selection strategy. In his motion to set aside the verdict and grant a new trial, the defendant charged that the court erred in dismissing several potential jurors from service "when they answered that their knowledge of Indian character would prevent them from giving sufficient credit to Indian testimony when unsupported by other evidence to return a guilty verdict." The court turned down the motion and sentenced Parsons to four months in the Port Townsend jail and fined him $200.[33]

Sentencing data bear out the decline in sympathy for liquor dealers. In the period before 1859, the average jail sentence in the sixteen cases that ended in conviction was only 100 days. During the 1860s, that average rose to 133.6 days, then to 234.4 days in the 1870s, before falling off to 162.5 days in the 1880s. The drop-off in severity during the later years signaled the development of what has been called "implicit plea bargaining" for those who pleaded guilty.[34] During the 1870s and 1880s, the average jail sentences for those defendants found guilty by a jury stayed fairly constant, at 260.2 days and 258.6 days, respectively. During the 1880s, however, the number of guilty pleas skyrocketed, and judges rewarded those who pleaded guilty with lower jail sentences. In the 109 cases that ended in a guilty plea, defendants received jail sentences averaging 122.3 days, more than four months less than those who took their cases to jury trials.[35]

Such changes in enforcement patterns are important because laws are more than mere rhetorical expressions of how society ought to be. Enforcement attaches real-world consequences to the normative statements of the law. Improved enforcement suggests more than improvements in the techniques of policing and prosecution; it also suggests increased popular acceptance of the ideological statements codified in the law.[36]

The liquor laws codified a set of white assumptions about Indians and alcohol. Joy Leland has labeled this set of assumptions "the firewater myth." This myth holds that Indians are, in Leland's words, "constitutionally prone to develop an inordinate craving for liquor and to lose control over their behavior when they drink." These beliefs regarding Indian drinking did not, of course, originate in Washington Territory, nor did all territorial residents share them, but they lay behind the efforts to deny alcohol to Indians.[37]

This ideology played an important role in the dramatic expansion of federal authority represented by the 1862 amendment to the Intercourse Act. Whites assumed that Indians had a racial vulnerability to alcohol that made it necessary to control their access to liquor not just in Indian country, but in all locations. "Whiskey everywhere seems to possess for the Indian an irresistible attraction," Commissioner of Indian Affairs William P. Dole wrote in 1861, "and having no just appreciation of values, he readily exchanges the most valuable of his possessions to gratify his uncontrolable [sic] desire for this stimulant." Indians thus depended on the benevolent protection of white law to remove the temptation and promote their well-being.[38]

In light of the social ills linked to alcohol abuse in past and present-day Indian communities, historians have often accepted the premises of the firewater myth. Francis Paul Prucha, for example, has stated that "ardent spirits" made "madmen of the Indians." Similarly, Norman Clark, in his study of liquor control efforts in Washington, states that "drunkenness encouraged an ugly streak of natural viciousness [among the Indians]." Over the last three decades, however, anthropologists, ethnohistorians, and other students of Indian drinking patterns have attacked the ideas underlying the firewater myth. In particular, they have sought to discredit the notions that Indians have a "natural" or biological craving for alcohol and that violence and mayhem inevitably follow from Indian drinking.[39]

Craig MacAndrew and Robert Edgerton's *Drunken Comportment* offers one of the most convincing and influential critiques of the fire-water myth. Using examples from various cultures around the world, they challenge the notion that alcohol had uniform effects on behavior and that its behavioral effects were uniformly bad. Instead, they stress the impact of culture on the way people behave when drunk. In their chapters on American Indians, they argue that Indians imported European ideas of drunkenness when they imported European drink. The Indians "learned" that drunkenness led to aggressive behavior, and thus began the behavioral "changes for the worse" that so many observers of Indian drinking noted. The corollary to that lesson, MacAndrew and Edgerton argue, is that drunkenness served as "time out" from prevailing social norms regarding aggressive behavior. In other words, Indians learned to behave aggressively when drunk and then learned to use drunkenness as an excuse for such behavior.[40]

The shift from biological explanations to cultural explanations of Indians' drinking behavior has neglected the importance of the law as a medium for constructing notions of cultural and racial difference. If Indians learned early on that drinking led to behavioral "changes for the worse," as MacAndrew and Edgerton suggest, the laws communicated the European idea that *Indian* drinking in particular led to behavioral changes for the *much* worse.[41]

The Indians' presumed lack of self-control explains why the indictment in *United States v. Charles Vogelsong* named Vogelsong and not Henry as the criminal agent in their transaction. The Indian buyers, such as Henry, were thought to be merely the victims of uncontrollable desires, unable to resist temptations offered by whiskey sellers without the aid of external controls. The liquor laws thus helped mark the boundary between the rational, self-controlled adult white male and the irrational, passionate savage.

As with habitual drunkards and minors, Indians' possession of alcohol did not constitute a crime. But the agents of the Indian Department did punish Indians' possession of alcohol. The reservation was supposed to be the "school" where Indians were taught self-control and civilized behavior. It was believed that racially inherent behavioral defects could be mitigated through a program of education and stern discipline. As the family disciplined the minor, the reservation disciplined the Indian. Writing of his successful efforts to control on-reservation drunkenness, for example, Tulalip Agent A. R. Elder lamented in 1867 that the Indians still strayed into some "town or logging camp" where they "fall into the snare of the tempter and become drunk, but they have learned better than to come upon the reservation in that condition." Similarly, Chirouse, who took over the Tulalip Reservation, commented in 1874 that after a three-week leave of absence, he returned to find only a few cases of drunkenness. "The Indians who have been guilty have been punished according to the regulations of the Reservation."[42]

Although some Indians did act as liquor sellers, legal officials overwhelmingly—and for the most part, accurately—described the traffic as white sellers exploiting Indian buyers. "The Indians should be protected from the rapacious conduct of the dissolute and unprincipled whites engaged in supplying them with whiskey," wrote J. W. Nesmith, superintendent of Indian affairs for Oregon and Washington, in 1858. This rhetoric of protecting the Indians from their own weaknesses provided an important justification for the attempted sequestration of Indians on reservations and the tight control exercised over them.[43]

The second major component of the firewater myth that underlay the liquor laws held that Indians' behavior changed for the worse when they were drunk. The laws aimed to prevent these behavioral changes for the worse. The agents in Washington Territory explicitly linked sobriety and docility among the Indians under their charge. Agent Simmons, for example, remarked in 1854 that the normally peaceable Indians of Puget Sound turned "saucy" when drinking, "twitting the whites with having stolen their land without any intention of ever paying for it." Similarly, E. C. Fitzhugh, the agent at Bellingham Bay in 1856, reported that "my Indians are drunk every where & seem to defy & laugh at my authority. . . . [N]ow that every house has become a grog shop, I can be of no use to Government."[44]

Fears of social disorder echo through the agents' reports. In their eyes, the disinhibitory effect of alcohol threatened to unleash the violence lurking in the savage heart of the Indian. The sale of liquor to the Indians, Simmons told Governor Stevens in 1854, "is the main if not the sole cause of any & all difficulties which ever occur between the whites & natives." Four years later, Simmons wrote in a similar vein that "my greatest fear is that some drunken Indian will murder a white man, and then the whites will kill some innocent Indian and thus an outbreak be brought about."[45]

As white settlement increased in various parts of the territory, the potential for interracial conflict likewise increased, especially as many Indians remained off the reservations. The Clallam Indians residing around the town of Port Townsend, for example, caused a great deal of concern to the white residents of the town and to the Skokomish agent charged with watching over the Indians. "I found the Indians about Port Townsend in a deplorable condition, drunk all the time, cutting and killing one another almost every day," Agent Knox wrote after a visit in 1864. "The citizens of the place complain loudly about the annoyance they are subjected to by drunken Indians."[46]

Settlers in other parts of the territory voiced similar complaints. C. C. Finkboner, farmer in charge of the Lummi Reservation, noted in 1865 as settlement began to spread into a nearby river valley: "The number of drunken Indians around the *Skagit River* is getting to be quite alarming and dangerous for white settlers and something ought to be done." In 1858, Agent Simmons commented that settlers near Grays Harbor along the Pacific Coast feared the Indians when the Indians were drinking. "They have no fears while the Indians are sober, but . . . this is so seldom that it is with dread that they leave home." Two years later, a Grays Harbor settler wrote to the superintendent of Indian affairs that "no one can live among them [the Indians] so long as whisky is coming into their country." When investigating settlers' complaints about Clallam Indians on the Elwha River in 1874, Agent Eells wrote that "when [the Indians are] drunk the whites could do nothing with them but were often abused by them." The whites all agreed, Eells said, that if whiskey could be kept from the Indians, "they would be peaceable enough."[47]

The liquor laws contributed to the idea that a drunken Indian was a potentially violent one. The white perception of drunken Indians as prone to violence existed despite the fact that few whites seem to have actually been attacked by Indians who had been drinking. Data from criminal cases involving Indian defendants in Washington support the general conclusion reached by MacAndrew and Edgerton in their analysis of Indians' behavioral "changes for the worse": Other Indians suffered most from the violence noted by white observers of Indian drinking bouts. The threat perceived by whites thus always resided in the potential for violence, rather than from direct experience of violence. The law helped heighten that fear of potential violence. By trying to keep alcohol out of Indians' hands, it expressed the idea that alcohol made Indians dangerous.[48]

Describing the assumptions behind the liquor laws as a firewater myth does not deny the real social and physical consequences to Indian drinking. The point is that the laws prohibiting the liquor traffic racialized these consequences. The laws conveyed the message that there was a big difference between Indian drinking and white drinking, despite the fact that many of the same negative consequences attached to both. Superintendent Milroy made this point in his first annual report in 1872. Milroy pointed out that alcohol had not only "occasioned the destruction of two-thirds of the Indian race of America . . . but is annually leading over 50,000 white men down to drunkards' graves." He therefore called for a national prohibition law as the only sure remedy for the problem.[49]

Milroy's call went unheeded, of course. Whites in Washington resisted efforts by temperance reformers to pass laws that controlled their right to buy and to drink alcohol. Describing the liquor problem some twenty years before Milroy, Agent Starling wrote that "it would be injudicious to attempt to prohibit its [alcohol's] importation and its use by the white settlers." Whites, unlike Indians, were thought to be masters of their appetites, and differential access to liquor served as a continuing reminder of the difference between the two races.[50]

Vogelsong did not contest the ideology behind the liquor laws directly. He did, however, contest the notion that one could easily tell the difference between Indians and whites and thus know to whom not to sell liquor. The existence of reliable markers of Indian identity lay at the very foundation of liquor-law enforcement. But in Washington, many of the conventional markers—phenotype, culture, geography—gave inaccurate signals. Intermarriage altered the stereotypical "Indian look"; integration into the territorial economy masked many of the visible signs of native culture and subsistence; and the failure of the reservation policy left Indians scattered all over the territory.

Vogelsong's brief for acquittal rested on his honest intention to buy a drink for a fellow white man; he had never intended, he claimed, to give liquor to an Indian. His lawyers charted this strategy in a set of jury instructions, intending to ask the judge to deliver them to the jury. The proposed instructions started from a noncontroversial point: The government had to prove all the essential elements of the indictment against Vogelsong beyond a reasonable doubt to justify a verdict of guilty.

One of those essential elements, they contended, was that Vogelsong knew the racial identity of Henry. If Vogelsong sincerely mistook Henry for a white man, then he had not willfully broken the law. "If a man acts honestly but is led into a mistake by appearances he should not be held liable criminally, and if the appearances of the man who got the liquor would indicate that under ordinary circumstances that he was not an indian under an indian agent Mr. Vogelsang [sic] would be justified in acting upon those appearances." The lawyers urged the jury to apply a reasonableness standard to Vogelsong's misperception. "Other men in like circumstances might be equally as honestly mistaken."

Vogelsong's lawyers further suggested that Henry had acted as the real agent in the whole transaction. He had duped Vogelsong into believing that he was a white man. "If the indian by any artifice on his part or deception lead [sic] or caused defendant to believe that he was a white man," then Vogelsong had acted reasonably upon appearances and was entitled to an acquittal, the lawyers argued.[51]

The uniqueness of Vogelsong's strategy lay mainly in its boldness, its assertion that reasonable people could not tell the difference between whites and Indians. But numerous other accused liquor sellers, in bids to save themselves jail time, questioned the legal definition of *Indian* itself. They argued that by observable political and cultural markers, some Indians were not really Indians and therefore did not fall under the exclusions of the Intercourse Act.

Prior to the 1862 amendment to the Intercourse Act, defining an Indian had not been much of a problem. At that time, the provisions of the Intercourse Act had been established according to the boundaries between Indian country and the rest of society. The 1862 amendment, however, included all Indians who were under an agent, both on and off the reservation, and suddenly the issue of Indian identity assumed more prominence.

The U.S. Supreme Court confronted this issue in *United States v. Holliday* (1865), when it upheld the 1862 amendment of the Intercourse Act. Holliday had been arrested under the Intercourse Act for selling liquor to Otibsko, an Ojibwa Indian living off the tribe's reservation in Michigan. Holliday challenged the indictment because Otibsko owned land, lived off the reservation, and had been granted suffrage and other civil rights upon severing his tribal relations, in accordance with state law. The Court ruled that despite this evidence of acculturation, Otibsko fell within the province of the Intercourse Act because the tribe to which he belonged still maintained political relations with the United States. Otibsko received an annual payment from treaty money paid to the tribe by the United States and an Indian agent oversaw the distribution of those funds.

In this case, the Court said, it had to defer to the judgment of the political departments of the government. "If by them those Indians are recognized as a tribe, this Court must do the same," it stated. No grant of civil rights by a state or local jurisdiction released individual Indians from the scope of a congressional law passed for their benefit. So long as Congress retained a political relation to a tribal group, then the law deemed all Indians of that tribal group under the authority of an agent. Only a formal renunciation of tribal relations by, paradoxically, the tribe itself, and the acceptance of such a renunciation by the federal government could end federal stewardship over individual Indians.[52]

The *Holliday* decision implied that individual Indians could not acculturate themselves to fully equal legal status. The case thus encapsulated many of the debates that would occur later over the distinction between civilized and uncivilized Indians relating to matters of citizenship. As part of the history of efforts to control liquor, the Court's reasoning implied that Indians' vulnerability to alcohol and resulting penchant for violence persisted despite outward changes in an individual's behavior.

Holliday made Indian identity a combination of racial and political factors. If the liquor buyer was an Indian "by blood" and under the authority of an Indian agent, which presumed that he maintained tribal relations, then the law made the seller of the liquor criminally liable. In Washington Territory, liquor sellers would challenge both the political and racial aspects of the Court's definition of Indian identity. The district courts, following *Holliday*, held the line against these challenges. These cases reveal the symbolic content of the liquor laws and their importance in marking racial boundaries. Indians themselves played only a small role in these courtroom debates; in the main, these were conversations between whites about Indians.

United States v. Charles Vogelsong

Accused liquor sellers disputed the political status of their Indian buyers by questioning whether an agent or superintendent actually exercised control over a particular Indian. Post-1862 indictments routinely stipulated this in their descriptions of the Indian buyers. As a material allegation in the indictment, defendants argued that prosecutors had to prove that the Indian Department had charge of the Indian in question. The defendants argued against the a priori assumption that every Indian in the territory was subject to an Indian agent, particularly since so many Indians in Washington resided outside of Indian country.

Defendant John McBride, for example, filed a bill of exceptions after being convicted for selling liquor to an unidentified Indian in Yakima County in 1871. Prosecution witness A. C. Warren testified that he saw McBride give whiskey to two Indians on the Columbia River, about ninety miles from any reservation. Warren said he did not know the tribe to which the two Indians belonged, and McBride's attorney urged the court to instruct the jury that there was no legal presumption that the Indians were under the charge of an agent or superintendent. The court refused, instructing the jury instead that there was such a presumption of law.[53]

McBride did not challenge the racial identity of the buyers, but whether that racial identity necessarily implied a politically subordinate position. At the very least, McBride argued, the jury should determine an Indian's political status as a question of fact. The judges disagreed. By defining the issue as a matter of law, they took it out of the hands of jurors suspected of sympathizing with the whiskey traders on trial. In those cases where written jury instructions survive, judges routinely admonished jurors that the law presumed all Indians living in the United States to be under the charge of an Indian superintendent or agent.[54]

Once they defined the issue as a rule of law, judges applied it to all Indians, irrespective of the actual facts of their political relationship to the government. They thus blurred the two aspects of the *Holliday* doctrine, for race became an indicator of political status and of legal subordination to Congress. Indians from Canada, for example, frequently crossed the border to work, visit relatives, and sometimes to smuggle liquor and other contraband. Judges in Washington Territory upheld the race-based restrictions on selling liquor to these Indians. In an 1880 case, authorities arrested Richard Fryer for selling liquor to three women, Kitty

Spencer, Annie Powers, and Louisa Hill. In her testimony at the preliminary hearing, Spencer identified herself as a Haida Indian residing in Seattle. At the trial in August, Fryer's attorney noted that Powers and Spencer were only temporarily sojourning in Seattle from their native British Columbia, and thus were neither U.S. citizens nor residents of any reservation in the U.S. The court ignored any claims as to the Indians' political relations with the government, and the jury convicted Fryer.[55]

Questioning a buyer's tribal relations offered a second avenue by which liquor dealers challenged the political aspects of Indian identity. Like Holliday, liquor sellers in Washington invoked the rhetoric of "civilization" utilized by policy makers to try and carve out exemptions from the laws for individual Indians. They attempted to persuade judges that acculturated Indians were autonomous individuals who lived and made decisions independently of the oversight of the Indian Department. Thus a King County defendant requested the judge in an 1885 case to instruct the jury that "the government must also have proved to you beyond a reasonable doubt that the Indian Sampson was at those times an Indian maintaining tribal relations." It was no crime, the defendant urged, to sell liquor to an Indian who had severed his tribal relations. The judge refused to give the instruction.[56]

In a similar case in Thurston County in 1880, defendant Charles Fisher requested the judge to instruct the jury that it must acquit if it found that the Indian in question had "severed his tribal relations by adopting the habits of the whites and . . . was living . . . as a civilized being." He requested that the jury take into account certain facts, such as whether or not the Indian resided on a reservation and whether he lived independent of the control of an agent or superintendent, in determining whether the law applied in a particular case. The judge refused, and Fisher was convicted and sentenced to six months in the federal penitentiary.[57]

One of the most interesting cases in this regard occurred in 1888 in the case of "Frank Joe," an Indian who was indicted on two counts of selling liquor to Indians—to Julia Rains and to a man known only as "Sam." Both of the buyers, according to the indictment, were under the charge of an Indian agent. A jury found Frank Joe guilty of the second count on June 7, 1888; on June 9, he filed a motion for a new trial. In the motion, Frank Joe played upon the distinction between a race-based definition of Indian and the race-neutral category of citizen. The motion charged that the trial judge had erred in sustaining the prosecution's objections to Frank Joe's attempts to prove that Sam was not an Indian under an agent, as charged in the indictment, but was a U.S. citizen.

Frank Joe stated in the motion that he and other Indians would have testified that Sam had "declared his intention to become a citizen of the United States—and had forever severed his tribal relations with the Nisqualla [sic] tribe of indians, and particularly the Nisqually tribe located upon the nisqualla [sic] reservation." When on the stand in his own defense, Frank Joe had been asked whether he knew if Sam lived in Indian country or under an agent or superintendent. The prosecution objected and the judge sustained the objection.

Frank Joe also challenged the legality of the indictment. A "material ingredient" of the offense charged in the indictment—but not dictated by the statute—was that Frank Joe was also an Indian under the charge of an Indian agent. "The defendant offered to prove that he was not under an Indian Agent," stated the motion, "but the court ruled that under law every Indian was under an Indian agent." The court overruled the motion and the defendant announced his intention to appeal to the territorial supreme court. No record of an appeal exists.[58]

If the courts meant to determine political status solely on the basis of race, then liquor dealers responded by challenging the blood quanta of their buyers. In the aforementioned case of Fryer, the defendant relied on the notion of blood to escape the strictures of the law. During the preliminary hearing, one of the women to whom Fryer had sold liquor identified herself as a mixed-blood Indian. As a result, the prosecutor dropped the charge against Fryer for selling liquor to her. In testifying in his own defense, Fryer had told the magistrate, "I did know it was contrary to the law to give it [liquor] to Indians, but supposed I could give it to half breeds at any time."[59]

In other cases, judges refused to allow the jury to consider evidence regarding the blood quantum of the buyer. Isaac Jones, indicted in 1876 for selling whiskey to an Indian boy named George, contested George's Indian identity. He could produce witnesses who would prove that George was a mixed-blood. He asked the judge to instruct the jury that they must acquit if they found that "George the indian boy is a half breed indian having a white father . . . and that the mother of said George did not reside with the Indians or upon a reservation."

Jones also argued that George's behavior should exempt him from the liquor prohibition. "He was reared among the white people and not among the Indians," Jones stated in his request to the judge. If the jury found that "said George was at the time of the offense and for years prior thereto living with white people accustomed constantly to their habits and not adicted [*sic*] to the habits of the Indians," then the judge should instruct them to acquit. Judge Roger Greene refused to give the instruction, but the jury acquitted Jones anyway.[60]

Issues of blood, cultural behavior, and legal status came up repeatedly in the liquor cases. In *United States v. W. J. Wilson*, the defendant, like Frank Joe, juxtaposed Indian identity and U.S. citizenship to try and exempt his customer from the provisions of the liquor law. Wilson was convicted in 1874 on one count of selling liquor to an Indian called William at Wallula in Walla Walla County. The jury recommended mercy and the court sentenced him to twenty days imprisonment. On November 24, the day after his conviction, Wilson filed a motion to set aside the verdict. He had new evidence, he stated, that would show William to be a legal citizen of the United States. William's father and mother, according to the motion, "are both United States citizens and not Indians." The father was a white man who had legally married William's Indian mother, thus conferring citizenship on her. As a result, William was a legal citizen of the United States. If granted a new trial, Wilson stated, he could produce William's father, who would verify these statements. The court overruled the motion.[61]

Wilson's case shows how contact—in this case, intermarriage—blurred the boundaries set up by the law. The argument in the motion relied on notions of blood and on the recently created legal fiction of national citizenship to challenge William's Indian identity under the law. By stressing the legality of the marriage between William's father and mother, Wilson used law to establish an alternative identity for William that served Wilson's own interests.

In resisting such strategies, the judges of Washington Territory fought to uphold the category of Indian as self-evident, not allowing evidence of acculturation or alternate civil status to trump the fundamental category of race. And once they established the racial identity of an Indian, they took for granted the political fact of subordination to the Indian Department.

This hard-line interpretation of the law may have led Vogelsong's lawyers to flirt with their new line of defense—not to question Henry's blood quantum or legal status, but to deny that his racial identity could be established with any certainty. Ultimately, though, Vogelsong's lawyers lost confidence in their bold ploy for acquittal. On March 2, 1889, Vogelsong withdrew his not guilty plea and filed instead a plea of no contest, submitting the matter to the court for judgment. The judge in the case levied a $50 fine on Vogelsong and ordered him to pay the $40.80 in court costs, which he did that same day.[62]

Vogelsong's case thus ultimately ended in a typical fashion. By the late 1880s, faced with a good chance of conviction, fewer and fewer liquor dealers bothered to contest the charges vigorously, counting on "cooperation" with the court to get them a lighter sentence. The jury in Vogelsong's case therefore never heard the jury instructions that the lawyers prepared. Indeed, Vogelsong might have changed his plea because his lawyers realized that no territorial judge would instruct a jury along the lines they proposed. Preserved in the case file nonetheless, the instructions reveal just how slippery the issue of Indian identity had become.

Vogelsong and his fellow liquor traders were not, of course, crusaders for social justice. They were not arguing a principled position of equal rights for Indians, nor were they defending critical civil liberties. They voiced these arguments solely to avoid jail time. To save their own skins, they struck at the perceived weak points in the law, the notion that one could reliably tell who is an Indian and that Indian identity necessarily implies a certain political and legal status. In repelling these attacks, judges laid bare the role of the liquor laws in upholding racial identities and enforcing racial boundaries.

Interestingly, the position of the judges in Washington changed again just a few years later, marking another significant shift in white attitudes toward Indians and their legal status. After Washington achieved statehood, judges abandoned the hard line they had taken on Indian legal identity. Under the provisions of the 1887 Dawes Act, which provided for the survey and individual allotment of reservations, Indians who took up allotments became U.S. citizens. In an 1891 case, the U.S. district court for Washington ruled that Indian agents could no longer exercise control over allottees. Agents forecasted that a flood of newly licit liquor would flow to the Indians as a result of the decision.[63]

Where previously judges had upheld the race-based protection of Indians under the liquor law and the regulation of the Indian population within the territory, allotment signaled the dismantling of these forms of legal distinction. The rhetoric of the allotment period stressed the full assimilation of Indians into the wider society, where full and equal competition with whites would measure and test the importance of race. If blood mattered, it would allow certain groups to triumph "naturally" over others, allegedly free of the interference of law or policy.

The allotment period views on the liquor traffic mirrored in some ways the laissez-faire attitudes of the early territorial period. But the lax enforcement of the liquor law in the earlier period did not grow out of a judicial acknowledgment of Indians' privileges as citizens. Rather, it grew out of a popular feeling that Indians fell outside the law—a feeling reinforced by the exclusionary intent of the early territorial statutes. Thus, despite the protests of the "respectable" elements of territorial society, liquor sellers operated with little interference in the first decade or so of the territorial period.

In the later years, the strength of the firewater myth increased among the residents of the territory. The public-order consequences of an unrestrained liquor trade led to improved enforcement of the liquor law and tighter control over the Indian population. Perhaps not surprisingly, this shift coincided with the declining importance of the liquor trade in the broader territorial economy. Popular legal culture, then, increasingly fell into line with the legal culture of the territorial elites.

Chapter 5

TERRITORY V. JAMES CLOSE
INTERRACIAL CONFLICT AND AMERICAN LEGAL CULTURE

Federal and territorial officials expected that reservations would preserve peace between settlers and Indians by keeping the two groups separated, thus limiting the opportunities for interracial conflict. Yet the porousness of reservation boundaries in Washington Territory gave rise to frequent disputes between settlers and Indians—over land, property, and acceptable behavior.

Territorial officials and officers of the Indian Department continually tried to push the settlement of such conflicts into the formal legal system. Even as they denied Indians full participation in that system, they insisted that the rule of law and formal due process should be the exclusive means for resolving interracial conflicts. In the early years of the territorial period, however, incoming settlers sought to preserve room within the legal structure for the exercise of private discipline against Indians, including summary execution. They resisted efforts by territorial officials to prosecute such illegal forms of private discipline, even as they had initially resisted efforts to enforce the liquor laws. But in a pattern that mimicked the settlers' response to the liquor trade, over time the formal mechanisms of law began to play a greater role in resolving interracial conflict, as territorial residents grew increasingly concerned with social order.

Mich-ki-a and Wal-sut-ut, two Indian men from the vicinity of Wallula, a railroad junction in Walla Walla County, blundered fatally into one such dispute on the evening of September 27, 1885. The two men entered the camp of James Close—a French Canadian only recently arrived in the territory by way of the mines at Leadville, Colorado and Coeur d'Alene—who was working as a woodcutter along the Columbia River north of Wallula.

Close's encounter with Mich-ki-a and Wal-sut-ut is a model of misunderstanding. The two Indians first helped themselves to a bottle of whiskey that Close had tucked beneath his bed. Close demanded that they put the bottle down. Mich-ki-a replied, "*Heap skookum,*" meaning "very strong" in Chinook Jargon. But Close spoke neither the Indians' language nor the Jargon, so the words meant nothing to him. Mich-ki-a then made a motion to Wal-sut-ut, which Close interpreted to be instructions for Wal-sut-ut to cut Close's throat.

Frightened, Close ran the short distance from his camp to the river, where his partner Gus Benoit lay asleep on a raft. He woke Benoit with cries of alarm and told him that the Indians were robbing him. Close was "about crying," Benoit stated later, because "he was so scared." Benoit urged Close to stay on the raft with him, but Close only remained fifteen to thirty minutes, explaining that he could not allow the Indians to take everything he owned. Close wanted Benoit to return to the camp with him, but Benoit refused. "I was afraid to go myself," he said later.

Close took Benoit's gun and returned to the camp. The Indians were still there, lying on Close's bed. As Close approached, he told them to leave. When the Indians gave no indication of their intention to comply, Close fired, sending a bullet into Mich-ki-a's shoulder, from whence it passed through his body and came out the other shoulder, severing his major arteries. At that point, Close said, Wal-sut-ut got up and started to come after him, so Close shot him. The coroner's examination, however, showed that Wal-sut-ut was shot in the back three times, the bullets emerging from the abdomen. It is more likely that Wal-sut-ut, unarmed and fearing for his life, had been trying to flee when Close killed him.[1]

By protecting his property with lethal force, Close had exercised a white prerogative still cherished by many settlers. A close examination of white on Indian violence, as well as other aspects of relations between them, indicates that such actions often transcended simple lawlessness. Some settlers adhered to a legal culture that had little to do with the institutional and procedural formalities of American law. This culture stressed summary judgment over procedural formality and private administration over the intermediation of public institutions. Settlers saw a place for due process in their own legal affairs, but they believed that "civilized" law was the province of "civilized" people. As a subjugated and inferior race, Indians could not claim the rights of civilized law. Rather, they needed to be cowed by the exercise of superior force, apart from the work of judges, lawyers, and constables.

This legal culture was most evident during the first two decades of the territorial period. By the time Close shot Wal-sut-ut and Mich-ki-a, summary killings of Indians had become increasingly rare. By 1885 most settlers had accepted the formal institutions of law as appropriate for punishing perceived offenses by Indians, like the trespass committed by Mich-ki-a and Wal-sut-ut.

During the early decades, however, the vernacular legal culture drew nourishment from the cultural background common to many of the early American settlers. Many of these early migrants shared views on politics, law, and racial matters that were characteristic of the antebellum South. The fact that Close was French-Canadian and a transient laborer shows, however, that these views were neither distinctly southern nor unique to Washington Territory.[2]

Robert Johannsen, who has studied the politics and provenance of the settlers of the Pacific Northwest during the period before the Civil War, identifies Oregon and Washington as "transplanted border states" in their political culture. Thirty-nine percent of the settler population in Washington and Oregon in 1860 hailed from eight states: Missouri, Kentucky, Virginia, Tennessee, Illinois, Indiana, Iowa, and Ohio. The numbers are lower if one looks only at Washington Territory's population—out of a total population of 11,594, settlers from these eight states totaled 2,839, or 24 percent. Thus these eight border states accounted for the single largest chunk of Washington's settler population in 1860.[3]

Johannsen characterizes the political culture of antebellum Washington and Oregon as strongly Democratic, favoring Stephen Douglas's doctrine of popular sovereignty for the territories. Settlers in the Northwest disliked slavery, despised blacks, and fervently endorsed local self-government for white people. Other sources have noted the prominence of southern Democrats among the early settlers in Washington Territory. John J. McGilvra, a prosecuting attorney in the territory, noted in his memoirs that "at the beginning and all through the War of the Rebellion there were a great many Southern men and Southern sympathizers scattered all through this country."[4]

The political views carried west by these settlers corresponded to a set of attitudes about the law. Forged in the crucible of chattel slavery, antebellum southern legal culture differed markedly from the legal culture of the antebellum North. The "culture of honor" in the South disprized recourse to the law for settling disputes. It elevated private resolution over public in such matters and was hostile to government intrusion into private matters. In the area of interracial relations, it brooked little interference by any authority other than the slaveholder, although the duty of policing non-whites fell equally upon all white citizens.[5]

Few Washington residents were former southern slaveholders, of course, and Indians cannot be made to stand in for black slaves in this schema. Nonetheless, as Johannsen's work suggests, southern culture shaped the views of many residents of the territory. Far from shucking off such ideas as they moved west, they adapted them to the new environment, limiting the reach of the law and expressing a diffuse sympathy for the administration of summary punishments to control unruly Indians.

The settlers introduced whipping, for example, to punish Indians who committed less serious infractions.[6] In one instance from 1857, a young slave belonging to a headman from one of the northern Coast Salish groups broke into a settler's house in the town of Whatcom. The owner of the house wanted to send the boy to Port Townsend for trial, but another settler advised the homeowner to give the slave "a good thrashing and let him run and not put the Govt [sic] to expense." Instead the whites first asked the headman to discipline the slave, but the headman refused, saying that if he whipped the boy, the slave might run away. He told the whites, however, that they could whip the boy "as much as they please." The two settlers, in apparent collaboration with the local Indian agent (a Virginian who later fought for the Confederacy), gave the boy "a good thrashing."[7]

In another case from 1857, settlers apprehended a group of Indians burglarizing the residence of a Dr. Williamson in Seattle. The settlers selected a German immigrant named Williams to whip the Indians. Williams administered the punishment and was later reported killed by the Indians in revenge. Another whipping occurred in 1858, when a

Steilacoom storekeeper named McCaw apprehended an Indian attempting to take two coats. He beat the Indian with an axehandle and then whipped him with a three-foot length of rope. "The punishment was severe," commented a local newspaper, "but well merited."[8] The settlers saw whipping as, in part, a pragmatic response to a weak law enforcement infrastructure. In 1857 a local newspaper praised whipping as "the only punishment, from want of proper places of confinement, that can be inflicted on the Indians, and at the same time the most effectual and beneficial."[9]

In the eyes of many federal and territorial officials, however, whipping usurped proper legal authority, and they feared that such usurpations poisoned Indian-white relations. Commenting on the frequency of whipping in 1853, Agent E. A. Starling wrote that it "makes them [the Indians] revengeful, and causes innocent persons to be ill treated by them . . . for the willful and injudicious conduct of others." Better for whites to "govern their passions," Starling wrote, "and consent that punishment should be inflicted by proper authority." He recommended that Indians guilty of "any misdemeanor" should be taken to a military post and punished there.[10]

Summary killings of Indians by whites constituted an even greater usurpation of authority. While some of these killings can be attributed to simple racial hatred and exterminationist sentiment, others had more complex motivations. Settlers exercised a racial privilege to mete out private discipline for perceived offenses perpetrated by Indians. Racial hatred did play a role in these killings, but settlers often argued that their grievances against the Indian victims justified such punishment.

Close used this line of argument when he justified his actions as self-defense. He claimed that his knowledge of Indian character generally and his particular knowledge of Mich-ki-a's and Wal-sut ut's "bad" character legitimated the two killings. At his trial for the murders two months later, Close argued that, subject to a "ferocious attack" by the deceased and with knowledge of "the quarrelsome and ferocious and drunken character" of the Indians, he legitimately feared for his life and thus had to strike first.[11]

Close hardly stood alone among accused Indian killers in arguing that the Indians had asked for it. For example, George Wood, a settler in the coastal town of Grays Harbor, shot and killed an Indian called Cox, because he suspected the Indian of stealing. Wood believed that three

Indians—Cox, Riley, and Annie—stole a demijohn of whiskey and some powder and lead from him. Wood first threatened to shoot Riley if the Indian did not return his belongings. Riley returned a portion of the missing material, whereupon Wood punished him by beating him with a stick. Later, Wood shot and killed Cox. "I have heard him [Wood] remark that . . . if they [the Indians] did not stop stealing from him he would shoot some of them," testified the principal witness at Wood's preliminary hearing.[12]

More Indians were killed in the immediate aftermath of the Indian wars of 1855–56. Numerous whites avenged the wartime deaths of friends or relatives by killing Indians suspected of engaging in the hostilities. Two territorial volunteers, for example, killed an Indian called Mowitch on May 17, 1856, while they held him in their custody. Joseph Brannon and James Lake were transporting Mowitch to Seattle, where he was supposed to stand trial before a military commission for his participation in the war. On the way, Brannon shot Mowitch in the head, and Lake killed him with a second shot to the head.

A military tribunal brought up the two militiamen on charges of "conduct subversive of good order and discipline." At his hearing, Lake stated that he was "firmly convinced that the Indian Mowitch was concerned in the depredations perpetrated . . . last fall, murdering defenceless women and children. . . . Besides I was satisfied that he was concerned in shooting my brother and driving off my cattle, and I was determined that no such savage monster should escape the fate he so richly deserved." Lake thus expressed his distrust that a formal trial would convict and punish Mowitch sufficiently, justifying his actions by claiming his prerogative to enforce the law.[13]

Other postwar killings of Indians stemmed from similar motivations. Quiemuth, one of the Native leaders during the Puget Sound War, turned himself in to the territorial authorities as the hostilities drew to a close. As with Mowitch, officials planned to put Quiemuth on trial for his actions during the war. While under guard in Governor Stevens's office, however, he was assassinated by a group of whites, some of whom had lost relatives in the war. Suspicion fell on Joseph Bunton, whose father-in-law Quiemuth had supposedly killed, but a local magistrate examined and released Bunton. The *Olympia Pioneer and Democrat* was "not prepared to say" that Bunton was guilty, but labeled it a "melancholy fact that those who have lost near and dear relatives by assassination or treachery on the part of the Indians, seem determined to enforce the old Levitical law wherever and whenever an opportunity presents itself."[14]

Many whites feared that such summary action would only intensify conflict with the Indians. During and immediately after the war, for example, numerous critics pointed out that the settlers had brought the war upon themselves by mistreating the Indians. But territorial officials disputed this representation, describing these acts of violence as atypical outbursts of lawlessness and stressing the generally law-abiding nature of the white populace.[15]

A militia officer wrote to the *Olympia Pioneer and Democrat* in September 1856 that he knew of only one Indian killed by whites prior to the outbreak of the war. Although acquitted, the killers had been forced to leave the territory through the force of public sentiment. Governor Stevens declared that the territory's citizens "universally regretted and reprobated" two murders of Indians that took place immediately after the war, stating that they had occurred only after "extraordinary provocation."[16]

Each new attack disturbed this image of a settlement ordered by law, where the guarantees of due process afforded impartial justice to Indians and whites alike. Local Indian Agent Sidney Ford branded the killing of Quiemuth, for example, "an outrage upon all law and order. . . . It would cast upon the people of the Territory an imputation of lawlessness (with which we already stand charged)." The *Olympia Pioneer and Democrat*, a staunch Stevens supporter, portrayed the governor as "exceedingly mortified at the occurrence," adding that "the community generally . . . are positive in their condemnation of the act—the more so as having occurred in the governor's office, and after the Indian had surrendered himself for trial."[17]

In their condemnations, officials called on settlers to let the law do its work. In 1857, when a settler shot and killed Yelm John, an Indian living on the Nisqually Reservation who had been involved in the war and surrendered himself to the authorities, local Agent Wesley Gosnell wrote a letter to the Olympia newspaper denouncing the act as "not to be justified upon any principle known to civilized people." If the Indian was guilty of some offense, Gosnell said, "the civil courts are open for his conviction, and the strong arm of the law ready to execute the sentence." The killing—by men motivated by "a petty desire of personal revenge"—

would bring further "discredit upon the territory," whose people had already been "stigmatised abroad as Indian exterminators."[18]

Gosnell also argued that officials represented the law to the Indians as a universal mechanism for the settlement of interracial conflict, and summary killings in retaliation for perceived offenses undermined that representation.

> The Indian service has uniformly labored to impress upon the mind of the Indian that it was the duty of both whites and Indians to be governed in all things by law—that all grievances must be redressed by law—that to be a good people they must be a law-abiding people, and as such their rights would be respected. Was it not right to instruct them thus?—could government teach them otherwise? And yet what reasonable hope can we entertain that they will respect our laws, when they see white men ready to violate them and trample under foot the rights of the Indian?[19]

In consonance with their emphasis on due process, territorial officials prosecuted the most egregious offenses committed against Indians. "I am determined," Stevens wrote in June 1856, after three Indians were killed by a former militia volunteer, "to apply the whole force at my disposal to bring to punishment the infamous perpetrators of such crimes." Overall, however, only a small number of whites faced charges for offenses against Indians. James Close was one of just thirty-five non-Indian defendants prosecuted during the territorial period for crimes against Indians.[20]

Like Close, most of the defendants in these cases faced murder charges. Of thirty-six total cases (Close stood trial twice, once for each victim), twenty-three involved murder or manslaughter charges. Unlike Close's case, most of the murder prosecutions occurred in the first dozen years of the territorial period. Fifteen of the twenty-three cases occurred in the years between 1853 and 1864. The number of prosecutions dramatically underestimates the actual number of Indians killed by whites, for it does not include cases such as the killing of Quiemuth, where whites were examined and discharged after a preliminary hearing, or cases that sparked no legal action at all.[21]

Territory v. James Close

The exclusion of Indians from participation in the legal system during the early territorial period clearly had an effect on the number of prosecutions. Since Indians could not directly initiate cases against whites until 1873, numerous white crimes against Indians went unprosecuted.

Furthermore, the cases that did make it to district court generally failed. Among the twenty-three murder cases there were just three convictions (13 percent)—with Close accounting for two of them. From the total of thirty-six cases, there were but five convictions. More than 60 percent of white defendants got off through acquittals, dismissals, or flight before arrest. The result in nine cases is unknown.

By some lights, Close's case could be seen as a victory for American justice. Surely it meant something that a jury convicted a white man for killing an Indian. Juries during the early territorial period had routinely acquitted whites accused of killing or assaulting Indians, severely limiting the reach of the formal institutions of law into the areas of private discipline exercised by settlers. "It would perhaps be impossible in this country to obtain a jury that would find a bill against a white man for killing an Indian," a local newspaper stated after a grand jury acquitted a soldier accused of murder. Three years later, after a fruitless coroner's inquest into the death of an Indian woman, the newspaper commented that "a lawyer can find, any day, twelve men who will say under oath that killing an Indian is not murder, because the dust of the earth of which a white man is made is of a little better quality than that of which an Indian or negro is made."[22]

In fact, a glaring contradiction lay at the heart of the official ideology that formal legal procedures guaranteed equal justice. Officials held up law as a neutral and almost autonomous mechanism for ascertaining and punishing guilt. Thus, they could promise equal justice under the system, while legally excluding Indians from participation in that system. In the context of the civil disabilities imposed upon Indians, reliance on formal legal procedures only ensured that the reigning popular legal culture ruled in the jury box.

Close doubtless counted upon the prejudiced popular sentiment of earlier days to spare him from punishment. After the shootings, he had returned to the raft and informed Benoit that he had just shot two Indians. Benoit told him to give himself up and things would be "all right." The two began walking to Wallula, reaching the town at about sunrise on September 28, 1885. Close turned himself in to the justice of the peace, who bound Close over on $2,000 bail to appear before the grand jury. Failing to make bail, Close waited in jail for the next term of court.

By turning himself in, Close betrayed his own confidence in Benoit's assertion that things would be "all right." He counted, in other words, on the sympathies of the community.[23] But the community had undergone significant change over the previous twenty years. The earlier legal culture, while not gone, was now tempered by an increasing willingness to submit Indian-white conflicts to the courts, rather than resolve them privately. Even minor offenses committed by Indians—which earlier might have been punished by a whipping or beating—were brought by settlers to the courts for adjudication. In other words, many settlers had come to terms with the legal formalism urged on them by territorial officials. Close's decision to surrender, despite the clear expectation that he would be exonerated, reflected this acceptance of the role of law; Benoit knew that the law would be brought into the matter, so he urged Close to bring it in himself.

In his decision to submit his actions to formal legal judgment, Close followed a precedent established by another accused Indian killer. Several months prior to the Close incident, a Walla Walla County rancher named Henry Roff had shot and killed an Indian named Me-ats. Me-ats and a companion had appeared at Roff's ranch and assaulted John Linn, Roff's hired man, after Linn refused to give the men some matches. Roff intervened, whereupon the Indians threatened him with a knife. Roff retreated to his house and waited for the Indians to leave. When they did, Roff followed them, armed with a shotgun and intending to arrest them. When the Indians resisted Roff's efforts, he shot Me-ats in the head.[24]

Like Close, Roff proceeded to the nearest town, Waitsburg, and turned himself in to the justice of the peace. He also filed a complaint for assault with a deadly weapon against Me-ats's companion. His surrender, like Close's, evinced not only his confidence that his motive for killing Me-ats would stand up to the legal scrutiny of a jury of his neighbors, but also his acceptance of the law's ultimate role as the arbiter of legality.[25]

This growing acceptance of the role of law reflected demographic and cultural shifts within the settler population, which facilitated the extended reach of formal legal institutions. The makeup of the settler population in

1880 differed significantly from its makeup in 1860. The non-Native population rose from 11,594 to 70,711, and the sex ratio became more balanced, from 2.82 men for each woman in 1860 to 1.63 men for each woman in 1880. As the population became more dense and more settled, there was a greater reliance on the formal institutions of law.[26]

Although the top ten states of origin for the 1880 population differed only slightly from those of the 1860 population, migration from other areas diluted the influence of the border states. More importantly, the Civil War had overturned many of the cultural assumptions of the early years. The territory's residents, for the most part, supported the Union during the war and viewed suppression of the Confederacy as part of the government's duty to enforce the law. When noting the Republican victories in Washington's 1874 local elections, for example, Bancroft commented that "the class of voters which in 1862–64 overflowed from the south-western states upon the Pacific coast was being either eliminated or outnumbered."[27]

The postbellum view of government authority colored settlers' attitudes toward local law enforcement. Residents looked to formal legal institutions to police society and enforce order more consistently than they had in the first two decades of the territory's existence. The Republican appointees who occupied the district judgeships during these decades gave added force to this view of the law.[28]

The extended reach of legal institutions into Indian-white conflicts was apparent in the type of offenses for which Indians faced trial. During the later period, settlers routinely charged Indians with lesser crimes against persons and property. Of forty-five cases in which whites charged Indians with larceny or burglary, for example, only four (9 percent of the total) occurred in 1853 64. During the last twelve years of the territorial period, on the other hand, there were twenty-eight such cases (62 percent).

Increased white settlement east of the Cascades explains part of this increase in charges against Indians for property crimes. The settlers brought more horses and stock into the territory, and horse theft prosecutions account for twenty-three (51 percent) of the larceny and burglary cases. Nineteen of those occurred east of the mountains. Given the cultural importance of the horse among the Native groups on the Plateau, it is not surprising that Indians targeted settlers' horses for expropriation.

Rather than administer the same type of private discipline that held sway in the early territorial period, settlers turned to the legal system to enforce their property rights. These prosecutions served symbolic as well as functional ends. They announced the arrival of American notions of property rights and served warning that Indian actions would be subject to review and judgment in American courts. Adherence to American standards of due process legitimated the proceedings as fair, which allowed questions of power and sovereignty to be ignored.

Conviction rates for Indian defendants in these larceny and burglary cases provide evidence that whites did respect due process rights. Fifteen of the Indians (33 percent) charged with these crimes were convicted or pled guilty. Of the remaining cases, twenty (44 percent) ended in either acquittal or other form of discharge; the result in ten cases is unknown.

Prosecutions of Indians for assaults show similar patterns. Of twenty-one assault prosecutions, only four (19 percent) occurred in the first third of the territorial period. In the 1878–89 period, by contrast, prosecutors brought fifteen cases of assault (71 percent). Such figures indicate, not a general increase in the level of white-Indian violence, but the changing views of white settlers regarding the usefulness of the legal system in controlling Indians.

An example that captures these changing views occurred in March 1885. Charles Vader, a settler on the Green River in King County, had a run-in with an Indian called Alverds Bob, also known as Bob James. Vader had hired Bob's cousin, the son of a headman called King George, to clear a field, promising to pay him fifteen dollars. On March 9, Bob had demanded payment from Vader for doing part of the work. Vader told Bob that he had not hired him and that he would have nothing to do with him, but Bob maintained that he had done half the work and deserved half the pay. After several minutes of confrontation, Vader returned to his house; a few minutes later, he saw Bob approaching with an axe in his hand. Bob asserted that he intended to take Vader's canoe as security for payment. Vader told him to leave, at which point Bob stepped close to Vader, still holding the axe, and, according to Vader's account, threatened to kill Vader. Bob later admitted that he had threatened to take the canoe, but denied ever threatening Vader's life.

How did Vader respond to such a threat? Rather than administer his own summary punishment, Vader filed a complaint against the Indian for assault with a deadly weapon. The justice of the peace found sufficient evidence of wrongdoing to bind Bob over for the next term of district court. Unable to make bail, Bob sat in jail from March 12 until April 6, at which time the grand jury refused to indict him and he went free.[29]

Whether Bob actually threatened Vader is impossible to know. What is clear is Vader's reliance on the legal system to quell a perceived threat from Bob. Moreover, the perceived threat was fairly minor; although arrested on a charge of assault, Bob had not harmed Vader. Nonetheless, Vader perceived the law as sufficiently accessible and sufficiently powerful to restrain any hostile intention Bob might have harbored. Although the grand jury eventually acquitted him, the month in jail awaiting trial probably served Vader's purposes.

Settlers like Vader increasingly viewed the legal system as a tool to harass Indians perceived as too aggressive or assertive. Perhaps the best example of such manipulation aimed at a recalcitrant Indian came in the legal harassment of the Columbian chief Moses, who had long refused confinement on any reservation and in the 1870s actively campaigned for a separate reservation for his people. In 1878, with the outbreak of the Bannock-Shoshone war in Idaho, the settlers in Washington Territory regarded Moses with a great deal of suspicion. They suspected him of having colluded in the killing of a male settler named Perkins and his wife, and they feared his efforts to remove another block of land from the public domain.[30]

Moses agreed to help a Yakima County posse locate the true murderers of the Perkins, but after a series of missed rendezvous and rumors of a double cross, the posse arrested Moses and nine other men and confined them in jail at Yakima City. The agent for the Yakima reservation succeeded in getting Moses out of jail and kept him confined to the reservation for three months, until the OIA finally granted him permission to visit Washington, D.C. to negotiate a separate reservation.

As he began his journey, however, Moses was apprehended by the Yakima County sheriff and another posse of local settlers. Arraignment on a charge of accessory to the Perkins murder kept Moses in jail, and the prosecution delayed trial for eight successive days. It became clear to the agent that the prosecutor wanted a continuance until the next term of court, thus preventing Moses from journeying to Washington, D.C. Finally, the agent arranged to post bail for the chief, who then traveled to

Washington and succeeded in obtaining a separate reservation. On his return journey, he had to ask the regional military commander for protection against possible attack. When a grand jury finally investigated the charge of accessory to murder, it refused to indict and the case was dismissed.[31]

In Moses' case, it is difficult to assert that the law simply served as an instrument of white domination, since Moses was eventually acquitted. Rather it seems that the settlers used the formal routines of the law—the very procedures supposed to guarantee the neutral administration of justice—to hinder Moses' efforts to secure a separate reservation for his people. Such manipulations of formal procedures stand apart from the direct action—shooting, beating, whipping, etc.—adopted by settlers earlier in the period, and they illustrate the settlers' changed perceptions of the law.

A decline in white-on-Indian homicide provides another sign of the change in the settlers' legal culture. While the murders committed by Close, Roff, and others in the 1870s and 1880s showed that summary killings did not stop occurring, nonlegal sources such as agents' reports and newspaper accounts suggest that they did become less frequent. That only six whites were prosecuted for killing Indians during the last third of the territorial period stemmed only in part from the existing bias against tough enforcement for such crimes. A larger part of the explanation lies in a real decline in interracial violence, as settlers began to use the law, rather than firearms, to punish Indians.

When summary killings of Indians did occur in the later part of the territorial period, they differed from earlier killings in that they were not seen as substitutes for the law as the best vehicle for maintaining order. These episodes accepted the role of law in controlling disorder, and further, they indicted the process for not adequately carrying out that role. They often interrupted legal processes already underway, removing their victims from jail cells, for example, where they awaited trial. During the troubled summer of 1878, the year of the Bannock-Shoshone war, a local paper reported that one Indian, charged with assault against a white woman in Yakima County, "came very near" being taken forcibly from jail and given "the fatal punishment the extremely cruel brute deserved." Three weeks later, the same paper published a letter from "Young America" that reported another Indian removed from a jail cell in Yakima

County by a white mob. "We don't know what the result was—but hope there is one good redskin," the letter stated.[32]

Furthermore, such episodes of vigilantism did not only target non-whites. In the 1880s, a more general concern with the problems of social order led to episodes of vigilantism against white transients and criminals, particularly when law enforcement appeared to be "soft" in certain areas. Thus in 1882, a Seattle mob lynched two itinerant laborers accused of killing a local citizen, and newspapers up and down Puget Sound applauded the action for striking a blow for law and order. In 1887, a mob attempted to lynch an accused murderer in Goldendale, the county seat for Klickitat County. In 1889, the Yakima newspaper reported the lynching of an accused killer in the town of Roslyn, a mining community in Kittitas County.[33]

Changes in the pattern of prosecutions of whites charged with offenses against Indians also testifies to the larger role accorded to the law. As with crimes charged to Indians, one finds more prosecutions of minor offenses committed by whites in the later period. Five of the eight white-on-Indian assault prosecutions and three of the four property-crime prosecutions took place in the 1878–89 period. While small overall, the numbers suggest a growing role for the law in policing Indian-white relations and an increasing concern with social order among settlers. The routine and long-ignored abuse of Indians, which had marked the earlier period and had exacerbated tensions between the two groups, increasingly found its way into the courts.

Juries certainly did not lose all of their sympathy for whites charged with crimes against Indians, however. Despite the evident changes in popular legal culture, despite the removal of the prohibition on Indian testimony in criminal proceedings involving whites, prosecutors still found it extraordinarily difficult to find a jury that would convict a white person for an offense against an Indian. In Roff's case, for example, the prosecutor dropped the charges after Roff defaulted on his bail because "it would probably be impossible under the circumstances of the case ever to convict the defendant before a jury."[34]

At his trial, Close drew a jury that was sympathetic, but that simply could not overlook the mountain of evidence against him. Indicted on two separate charges of manslaughter, Close stood trial in December 1885 for the killing of Wal-sut-ut and in May 1886 for the killing of Mich-ki-a. At his initial trial, he introduced a number of witnesses who testified to the Indians' reputation for drunkenness and violence. On the stand in his own defense, Close stated that Benoit had pointed the two Indians out to him in Wallula and remarked on their bad character.[35]

Unfortunately for Close, he could not establish with certainty that he had killed these particular "bad" Indians on September 27. Close said he recognized them as the same Indians because of their size, but said they were not otherwise particularly distinguishable from other Indians. Benoit did not do much better. "All Indians look black to me," he stated. He did identify Mich-ki-a as the brother of an Indian called "Juanista," but he could not specifically identify Wal-sut-ut. "I never took notice of the other one[.] It is not my business to size dead Indians," he stated.

Guided by the judge, the jury rejected Close's broad plea that the character of the deceased men warranted their murder. In his final charge to the jury, the judge emphasized a more traditional notion of self-defense. "Consider all the evidence as to what danger if any was impending and about to fall upon the defendant *at the time* the fatal shot was fired. . . . Any danger which had passed by before the shot was fired, ought not to be considered." If they were not in self-defense, the judge told the jury, then were the killings a legitimate defense of property? He cautioned them that "a mere trespass upon property does not excuse the killing of the trespasser." Finally, contrary to the defense's portrayal of a "ferocious attack" committed by the deceased, the judge asked the jury to consider whether the Indians had even committed a felony. Taking whiskey was not a felony, he told them, nor was a threat to take thirty dollars worth of goods from the camp a justification for killing.[36]

The jury, torn between sympathy for Close and the nature of the evidence, chose a compromise. At the initial trial, the jury convicted Close of assault and battery upon Wal-sut-ut, "with the understanding that the prisoner was to be tried on the second indictment," according to the *Walla Walla Union*. "Among thinking people," the *Union* continued, "the verdict, to say the least, is a strange one." The judge took what he could get, sentencing Close to seven months in the county jail. At sentencing, the judge noted the absurdity of the jury's conclusion, since the "assault terminated in the death of two human beings."[37]

At Close's second trial, the judge made a point of including in the jury instructions the admonition that assault and battery was not a lesser offense included with manslaughter. An assault that ends in death, the judge told them, is a homicide. As a result, the jury in Close's second trial found him guilty as charged, but requested clemency in punishment. The judge sentenced Close to one year in the territorial prison and a five-dollar fine, the prison sentence to begin on July 3, 1886, the date his seven-month term in the county jail expired. Shortly before he was to be moved to the prison, however, Close broke out of the county jail and escaped to Oregon.[38]

Despite the jury's absurd verdict in the first trial and the very slight punishments meted out, the verdicts did reflect the changes in the settlers' legal culture since the early territorial days. Although they made it clear that the community did not view the killing of an Indian with a great deal of concern, the jurors had to accord the formal procedures of law a certain grudging respect.

According to the rhetoric of territorial officials, such formal proce-dures had always governed conflicts between Indians and whites. But official rhetoric had clashed repeatedly with a popular legal culture that reserved space for the private punishment of Indians administered by settlers. When officials tried to control such private punishments by bringing settlers to trial, early juries nullified their efforts.

But Close discovered that by 1885 whites could not absolutely count on this popular sentiment to pardon abuses against Indians. The popular legal culture changed as the broader cultural and demographic character of the population changed. The Civil War had challenged many of the assumptions behind the vernacular legal culture, and settlers came to accept the formal institutions of law as the proper vehicles for punishing Indians charged with crimes against whites. Many traces of the popular legal culture remained, but by the end of the territorial period, settlers had come to accept the official legal culture of due process of law.

Chapter 6

ROBERT SULKANON V. DAVID LEWIS
INTERRACIAL CONFLICT AND INDIAN LEGAL CULTURE

Like the settlers, Indians disagreed with territorial officials over the appropriate means to resolve interracial disputes and resisted efforts to channel disputes into the formal legal system. Like the settlers, many Indians believed the courts could not deliver justice, though the Indians' description of justice differed dramatically from that of the settlers. Yet both settlers and Indians found the formal apparatus of law exerting greater control over their disputes as the territorial period wore on. As territorial law extended its reach, Indians began to mobilize it in their efforts to preserve their autonomy against the encroachments of settlers and even against the power of the Indian Department.

In 1885, the same year that Close killed Wal-sut-ut and Mich-ki-a, Robert Sulkanon, a Nooksack Indian, became embroiled in a dispute with a settler west of the Cascades. Between December 1883 and April 1885, Sulkanon's land was forcibly occupied on three separate occasions by a white man named David Lewis. Each time, Lewis abandoned the land after a short period. During the third incident, Lewis and his partner Adolph Ridderbjilke plowed up Sulkanon's oat crop and took possession of three thousand fence rails owned by Sulkanon. Unlike the dispute between Close and the Indians on the Columbia, this dispute ended not in bullets and backshooting, but in a lawsuit. On May 5, 1885, Sulkanon filed a writ of forcible entry and detainer against the two men.

Sulkanon benefited directly from the post–Civil War changes in Washington's legal regime. As their first line of defense, Lewis and

Ridderbjilke challenged Sulkanon's standing in court. On May 13, they demurred to Sulkanon's complaint because, they stated, the plaintiff "is an Indian of full blood and has no legal capacity to sue." By making an issue of Sulkanon's racial identity, Lewis played on common white assumptions about Indians' racial inferiority and presumed legal incompetence. Prior to 1873, this strategy would have worked, for territorial law would have barred Sulkanon from pursuing a case against a white person. But in 1885, given the changes in Indians' legal standing in the territory, the justice of the peace in the case had no choice but to overrule the demurrer. Sulkanon would have his day in court.[1]

Under the exclusionary legal regime of the early territorial period, many other Indians also had their days in court, but almost always as defendants charged with crimes against whites. From the earliest period of American settlement in the region north of the Columbia River, officials tried and punished Indians for offenses committed against whites. Under federal law, interracial offenses occurring inside Indian country fell under federal jurisdiction; those occurring outside Indian country fell under local jurisdiction. During the thirty-seven-year history of Washington Territory, prosecutors filed charges against Indian defendants in 106 cases of interracial conflict, almost all of which occurred off the reservations, outside Indian country. These cases arose out of the ongoing contact between Indians and settlers in the territory; as Indians and whites worked and lived in close proximity to each other, their interests inevitably clashed.[2]

Throughout the territorial period, officials had told the Indians, as they told the settlers, that interracial disputes should be handled by the appropriate legal authorities. They preached that the law would punish fairly both whites and Indians, in spite of the numerous restrictions on Indians' participation in the legal process.

Before 1873 Indians could not mobilize the law, as Sulkanon did, against whites who committed abuses against them. As a result, they relied on their own sanctions, including violent retaliation. Such recourse explains why most of the murder and manslaughter cases against Indians occurred early in the period. Murder cases accounted for twenty-seven (49 percent) of the fifty-five violent crime prosecutions against Indians; twenty of these occurred in the 1853–72 period. By contrast, most of the lesser offenses charged against Indians—property crimes and assaults—

occurred during the later years of the period, as settlers increasingly turned to the courts to punish such offenses (see graph 2).

The power to try Indians in American courts flowed from the presumption of American sovereignty over the territory. This presumption of sovereignty rested not on any cession by the Indians, but on the doctrine of discovery. This doctrine of international law recognized the Indians' rights to occupy the land, but reserved sovereignty for the non-Indian nation that claimed "discovery." The Indians could only cede their occupancy rights to the nation recognized as sovereign over the territory. By the 1846 treaty with Great Britain, which had initially claimed most of the Pacific Northwest region, the United States secured its own claim to sovereignty over the region south of the 49th parallel.[3]

The assumption of jurisdiction over conflicts between American settlers and Indians symbolized this claim to sovereignty. The trial and punishment of Indians who committed crimes against whites testified to the ability and the right of the United States to protect its citizens from harm. Similarly, the trial and punishment of whites who committed crimes against Indians testified to the dominance of the United States over the Indians, for it asserted U.S. law's superiority over the "barbarism" of Native law.[4]

The form that these legal prosecutions took also symbolized American sovereignty. Adherence to the formal routines of law in prosecutions of Indians justified the American occupation of Washington Territory. The emphasis on "the rule of law" identified the fledgling settlement as a civilized outpost, distinguished not only from the "barbarism" of the Indians, but also from the uncivilized practices of the Hudson's Bay Company. Although the treaty with Britain gave the United States sovereignty over the area north of the Columbia, the company continued to exercise a great deal of influence until the end of the Indian wars.[5]

Before the formal organization of the territory, relations between the Natives and the company resembled the "middle ground" model that Richard White has used to describe Indian-white relations in the Great Lakes area during the seventeenth and eighteenth centuries. In White's study the term *middle ground* denotes an area of shared meaning created by two distinct cultural groups interacting with each other on relatively equal footing. In this model each group communicates its desires to the other group in ways that it believes will be understood, but each group

Robert Sulkanon v. David Lewis

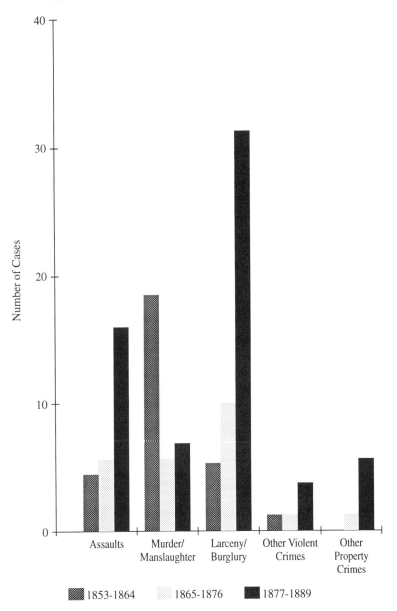

GRAPH 2
Indian-on-White Crimes Prosecuted during the Territorial Period

Number of Cases

Assaults   Murder/   Larceny/   Other Violent   Other
            Manslaughter   Burglury   Crimes   Property
                                                  Crimes

■ 1853-1864   □ 1865-1876   ■ 1877-1889

also tends to interpret these messages in the way that most clearly serves its own ends, resulting in misunderstanding and conflict.[6]

In the region that was to become Washington Territory this ongoing process of communication and miscommunication created certain shared rituals and patterns of behavior that were neither wholly Native nor wholly European. "As Hudson's Bay men and local people married, traded, and tried to ascertain and respond to each other's expectations without forfeiting their own," one student of the Puget Sound area has noted, "they figuratively cleared and gradually expanded an arena for their joint activities—a cultural space where people of different cultures could serve their separate interests by observing a common, specialized set of rules."[7]

Dispute resolution constituted one arena of interaction where such specialized rules operated. The rules drew heavily from Native law-ways of reciprocity, compensation in atonement for wrongs, and retaliation when such compensation was not forthcoming. John Phillip Reid, who has studied the settlement of homicides among the fur traders and Indians of the Far West, concludes that the fur traders "employed words derived less from British ways of speaking than from a pan-Indian legal vocabulary."[8]

The company therefore retaliated when Indians killed one of its officers or traders. For example, company officers avenged the killing of Samuel Black, chief factor at a company post on the North Thompson River, by killing the young Shuswap suspected of murdering him. Similarly, when William F. Tolmie served at Fort Nisqually in the 1830s, he described in his diary a conflict with a group of Clallams over the price of furs. When the Indians threatened him, Tolmie warned them that "the smallest violence . . . would be severely avenged by the Whites." As Reid observes, "always, they [the traders] spoke of vengeance."[9]

The presence of the Hudson's Bay Company twisted Native concepts of compensation and reciprocity, however. The company would not accept compensation as settlement for the killing of one of its officers, although it would pay out compensation to the kin of Indians killed by its employees. John McLoughlin, chief factor at Fort Vancouver, emphasized that economic interest lay behind the Hudson Bay Company's acquiescence to demands for Native justice. "We are traders, and . . . all traders are desirous of gain," he wrote in 1843. "Is it not self evident we will manage our business with more economy by being on good terms with Indians than if at variance."[10]

Incoming American officials sought to replace the Hudson's Bay Company system with one that seemed "legal," at least by non-Indian standards. During the political conflict over the possession of the area north of the Columbia River, American polemicists attacked the company for its brutal treatment of the Indians in the quest for vengeance. American officials called for the extension of American law over the Indians and the recognition of Indian rights to a fair trial.[11]

In 1849, proceedings against a group of Snoqualmie Indians who killed Leander Wallace, an American settler, clearly showed the difference between the legal approach of the Americans and that of the Hudson's Bay Company. Wallace was killed during a conflict between the Snoqualmies and a group of Nisqually Indians over the mistreatment of a Snoqualmie woman by her Nisqually husband. The Snoqualmies pursued the Nisqually, seeking to punish them, and the Nisqually fled for protection to the company's Fort Nisqually, where chief factor Tolmie tried to dissuade the hostile Snoqualmies from their purpose by offering them presents. After several hours of discussion, the Snoqualmies fired on the fort, inadvertently killing Wallace. A return volley from the fort killed one of the Indians.[12]

Since Wallace was an American, and since the area north of the Columbia was part of Oregon Territory, the Americans insisted on the apprehension and trial of the Snoqualmie suspects. After negotiating with the Snoqualmies and eventually paying them eighty blankets, American officials secured the arrest of six Snoqualmie men. In October 1849, at Fort Steilacoom—the only American outpost on Puget Sound at the time—American officials held the first-ever district court session in what was to become Washington Territory. Chief Justice William Bryant of Oregon presided, and the jury convicted two of the Snoqualmie—Kussass and Quallahwowt—and released the other four. The convicted men were hanged.[13]

The difficulties of holding a trial with an American jury and American lawyers proved immense. Bryant allowed the prosecutor and defense attorney $250 each for their services, as "they had to travel two hundred miles from their respective homes, camp in the woods, as well as the rest of us, and endure a great deal of fatigue in the manner of travelling."

Grand and petit jurors had to be summoned from as far away as Oregon City, the territorial capital, some two hundred miles distant, because of the sparseness of white settlement on Puget Sound. Bryant admitted in a report to the governor that it would have been cheaper to bring the accused and the witnesses to Oregon City for trial, but believed "the policy pursued here more than repaid any additional expense that may have been incurred."[14]

This policy was to bring American law to the areas of American dominion. "The effect produced by the trial was salutary," Bryant wrote, "and I have no doubt will long be remembered by the tribe. . . . [T]hey were made to understand that our laws would punish them promptly for every murder they committed." Thus the trial and hanging of Kussass and Quallahwowt was meant to announce that punishment mediated by law would replace punishment based on retaliation and compensation, which had marked the "middle ground" between Indians and the Hudson's Bay Company. The intended message may have been lost, however, since to the Indians the two hangings must have looked quite similar to retaliation. In addition, the Americans had to compromise with the existing system, paying compensation of eighty blankets to the Snoqualmies in exchange for their surrender of the accused.[15]

Even where they had to compromise, however, American officials tried to alter the vocabulary in the direction of Anglo-American legal terminology. Investigating a break-in at a settler's house in Seattle by a party of Duwamish in 1855, Puget Sound District Agent Simmons compelled the group to make restitution. The Indians had stolen a small amount of hard bread and sugar, and Simmons assessed them ten dollars, "not to satisfy the value of the depredation committed, but as a fine or punishment of the wrong doer." Like the insistence on the formal procedures of trial before punishment in the case of Kussass and Quallahwowt, Simmons's emphasis on the vocabulary of Anglo-American law differentiated the American settlement from the Native society and from the regime of the Hudson's Bay Company, at least in the eyes of American officials.[16]

The stress placed on due process is revealed in the number of murder cases that convicted Indian defendants appealed to the territorial supreme court. The high court heard twenty-six appeals of murder convictions during the entire territorial period, representing about 9 percent of all murder cases heard in the district courts. Five of these appeals involved Indian defendants. These cases are concentrated in the early part of the territorial period; all five occurred between 1856 and 1864, when the high court heard only two murder appeals from non-Indian defendants.[17]

The high court used these appeals as opportunities to praise the fairness of the American justice system and its evenhanded treatment of Indian defendants. In overturning the murder conviction of an Indian man called Elick in 1861, Justice John Wyche made clear the link between due process and American sovereignty. "The Constitution of the United States is co-extensive with the vast empire that has grown up under it, and its provisions securing certain rights to the accused in criminal cases, are as living and potent on the shores of the Pacific as in the city of its birth. In the matter of these rights it knows no race. It is the rich inheritance of all, and under its provisions in the Courts of the country, on a trial for life, the savage of the forest is the peer of the President."[18]

The American emphasis on respect for due process emerged most strongly during the murder trials of Indians who had participated in the 1855–56 Puget Sound War. The territorial district courts tried at least four Indian leaders for their participation in the war, and military commissions tried many Indians during and immediately after the war.

Given the criticisms leveled against the territorial administration and the settlers during the course of the war, respect for due process during the trials that followed worked as a legitimating ideology for punishing the Indians involved in the hostilities and thus helped legitimate the war itself. During a quarrel with General John Wool, the regional commander of the regular army and a harsh critic of the territorial regime, Governor Stevens made a point of emphasizing the scrupulousness of the legal proceedings by which Indian involvement in the hostilities was judged "When a military commission, composed of a majority of volunteer officers, tried . . . eight Indians, only one was convicted, and . . . the sentence of death passed upon him has not not [sic] yet been executed," he wrote to Wool. Such respect for due process proved the validity of these proceedings, Stevens argued.[19]

Other members of the territorial establishment echoed this sentiment. In a letter to a local newspaper, a militia officer wrote that, contrary to accusations against the volunteer troops for abusive treatment of Indians, the troops executed only those Indian prisoners proven guilty of participating in the murders of white citizens. When there was not compelling proof of guilt, the volunteers released the Indians to reservations.[20]

It is worthy of note that there was little discussion of fairness or legality when Colonel George Wright and other regular army officers summarily executed Indians east of the Cascades in the fall of 1858. These executions do not appear to have followed any formal proceedings—in the form of arrests, empaneling of judges, or review by the governor or commanding officer. In September 1858, after the two major battles of his campaign, Wright executed one member of a group of Spokane men who came to seek terms with the army. Jesuit missionaries persuaded Wright to follow a softer line with the Coeur d'Alenes and Spokanes thereafter, but the colonel pursued a "policy of hanging" with the other Plateau tribes.[21]

When the Yakima war leader Owhi rode into Wright's camp to ask for peace, Wright seized him and threatened to hang him unless he persuaded his son Qualchin to surrender. Qualchin arrived with his wife on September 24, their horses "gaily caparrisoned," according to a newspaper correspondent with Wright's command. Fifteen minutes after his capture, "it was determined that he should prowl the country no longer," and Wright had him hanged from a nearby pine tree. Owhi, held as a prisoner and doubtless headed for a similar fate, was shot while trying to escape ten days later.[22]

Before leaving his camp at the aptly named Hangman's Creek, Wright hanged six Wallawallas who, encouraged by the lenient treatment offered the Coeur d'Alenes and Spokanes, had come in to surrender. Heading south to Fort Walla Walla, Wright met in council with a group of Palouse and Nez Perce Indians. He demanded the surrender of men who had killed two miners in April; they were immediately hanged. He then secured the surrender of two men who had reportedly stolen government cattle in July. They, too, were hanged. On October 5, at a council with the Wallawallas and Cayuses, Wright hanged four more men who had acknowledged their participation in the hostilities.[23]

Wright's actions stand in contrast to the formality of the proceedings west of the mountains. The orders convening a military commission for the trial of a group of Duwamish men in May 1856, for example, specified that the presiding officer of the commission "keep a clear record of all the proceedings of the Court and forward them for revisal [sic] approval or other action to the Commander in Chief." Indeed, the existing records of

Robert Sulkanon v. David Lewis

three military commissions convened to prosecute hostile Indians, dating from November 1855 to June 1856, all show that the proceedings were forwarded to the territorial executive for review and approval.[24]

The greater stress laid on formal procedures west of the mountains shows the ideological import of due process. East of the Cascades, the small number of settlers and the resulting absence of political controversy freed Wright from the need to justify his actions. Authorities to the west, blamed for the war and accused of abusing the Indians, had to prove their own innocence by adhering to all the formalities of a fair hearing, even for hostile Indians.

This emphasis on due process emerges even more clearly in the civilian trials of the war leaders Leschi, Wahoolit, Kitsap, and Winyea. The best known of these is the murder trial of the Nisqually leader Leschi, the only "war trial" in district court that ended in conviction and execution. His trial was also marked by a heavy ideological emphasis on due process, notwithstanding numerous doubts about the evidence linking Leschi to the crime in question. Leschi was convicted on March 19, 1857, and his lawyers almost immediately appealed his case to the territorial supreme court. At its December 1857 term, the high court upheld the lower court's decision and confirmed Leschi's death sentence.[25]

"It speaks volumes for our people," the high court said in turning down the appeal, "that, notwithstanding the spirit of indignation and revenge, so natural to the human heart, incited by the ruthless massacre of their families, that at the trial of the accused, deliberate impartiality has been manifested at every stage of the proceedings." On December 18, 1857, the supreme court commanded the sheriff of Pierce County to keep Leschi in custody until January 22, 1858, and then hang him.[26]

On the scheduled date of execution, however, a collection of military officers and lawyers, who believed Leschi had been unjustly convicted and were equally eager to discredit the Stevens administration, arrested the sheriff on a charge of selling liquor to the Indians. Detained, the sheriff could not carry out the execution within the time specified in the writ. This ploy did not amuse the supreme court. "For reasons which may not be understood by this court the sentence . . . has not been carried into effect," it stated at Leschi's resentencing. The court then addressed Leschi directly:

You have had the benefit of a trial by a jury of twelve men who after hearing all the evidence and the arguments of counsel in your behalf say you are guilty. Your case has been reviewed by the Supreme court and no substantial error has been found. The executive clemency has been appealed to, which although not bound by the inflexible rules of law yet finds no reason why you should not suffer the penalty of the law. Whatever may be said of the *probability* or *possibility* of your innocence one thing is quite certain you have had the benefit of all the forms of law that the most favored of our own raice [*sic*] have in trials for murder.

After receiving such assurances, Leschi was hanged on February 19, 1858.[27]

Numerous commentators—both at the time of the trial and subsequently—have noted the dubious legality of Leschi's conviction. They have raised serious doubts not only about the evidence but also about the underlying legality of trying a war leader for murder. At his resentencing, Leschi himself reportedly raised this issue. "I have supposed that the killing of armed men in war time was not murder," he declared. By emphasizing the legality of Leschi's conviction, the courts meant to lay such doubts to rest.[28]

The trials of Indian war leaders and the proceedings of the various military commissions served to individualize and criminalize actions taken by hostile Indians. The proceedings sought to deny the legitimacy of Indian resistance to white occupation. "We are not willing to express the opinion that Indian tribes . . . have such a national character that they can, at their will, make war, and claim immunity for acts of indiscriminate and barbarous murder," the territorial supreme court stated when deciding the case of Wahoolit, another war leader. Similarly, a military commission convened in May 1856 charged Indians with waging "*unlawful war* upon the white inhabitants of Washington Territory" (emphasis added).[29]

Critics of the war trials emphasized the distinction between war, a collective act of violent resistance, and crime, an individual antisocial act. Trying Leschi for murder was illegitimate because the killings for which he was supposedly responsible occurred in wartime. But in the context of U.S.-Indian relations *wartime* tends to be defined by white authorities and historians, who limit it to a particular period of organized Indian resistance. Such distinctions obscure the political character of many Indian acts identified by whites as crimes during the territorial period.[30]

One example is the Indian response to the work of government surveyors, since surveys represented a direct abridgment of Indian claims to the land. In July 1857, a group of Homamish—one of the signatory bands of the Medicine Creek treaty—followed a government surveyor who was running lines near Henderson's Bay and pulled up his stakes. When confronted by the agent, they expressed concern about the survey, seeing it as preparatory to settlement of their country. "Although they are willing to receive the benefits of their Treaty," the agent reported, "they do not wish their country to be settled by the whites."[31]

About a year later, a party of Swinomish Indians shot and killed a surveyor named Dominick Hunt on Whidbey Island. Authorities eventually arrested five Indians in connection with the killing, but the grand jury indicted only two. A special term of district court convicted and sentenced them to death, and both were hanged on December 10, 1858. The taking of two Indian lives for the killing of one white man doubtless struck many Natives as unjust, but from the perspective of white officials, the ideology of due process justified the sentences. As a local newspaper commented, "They are said to have had a very fair trial, and every proper indulgence shown them in the presentation of their evidence and defense."[32]

Trying Indians who imposed their own sanctions on abusive whites also denied the legitimacy of Indian law and Indian sovereignty. In September 1857, John Roberts, a white man of "notoriously bad character," shot and either killed or wounded a Clallam man at a village near New Dungeness, on the Strait of Juan de Fuca. As Roberts retreated from the village, two Indians attacked him, shooting and stabbing him to death. The two men, along with two others who incited them to take action, were indicted for murder in August 1858. The prosecutor eventually had to drop the charges, however, as the Indians involved fled the region.[33]

Other "crimes" charged to Indians had a more distinctly political character. When Agent Simmons and several of his subordinates tried to break up a gathering of Snoqualmie Indians in September 1858, for example, they were repulsed by force. Simmons had intervened because of reports that the Snoqualmies intended to attack the Snohomish Indians in the area. The Snoqualmies clearly viewed this as an unwarranted intrusion into their affairs. They refused to parley with the agent, and when the officials persisted, the Snoqualmies attacked them, forcing the small party to retreat.

Aided by the local military and the Lummi Indians, Agent Simmons arrested seven of the supposed culprits. The court released five for lack of evidence, but the grand jurors returned at least three indictments against the remaining defendants for assault with intent to kill. The petit jury later acquitted them.[34]

The agent thus used the law to quell a clear challenge to his authority and to label such challenges as crimes. The jury's decision notwithstanding, the Indians' trial was inextricably bound up with the U.S. government's claim of power over the territory and over the Indians. This does not mean that the Indians were railroaded, as the acquittal made clear, or that the law was bent to justify American domination of the Indians. Rather, it means that the trial of these defendants, legal by American standards, provided a way to deny Indian claims to sovereignty, display American power, and reinforce American authority.

The rhetoric of due process served ideological purposes by making such proceedings seem fair. But it was more than just rhetoric. The relatively low conviction rates of Indian defendants charged with offenses against whites indicates that officials did respect procedural formalities. Once Indians were within the white legal system, in other words, the law mostly adhered to its own standards and procedures. Prucha has found similar adherence in territorial Wisconsin. "Far from acting on the premise that the savages had no civil rights," Prucha concludes, "the government tried them in the same courts and by the same processes that were accorded whites."[35]

In Washington, of the 106 cases with Indian defendants, prosecutors obtained a guilty plea or a guilty verdict in 37 (35 percent). Fifty-two defendants (49 percent) went free either through acquittal, dismissal, or flight before arrest. In seventeen cases, the result is unknown. Conviction rates rise when looking at only the homicide cases—the most emotionally charged prosecutions—but the general conclusion still holds. Of twenty-seven cases in which Indians were charged with killing non-Indians, twelve (44 percent) ended in a conviction or a guilty plea. Thirteen Indians (48 percent) were not convicted, and the result in two cases is unknown.

Robert Sulkanon v. David Lewis

A review of white-on-white murder cases from Jefferson County, at the southwest corner of the intersection of Puget Sound and the Strait of Juan de Fuca, shows that these figures are roughly equivalent to the conviction rates among non-Indian defendants charged with killing non-Indian victims. There were thirty-four such cases in Jefferson County during the territorial period. Fifteen (44 percent) ended in either a conviction or a guilty plea. The non-conviction rate was 47 percent, and the results in three cases are unknown.

This suggests that an Indian accused of killing a non-Indian faced no greater chance of conviction than a non-Indian charged with the same offense. The fairness of proceedings against Indians doubtless helped justify the harsher sentences received by those convicted. Indians who killed whites were hanged more frequently than whites who killed other whites. Of the twelve Indians convicted, five (42 percent) were hanged. Only four whites (27 percent) of the fifteen convicted in Jefferson County went to the gallows.

For many years prior to Sulkanon's suit against Lewis, therefore, Indians had tested American justice. Unlike Sulkanon, however, most of these Indians did not willingly invoke the law. Dragged into court by officials intent on demonstrating the majesty and fairness of American law and unable to mobilize the law against whites, these Indian defendants were merely spectators to the proceedings unfolding before them.

Indians responded to this situation by invoking their own sanctions and standards of legality. They continually struggled to exercise their own law-ways in disputes with whites. This led them, like the settlers, to seek alternatives to the formal legal mechanisms sanctioned by American officials. Whites who abused Indians often escaped punishment—either through acquittals or through non-prosecution of the offense—a tendency that did not go unnoticed by the Indians. As a result, they tried to convince the Americans to follow the tit for tat that had typified their relations with the Hudson's Bay Company. In place of due process, they advocated a rough equivalence of sanctions, offering to "swap" Indian lives for white lives. After Leschi's capture, for example, various Indians campaigned for his release on the grounds that the earlier assassination of Quiemuth by a group of vengeful whites had evened the score. "The general opinion of the Indians under my charge," wrote Agent Sidney Ford to Governor Stevens, is "that Quiemuth having been killed, it would be but fair and just that Leschi should go unpunished—that they will be satisfied to let the matter thus drop and consider it even—but if Leschi is executed they will not consider it right."[36]

A Native headman called Shelton offered a similar swap in late 1860 when a white man shot and killed one of his relatives, an Indian called John. At about the same time, a group of Indians had killed a white trader named Carter. In February 1861 a vigorous manhunt for Carter's killers resulted in the arrest of two men, Peeps or "Charley" and Elick, also known as Phames or Harry Peeps. In September, Shelton planned to visit the superintendent of Indian affairs in Olympia to discuss the two cases. "He says that if a white man is permitted to kill an Indian when ever they please and go unpunished," the agent wrote when advising the superintendent of the visit, "then the same rule ought to prevail in cases where an Indian kills a white man. He thinks that a fare [*sic*] swap would be to let young Phames go free in case the white man is turned loose."[37]

The negotiations with the superintendent yielded nothing, and events more or less followed the course Shelton had expected. No extant district court case file shows that anyone was ever prosecuted for the killing of John, while Elick and Peeps did face trial. The prosecution dropped the charges against Peeps, but a jury convicted Elick and sentenced him to hang on August 17, 1861. His conviction was appealed to the supreme court, which reversed it in December 1861 and ordered a new trial.[38]

After giving American law a chance, the Indians now simply refused to countenance any more proceedings. When it failed to empanel a jury at its February 1862 term, the court released Elick into the custody of three headmen from his tribe. The chiefs made a pledge to "the Great Father" that they would deliver Elick at the next term of court, as they had done prior to his initial conviction. This time, however, they did not live up to their promise and refused to produce him in court. "A number of warrants have been issued . . . and have been returned that the prisoner is not to be found," a clerk's note stated.[39]

The Indians' regard for white legal proceedings eroded steadily as whites accused of assaulting or killing Indians went unpunished. Their own sanctions seemed more effective and more just. When a settler named Collins killed three Duwamish men in early June 1856, the local Indian agent discovered three of the Indians under his charge urging the relatives of the victims "to take revenge on the whites and kill three of

Robert Sulkanon v. David Lewis

them." The agent immediately arrested the men for inciting the others to violence and sent them to Olympia so that Governor Stevens could punish them.[40]

Native headmen, constantly told by white officials that American law would protect their people, found themselves in an untenable position. According to an agent's summation of one headman's views: "He thinks that trying a white man for killing an Indian is a Humbug and if things go on as they have heretofore it will be out of the power of the Indian Tyees [chiefs] to keep the other Indians from applying their old rules to white men as well as to Indians in cases where they kill one of their tribe. [H]e himself is for prosecution by the courts but many are not."[41] Where white law failed, in other words, Native legal principles of retaliation or compensation paid by the perpetrator would be invoked.

For the most part, however, Indians realized that to kill whites in retaliation for killing Indians would only result in the surrender and trial of those who had killed the whites, as happened with the Clallam men who killed Roberts. When George Wood—a settler who had earlier gone unpunished for killing an Indian called Cox—threatened a band of Chehalis Indians, officials of the Indian Department took notice of the Indians' forbearance. "Were the life of a white person thus threatened he would of course have no hesitation in taking the life of the party so threatening and would be fully justifiable in so doing," the agent wrote to the superintendent of Indian affairs, "but the Indians knowing well the prejudice against them, and the partiality so invariably shown to white men in the trial of these cases dare not exercise even the privilege of self defense."[42]

If retaliation proved untenable, compensation did not. The Indians often succeeded in getting the authorities to pay compensation to "cover" the dead and resolve disputes. The Indian Department eventually covered the murder of Cox, for example, by paying twenty blankets to his relatives. The case of the three Duwamish murdered by Collins was settled by a Snoqualmie headman, who was related to the deceased, in direct negotiation with Governor Stevens. The local agent provided Stevens with a kinship diagram for the deceased and reckoned that "one hundred or one hundred and twenty blankets will probably settle the affair." When a storekeeper named Grennan flogged an Indian "rather unmercifully" over a trivial matter in 1856, the agent settled the matter by having Grennan pay some fifteen dollars in goods to the Indian.[43]

Pressured by the Indians either to make or to arrange such compensation, agents entertained serious doubts about the legality of such payments, given the official emphasis on resolving interracial conflicts through the courts. After three whites killed an Indian near the Columbia River in 1858, Agent R. H. Lansdale reported that, while he was attempting to apprehend the suspects to bring them to trial, "the friends of the murdered Indian demand of me pay for his life according to the Indian rule." Lansdale acknowledged that his predecessor had made such payments and that Lansdale's own "sense of justice" inclined him to the same course. But he had "some misgivings" about whether the superintendent would approve of such payments.[44]

Indians also occasionally offered substitutes when the authorities called for the surrender of those responsible for a crime. A group of Clallam headmen, facing a demand from the white authorities for two men suspected in the 1853 murder of a settler named Albert Pettingall, surrendered an eighteen-year-old Twana boy, naming him as the murderer. The boy's relatives told the Indian agent, however, that the boy had no part in the killing. "Not being a Sklallam [Clallam], they [the chiefs] have given him up hoping, thereby, to satisfy the whites & prevent any further inquiries." Such a practice accorded with the notions of reciprocity of the Indians' "middle ground" with the Hudson's Bay Company, but it contravened American notions that punishment should be visited only upon the guilty party.[45]

In various ways, then, Indians attempted to nudge dispute settlement back to a form that was more familiar to them. Pressured by authorities to let American law arbitrate their conflicts with the settlers, the Indians quickly perceived that such a system offered less in terms of substantive justice than had the legal regime of the fur trade. While the Americans emphasized the fairness of the process, the Indians focused on the inequity of the results. The American legal system promised to punish both whites and Indians without discrimination; through evenhanded administration, it promised to deliver the same type of reciprocity that had been achieved under the fur-trade regime. When it failed to deliver those results, the Indians sought to restore balance by advocating a return to an earlier model.

Over the course of the territorial period, however, the viability of the "middle ground" of compensation and retaliation weakened. As we have seen, retaliation only invited arrest and trial. Moreover, as settlers increasingly relied on the law to police the Indians, the merest threat of retaliation or the first sign of hostility also invited arrest and trial. As settlers brought American law into more disputes with Indians, the Natives found that traditional sanctions had less room to operate.

The dramatic decline in the number of Indians charged with killing whites during the later part of the territorial period signaled the weakening of the earlier model. From 1873 to statehood in 1889, only seven Indians faced charges of murder or manslaughter of a non-Indian, compared with twenty in the first two decades of the period. The practice of retaliation waned as Indians became increasingly aware of the power and predisposition of American law to punish such acts.

The alterations in territorial law triggered by the Civil War caused a similar narrowing of legal options. As Indians gained the right to initiate lawsuits and testify against whites, the Indian Department increasingly answered demands for compensation with scorn or with advice to pursue legal redress. As traditional avenues of dispute resolution closed down, Indians turned to the courts. Sulkanon's suit against Lewis thus came out of a long and complex set of legal-historical developments.

The image of law-savvy Indians working the territorial courts to their advantage perturbed some whites. In 1863, James Swan, the teacher on the Makah Reservation, reported that he had witnessed Makah men making death threats against certain whites. They expected to get away with the murders because of the American emphasis on punishing only the actual culprit. "The Bostons [Americans] said they only want to punish the individual who commits a murder," the Makahs told Swan, "so we will set our slaves to shoot the white men, and then when the Bostons come here with their man of war, the chief will give the slaves to be hung, and themselves with their people will go clear." Seven years later, the Oblate missionary on the Tulalip Reservation painted an even more disturbing picture of the "bad Indians" among his charges. They persistently denied that the agent had authority to punish them for any wrongdoing, he said. "And some are going even further and say that they can kill white men also with impunity and save the lives of murderers by feeing a *good lawyer*."[46]

Mobilization of American law by Indians, however, never proceeded as easily as these white observers feared. It required financial and social resources that many Indians did not have. As a result, the district courts heard only a small number of cases initiated by Indians against whites. But while the number of such cases is insignificant as a proportion of the total, they offer important insights into Indian use of American law to preserve individual autonomy in the face of a hostile dominant culture. Indians were increasingly aware of American law's potential as a tool to punish settlers for abuses, bring exploitative employers to heel, and resist the encroachments of an increasingly intrusive Indian Department.

A small number of Indians, for example, filed criminal complaints against whites who committed offenses against them. On October 29, 1884, a Makah man called Andy Johnson filed a complaint for assault with a deadly weapon against a Clallam County settler named Ephraim Pullen. On September 17, Johnson had been trying out a new rifle by shooting at some ducks on the Quileute River, oblivious to Pullen's presence on the opposite bank. Angered, Pullen crossed the river and accosted Johnson. "He came to me and presented his pistol to me . . . and said what are you doing, what are you shooting at me for," Johnson stated in a deposition before a local justice of the peace.

Pullen proceeded to use "very bad language," Johnson stated. "Mr Pullen said he did not care for the Indians and did not care if he did kill one, shaking his pistol." Pullen then took Johnson's rifle and went home. Johnson procured one of the Indian policemen from the Makah Reservation to go to Pullen's home, but Pullen only told the policeman to send Johnson back to Neah Bay or Pullen would shoot him. Johnson did return to Neah Bay, but then left the reservation to travel to the town of Dungeness, where he filed a complaint with the justice of the peace.[47]

Not to be outdone, Pullen responded three weeks later by filing his own complaint against Johnson for assault with intent to commit murder. He told substantially the same story as Johnson, but denied that there were any ducks in the area, accusing Johnson of shooting at him.

In his response to Pullen's deposition, Johnson accused the white man of telling "an untruth." He also gave evidence of his reasoning for pursuing a legal remedy against Pullen. "The Indians at Neah Bay have an Indian agent a white man; and that agent does not want us to fight or kill with anyone [sic]," Johnson stated. "Our agent . . . tells us that if we kill anyone, we shall be hung." His statement, intended to cast doubt on Pullen's assertion that the Indian was trying to kill him, also testifies to the ascendance of white law in the territory and the pressure for Indians to pursue sanctions through formal legal channels.[48]

The justice of the peace bound Johnson over to district court on $1,000 bail, which the Indian agent posted. Pullen was bound over on $500 bail, which two other white men posted. The grand jury heard both cases on February 26, 1885 and refused to find a true bill in either case. The justice of the peace ordered Johnson's rifle returned.[49]

It is difficult to say who won this legal battle. Johnson got his rifle back, but Pullen avoided punishment. Pullen saw his antagonist acquitted and re-armed. What is clear is Johnson's willingness and ability to use the courts to protest the unjust seizure of his rifle by a white settler. Legal authorities had brought white settlers into court for crimes against Indians before, but in this case the Indian victim of the assault mobilized the law in his own interest. This recourse to the legal remedy evidences changing Indian perceptions of the law.

A similar mobilization by an Indian victim of white violence occurred about a year later in Whatcom County, which lies on the eastern side of Puget Sound near the border with Canada. In October 1885, a white settler in Whatcom bought a horse from two Indians. Later the horse was claimed as stolen by a settler from Sumas, British Columbia. Local settlers suspected a Nooksack Indian named Jimmie Poole of having knowledge of and possibly participating in the theft so, on October 24, 1885, a group of about thirty whites seized Poole and attempted to lynch him. Through the intervention of George Olosens, the Indian with whom Poole lived, and a white man named W. R. Moultry, who evidently had second thoughts about his participation in the proceedings, Poole was cut down and released. According to Jennie Olosens, George's wife, Poole "was sick in the throat" and "could not eat for two days" as a result of the attack.[50]

The attempt to lynch Poole showed the settlers' legal culture in action. The lynch mob took action against an Indian suspected of committing an offense. The *Whatcom Reveille*, the local newspaper, offered a nonchalant appraisal of the incident. It "regretted that the wrong Indian was maltreated," and counseled that "when people take the law into their own hands, they should be sure they are right."[51]

Against the "lawlessness" of the white settlers, Poole invoked American law. On November 2, 1885, Poole filed a complaint with the justice of the peace against at least three men involved in the attempted lynching on a charge of assault with a deadly weapon. The whites downplayed the incident; the *Reveille* reported that "no violence whatever was done the siwash. While the wisdom of this plan of obtaining information [i.e., attempted lynching] may be subject to criticism, yet there is probably not a person in Whatcom County who believes that the parties participating in the matter really meant to do violence." Nonetheless, the justice of the peace bound over the defendants on $500 bail. When the grand jury convened in March 1886, however, it refused to indict any of the accused.[52]

The case thus ended as did most prosecutions of whites for assaulting Indians. The result, however, should not obscure the significance of Poole's recourse to American law. As traditional Indian sanctions against whites were restricted, the Indians of Washington Territory mobilized white law to try and punish those who attacked them.

Indians were more successful in the handful of civil cases that they instituted against American settlers. For example, access to the law gave Indians a new weapon against the old problem of white employers who defaulted on their wage contracts. On January 7, 1879, two Indians, called Indian Jimmie and Indian Charlie, and a Chinese man named Yen Tey filed suit against W. B. Moore, a white man who had employed them in his logging camp. They charged that Moore had hired them to work in his logging camp in Snohomish County but had not paid them. Indian Jimmie claimed the largest amount. He charged that Moore had employed him from March 1 to December 14, 1878 at a rate of $55 per month and owed him $467.31 in back pay. The men sought a court-ordered sale of the logs owned by Moore, out of which their wages could be distributed.

The suit came fifteen days after a similar suit was filed by three white men who had also worked for Moore. The reason for the separate complaints is not indicated, but given the racial makeup of the two groups of plaintiffs, it may be that the white workers felt that the presence of nonwhite coplaintiffs would damage their prospects before a jury.

At any rate, the district court consolidated the two separate complaints into a single case. On March 13, 1879, the court judged Moore in default for not filing an answer to the charges. The decision awarded the plaintiffs the full amounts asked in the complaint, and the court ordered the sale of the logs to cover the award. The sale yielded $3,217, which was ordered distributed to the plaintiffs on May 15, 1879.[53]

Robert Sulkanon v. David Lewis

Indians also sued settlers for damages to property and attempted expropriations. When the steamer *Capital* crushed the canoe of an Indian named Henry Jackson against the piles of the wharf in Olympia in 1879, Jackson filed suit and was awarded half the damages by a justice court in Olympia. On June 21, 1888, a Seattle newspaper reported that Jimmy Claplanhoo, a Makah headman, had his schooner damaged by the steamer *Gretna* in the Strait of Juan de Fuca. The *Gretna's* master promised to repair the damage, but then put to sea before the job was done. "Jimmy put his case in an attorney's hands," the newspaper stated, "and the *Gretna* will find a libel awaiting her the first port she enters."[54]

Sulkanon's case fits into this pattern of legal mobilization by Indians. Like these incidents, Sulkanon's case arose in the general context of the failure of the reservation policy. According to white law, Sulkanon's people, the Nooksacks, had lost their right to occupy their lands under the 1855 Treaty of Point Elliott. But like many other Native groups in Washington, most of the Nooksacks never moved to the reservations created by the treaty, continuing to reside along the Nooksack River and its tributaries.

As increasing numbers of white settlers moved into their territory, Sulkanon and his Nooksack neighbors realized that they needed a more formal claim to the land than Native occupancy. So several of the Nooksacks approached the deputy county surveyor about marking out their lands. Sulkanon himself traveled to Olympia in 1881 to file a homestead claim on his tract. He knew that he had to be able to present and defend his claim to the land in a way that was legally acceptable in a white courtroom.[55]

Such legal formalities strengthened Sulkanon's case against Lewis. More broadly, these legal actions represented an effort by Sulkanon to forge a new identity for himself, an identity that would be more acceptable to his white neighbors. As the local newspaper reported, Sulkanon's family had lived on the tract "for generations" and Sulkanon's "ancestors are buried there," yet to hold on to his land Sulkanon had to reconfigure himself from an aboriginal occupant into an individual landholder and cultivator of the soil. Lewis's bid to disqualify Sulkanon on the ground that he was an "Indian of full blood" directly challenged this new identity. It reminded judge and jury just who the plaintiff was and threw into relief Sulkanon's effort to present himself in a way that would play well in a white courtroom.[56]

Sulkanon clearly won the support of his white neighbors. Whereas Lewis called one witness in his defense against Sulkanon's charges, Sulkanon called fourteen witnesses, seven whites and seven Indians. On May 23, 1885, the jury returned a verdict in Sulkanon's favor. The court ordered Lewis and Ridderbjilke off the land and attached their goods to cover Sulkanon's cost of suit. The defendants filed an appeal, but dropped it six months later after Sulkanon agreed to pay the twelve dollars in witness fees for the Indian witnesses in the case.

Like the land survey and the homestead claim, Sulkanon's ability to produce reputable white witnesses clearly contributed to his successful mobilization of American law. Lewis himself acknowledged this when he told one of the witnesses that he doubted whether he could get the land from Sulkanon. According to the witness's account, Lewis told him "the Indian had been there a long time in that neighborhood, and he could probably prove anything he wanted to."[57]

One should not conclude that Sulkanon's success in forging an identity that worked in a courtroom meant that he had completely assimilated, forsaking his Indian identity for that of a "civilized" American homesteader. Sulkanon recognized the symbolic and substantive power of American law, and he knew how to activate the American legal machinery. But he used that machinery for his own ends, which derived from his status and identity as an Indian. He employed American law in order to retain a piece of the Nooksack homeland and to defend his personal autonomy in the face of a hostile act by a member of the majority population.

While Sulkanon successfully used the law to trump the power that white settlers assumed they had over Indians, other Indians tried to use the law to trump the power of the Indian Department. Like Sulkanon, they had to persuade American courts that they were civilized and autonomous individuals if they were to invoke territorial law as a counterweight to the department's sweeping assertion of power over Indian lives. And like Sulkanon, they had to recruit allies among the white community to sustain their causes.

The Indian Department, typically the staunch cheerleader of Indian assimilation, looked with disfavor upon efforts by Indians to use American law to hamstring the department's own powers. In October 1881, for example, Coot-ee-ak-een and some other Indians on the Yakima Reservation disagreed over ownership of a horse. The agent decided the issue against Coot-ee-ak-een, who promptly left the reservation and traveled to nearby Yakima City. There he hired a lawyer, filed a complaint against the other parties in the case and had them arrested. In justice court, however, the decision again went against Coot-ee-ak-een. The agent, pleased at this outcome, decided not to levy any additional punishment on Coot-ee-ak-een "for his contempt in appealing to a civil tribunal which had no jurisdiction."[58] Although Coot-ee-ak-een failed to gain redress through the courts, his actions and the agent's reaction show their mutual perception of territorial law as a potential offset to the Indian Department.

The mobilization of American law by Indians took other forms besides filing lawsuits. Indians used the law to gain legitimacy for their resistance to the power of the government, as Sulkanon did by filing a homestead claim. Such alternative forms of validation proved especially valuable when the reservation agents attempted to intensify repression of Indian activity. In May 1877, for example, a group of Nez Perces from Alpowa in Columbia County filed declarations of intention to become citizens in the Walla Walla County District Court, renouncing "all allegiance and fidelity" to James Lawyer, chief of the Nez Perce. As noted in the *Walla Walla Weekly Statesman*, "the land law authorizes Indians under these circumstances to enter lands and hold them upon the same terms as white men." By altering their status as "tribal Indians," these Nez Perces sought to use white law to secure their lands, and thus to resist pressures to move to the Nez Perce Reservation.[59]

In 1884, Robert Milroy, now serving as the Yakima agent, believed that the new lenient policy regarding Indian homesteading undermined his authority. He complained that a man named Major MacMurray was consulting with the Indians, showing them maps of vacant lands where they could take homesteads without payment of fees. Milroy wrote that MacMurray had told the Indians that "upon taking or accepting a home-stead, they would be released from the control of the agent and from surveillance of the Indian police, and could not be forced to go on the reservation or required to send their children to school." Milroy told the commissioner that the bulk of the Indians off the reservation were "wild anti-civilization Indians." In this case, the alternate legal status conferred by the Indian Homestead law frustrated the authority of the agent.[60]

The legal protection sought for the Indian Shaker Church provided probably the most renowned example of legal mobilization against the intrusions of the Indian Department in the Northwest. Inspired by the vision of John Slocum—an Indian who reportedly died and was restored to life in 1882—the Shakers emerged as an indigenous revitalization movement among the Indians of Puget Sound that still has numerous adherents today. The Skokomish agent tried to squelch the infant religion by arresting the leaders and throwing them in jail. In 1892, after Washington had joined the union, the Indians sought the assistance of a lawyer, who assured them of their legal freedom to worship without interference. According to Homer Barnett, who wrote the classic ethnography of the Shakers, these assurances were critical to the Shakers' determination to pursue "a course of open defiance of their persecutors."[61]

An earlier incident from the Skokomish Reservation shows not only the Indians' recognition of the law as a tool to counter the power of the agents, but also the agents' hostility to these acts of resistance. On April 2, 1885, an Indian man named David Charley left the reservation with Susie, an eighteen-year-old Indian woman, to come to Port Townsend. While there, the couple procured a marriage license from the auditor for Jefferson County, and a local probate judge married them. Although the couple had previously married on the reservation, Agent Eells had dissolved the marriage and refused to sanction their remarriage or their cohabitation. Faced with the intransigence of the agent, David Charley sought an alternative legal validation of his marriage to counter Eells' authority. "We was trying to get married here [on the reservation]," David Charley wrote in a letter to a white acquaintance and lawyer, "but they wont let us that the reason I and went down to fine [*sic*] some other place to get married."[62]

After their marriage, the bride and groom went to the home of Susie's father, George Henry. George Henry lived at Quilcene Bay on land that he had been homesteading since 1882. In an affidavit sent to the commissioner of Indian affairs, George Henry stated that he supported himself by farming and logging, paid territorial, county, school, and road taxes, and sent his children to the county's public schools.[63]

Upon learning of the marriage of David Charley and Susie, Eells dispatched a squad of Indian police to arrest the couple and return them to the reservation. "He said David had done a very bad thing to come up to Port Townsend and get married," stated William Pasper, another Skokomish Indian who appeared before a Port Townsend attorney and notary public to prepare an affidavit pleading David Charley's case to the commissioner. Eells ruled that David should spend seven months in the agency jail, pay a fine of fifty dollars, and that he and Susie should be separated.

The Skokomish chiefs protested the sentence. According to Pasper's affidavit, an Indian called Joe Dan complained that although Eells had told the Indians to marry only one woman and to marry for life, "[n]ow David & Susie are married and you say you can separate them." He accused the agent of trying to force Susie to stay in the reservation school, but argued, "[S]he is a woman and can marry. You have had her in your school a long time."

Eells responded to Joe Dan's charge, according to Pasper, by proclaiming that "he was *king* of all of the Indians and could separate them if he wished, that no lawyer or white man or Indian or any one else had anything to say about it but him." Eells clearly tried to delegitimate the authority of local law over the Indians and thus the legitimacy of David and Susie's marriage.

After a great deal of negotiation, Eells agreed to allow the couple to live together and to reduce David Charley's sentence to twenty-four hours, but only on the condition that David Charley pay the fifty-dollar fine and bring George Henry's eight-year-old daughter and three other children to the reservation to be enrolled in the reservation school. David Charley agreed to do so, but then he and his father-in-law immediately sought some form of legal redress against Eells' demands.[64]

In his affidavit to the commissioner, George Henry wrote that he was consulting two lawyers in Port Townsend about the case. "Both . . . tell me I have a right to keep my children, and that the Court will, on writ of habeas corpus, return them to me," George Henry stated. The lawyers did not work for free, however, and given the distances between the court, the reservation, and his house, he would need $100 to institute legal action—money he did not have. "So I am advised to lay the matter before you," he stated.[65]

According to George Henry's affidavit, Eells repeatedly warned the Indians about recourse to lawyers. "He says he can do as he pleases with me and my children and with all the Indians. That we need not complain to a lawyer or anyone else, as he has power to do as he pleases." Later in the document, George Henry stated that Eells had threatened fines or imprisonment for any Indians who complained to lawyers. The white lawyer and notary public in the case, D. W. Smith, noted in his own letter to the commissioner that Eells' hostility to lawyers was counterproductive. "Formerly when Indians were abused, they went to war," Smith wrote. "Now when abused, if, like the whites, they consult a lawyer, they are told, he can do them no good. He only wants their money—the Agent is supreme, etc." He went on to recommend that Eells' abuses be investigated and that the agent be replaced.[66]

David Charley's case shows both Indian perceptions of the law and the limitations of legal remedies. By emphasizing a set of individually held legal rights—the right to get married, the right to keep one's children around home—David Charley and George Henry challenged the authority of the agent to infringe upon their personal lives. George Henry validated his claim to these rights by pointing out his own cultural transformation into landowner and taxpayer. In the end, however, the financial cost of mobilizing the law prevented George Henry from effectively pursuing legal remedies. He was thus forced to appeal to Eells' superiors, an appeal he could make only because of his racial status as an Indian.

In David Charley's case, as in several others, agents used Indian police forces to extend their authority beyond the reservations. Established on various reservations around the nation in the 1880s, these forces became important vehicles for implementing the agents' policies. As extensions of the agent's power, the Indian police also became targets of lawsuits and other legal maneuvers by Indians subject to that power.[67]

A complex example of such mobilization occurred in the summer of 1884. The case grew out of the intense conflict over access to the Columbia River fisheries during the 1880s. Historians generally present this conflict as a battle between Indians seeking to exercise their treaty rights and white settlers seeking to deny Indians access to the fisheries. The case of *William Spedis v. Thomas Simpson, et al.* complicates the picture of that conflict, and illustrates the use of territorial law to contest the authority claimed by the agent over off-reservation Indians.[68]

In July 1884, William Spedis, an Indian man assigned to the Yakima agency but living at the Tumwater fishery on the Columbia River, sued several members of the Yakima police force for assault. Spedis sought $5,000 in damages, alleging that the police forcibly abducted him and removed him to the Yakima Reservation. The police had apprehended

Robert Sulkanon v. David Lewis

Spedis because he had forcibly prevented an Indian from the Yakima Reservation from taking fish at the fishery. Yakima Agent Robert Milroy claimed the man was being held by Spedis as a prisoner, and he dispatched the police to release the man and arrest the perpetrator of the assault. "The Indian (Speetas) [sic] resisted the Police, who were compelled to hand-cuff him, but were careful to use no further violence than necessary," reported Milroy. The agent examined Spedis but discharged him upon receiving word that the Indian "held prisoner" had been released.

According to Milroy, a white settler named Frank Taylor had purchased the land adjacent to the fishery and promptly restricted Indian access to the river. Spedis and other Indians residing at Tumwater apparently obtained continued access through a separate deal with Taylor, who sold them the exclusive right to fish there. Spedis's action against the reservation Indians who came to use the fishery indicated that he took the exclusive privilege quite seriously.[69]

Although the court records and correspondence generated by this incident offer precious little insight into Spedis's motivations, a possible explanation emerges from ethnographic work on the mid-Columbia Indians. According to one study, resident families owned prime fishing spots. Although the owners "felt bound to share their bounty with both relatives and strangers," such use was conditioned upon the permission of the owners. Perhaps Spedis conceived of the exclusive right purchased from Taylor as validation of his continued ownership of this particular fishing station. His action against the Indian man from the reservation may have resulted from the stranger's failure to ask permission before taking the fish. In Spedis's view, it may have been the agency police, more than Taylor, who disrupted the traditional prerogatives of a resident owner. Spedis then turned to American law to defend those prerogatives.[70]

Agent Milroy did not see it in that light. In Milroy's eyes, the case was about treaty rights guaranteed to the tribe as a whole. In defense of those rights, Milroy filed for an injunction against Taylor to prevent him from blocking access to the fishery. Milroy's vigorous defense of treaty rights eventually helped secure legal recognition of the Yakimas' rights to the fishery, culminating in the first of many fishing rights cases to come before the United States Supreme Court, *United States v. Winans*.[71]

According to Milroy, the lawsuit by Spedis formed part of Taylor's plan "to compel the Department to purchase his claim to the fishery, and pay him ten times its value." Taylor doubtless helped finance Spedis's appeal to the territorial courts following his arrest by the reservation police. Whether Spedis was simply manipulated by Taylor or whether he sought to uphold the traditional rights of a resident owner cannot be known with certainty. Questions about the motivations of Indian plaintiffs' white allies, however, do not necessarily lead to the conclusion that the Indian parties had no independent interests in the conflict.[72]

In the Spedis case, a jury assessed damages of $500 against one of the police officers, Klickitat Peter, on October 10, 1884. Three years later, the court clerk ordered the sheriff to seize the property of the defendant to satisfy the judgment. On May 28, 1887, a sheriff's sale of a wagon, harness, and other items resulted in a final tally of $156.76. Although it took three years and resulted in a judgment far less than his original claim, Spedis successfully mobilized American law to counter the authority of the agent and the Indian police.[73]

The actions of Spedis, Poole, Sulkanon, and other Indian plaintiffs demonstrate that by the end of the territorial period, the legal culture of the Indians in Washington Territory had undergone significant changes. The fur-trade regime, based on "middle-ground" principles of retaliation and compensation, had given way to the regime of legal formalism articulated by American officials. Like the settlers themselves, Indians responded to interracial conflicts by working increasingly within the confines of legal institutions, rather than seeking to step outside them. The costs of pursuing a legal remedy could be high, however, not only financially but politically. Recourse to the law accorded legitimacy to the claims of dominance by white institutions and required Indians to forswear their allegiance to Native forms of power.

American law, moreover, offered only limited protection to Indians. When Indians gained access to the courts, the results most often proved unsatisfactory. Indian litigants and victims of white abuse faced unsympathetic and prejudiced juries, as well as a judicial tendency to uphold the authority of agents and deny Indians the full protection of the law. But in some cases, particularly when individual Indians suffered abuse at the hands of private citizens, Indians could obtain redress from white courts.

It should be repeated here that Indians did not acculturate to the status of litigious Americans. Rather, in a period marked by the increasing power of American institutions, Indians tried to mobilize those institutions to serve their own purposes. In conflicts with both settlers and officials, Indians tried to use the law to protect and expand their freedom and autonomy.

Chapter 7

TERRITORY V. HARRY FISK

INTRA-INDIAN CRIME AND
INDIAN LEGAL CONSCIOUSNESS

In late March 1874, Harry Fisk, a man of mixed Indian and white parentage who worked as an interpreter for the Indian Department, stood trial for murder in the territorial capital of Olympia. He was charged with killing a Squaxin Indian shaman called Doctor Jackson on December 14, 1873. Fisk believed that his wife, Susie, had become ill because of Doctor Jackson's sorcery. According to a newspaper account, Jackson, at the behest of one of Fisk's enemies, "threw his masatchie tamanawas, or evil spirit," into Susie at a potlatch in Seattle earlier in December.[1] In payment for his services, Doctor Jackson received nine blankets. When Susie became ill, her husband called in other shamans to extract the spirit, but Doctor Jackson's power proved too strong. Fearing for his wife's life, Fisk concluded that only by killing Doctor Jackson could he save Susie.[2]

Fisk killed Doctor Jackson during the day and in the presence of numerous Indian witnesses. Under the pretense of arresting him, Fisk had handcuffed the shaman and transported him by canoe from Olympia to the Indian camp at Mud Bay, some five or six miles away. At Mud Bay, Fisk brought Doctor Jackson to the house where Susie lay dying. Five other Indians were present. From her deathbed, Susie urged her husband to kill Doctor Jackson. Fisk, armed with a Henry rifle, shot Doctor Jackson in the head. The doctor fell to the floor, mortally wounded, but apparently still alive. Fisk then produced a revolver and fired twice more.[3]

Fisk's trial for murder marked a turning point in Washington Territory's legal history. It was one of the first cases in which the territorial courts successfully asserted their power to regulate intra-Indian conflict. The courts had never before assumed jurisdiction over intra-Indian crime as they had over interracial conflict. On the contrary, the territorial courts tried to stay out of Indian affairs for the first twenty years of the period. But beginning with the Fisk case and a handful of others in the early 1870s, the courts increasingly interfered in Native disputes. Before 1873, only two cases of intra-Indian crime came before the courts—one in 1855 and one in 1868—and both ended in dismissal. From 1873 onward, the courts heard forty-eight such cases.

The increasing intervention of American law in intra-Indian disputes stemmed not from any change in the power or the jurisdiction of the territorial courts, but from a change in the local legal culture. The courts moved away from a racially defined notion of sovereignty and legal authority, from which Indians were largely excluded, toward one based on geography, which acknowledged and sought to regulate the presence of Indians within white society. In other words, jurisdiction was increasingly determined, not by the race of those involved, but by where the incident took place. At the same time, the courts sought to uphold and reinforce the social boundaries between the two races.

Given the large number of Indians living off the reservations or residing there only seasonally, the shift from a racially bounded conception of legal authority to a geographically bounded conception had dramatic consequences. It subjected intra-Indian affairs to the authority of American law, trumping Native law. American courts did not completely replace Native mechanisms of dispute resolution, but the increasing interference of white legal authorities did disrupt their functioning.

Historians and anthropologists have generally shown more interest in the development of tribal mechanisms of conflict resolution than in the role played by American law in intra-Indian disputes. Scholars usually treat the assumption of jurisdiction by American courts over Indian matters simply as white legal imperialism abrogating tribal sovereignty. But in some of these cases, Indians themselves brought white law into the dispute, complicating matters and undermining simple "legal-imperialism" arguments.[4]

Scholars who focus on the erosion of Native sovereignty direct their attention to developments within Indian country, namely, the steady narrowing of tribal criminal jurisdiction on tribal lands. The federal Indian Intercourse Act of 1834 restricted tribal jurisdiction to intra-Indian crime occurring in Indian country and declared interracial crime in Indian country the province of federal courts. This jurisdictional arrangement continued until 1885, when Congress passed the Major Crimes Act. Enacted in response to the Supreme Court's upholding of tribal sovereignty over intra-Indian crime in *Ex Parte Crow Dog*, the Major Crimes Act cut back drastically on tribal criminal jurisdiction. The act gave federal courts jurisdiction over certain crimes committed by one Indian against another inside the boundaries of Indian country.[5]

Historians generally view these legal developments in light of the federal government's policies aimed at breaking down the institutions of Native society and forcibly assimilating Indians into white society. Prucha calls the Major Crimes Act "revolutionary" and "a major blow at the integrity of the Indian tribes and a fundamental readjustment in relations between the Indians and the United States government." Sidney Harring refers to the Supreme Court's 1886 decision upholding the Major Crimes Act as "the judicial embodiment of Congress's policy of forcing the assimilation of the tribes, recognizing none of their sovereignty, none of their status as domestic nations."[6]

There is no doubt that the Major Crimes Act dealt a serious blow to tribal sovereignty and formed a key component of the assimilationist Indian policies of the late nineteenth century. The scholarly focus on Indian country, however, obscures a central truth about Indian-white relations in Washington Territory—the prevalence of Indians living off the reservations and the frequency of their contact with white settlers.

A great deal of intra-Indian conflict in Washington Territory—like Fisk's killing of Doctor Jackson—occurred off the reservations, outside of Indian country. Forty of the fifty intra-Indian criminal cases heard in district court took place off the reservation. Indeed, the Major Crimes Act had relatively little effect on the number of prosecutions that came before the courts. After the passage of the act in 1885, eighteen cases of Indian-on-Indian crime came before the courts. This is not dramatically higher than the number prior to the act. The courts heard fifteen cases in the five-year period before 1885 and fifteen more between 1873 and 1879. More significantly, only five of the post-1885 cases occurred on a reservation, reflecting the added jurisdictional scope of the act.[7]

This is not to deny the impact of the Major Crimes Act on particular reservations. The Yakima Reservation, especially, became a zone of conflict over the imposition of American law. Of the five post-1885 cases that occurred on a reservation, four took place on the Yakima Reservation. For example, in two of the earliest Major Crimes Act prosecutions, Dick Wyneco and Dan Planopleopike separately faced murder charges for killing shamans suspected of sorcery on the Yakima Reservation. When the men were arrested and taken to the county jail, the Yakimas demanded an explanation from the agent and were told, to their surprise, that the Major Crimes Act authorized punishment of such actions. Both men were convicted of manslaughter and sentenced to one year in prison.[8]

Neither the 1834 Intercourse Act nor the Major Crimes Act said anything explicit about Indian-on-Indian conflicts outside Indian country. Both acts implied, however, that local courts could apply state or territorial law to all criminal cases—without regard for the race of the parties involved—occurring off the reservations. In Washington Territory, however, the courts did not do this, at least during the first twenty years of the territory's existence. Instead the courts developed a philosophy of judicial restraint that kept them out of Indian disputes.

A jurisdictional muddle existed in Washington Territory during the 1850s. Before ratification of the Stevens treaties, all of Washington Territory remained Indian country from a legal point of view, and thus the tribes had authority over intra-Indian crime. Territorial officials tested these arrangements quite early. On June 7, 1855, a Skokomish man named Schotum stabbed and killed a Skokomish woman called Mayeotot. On October 1, a territorial grand jury indicted Schotum on the testimony of three Indian witnesses. On October 2, the attorneys for the defense filed a motion challenging the court's jurisdiction, arguing that both victim and defendant belonged to an Indian "nation treating with the government of the United States." "The offence charged in the Indictment was committed in their own country, and . . . this court cannot take cognizance of, or try the cause."

It is not certain where the incident occurred, but legally that did not matter in deciding the issue of jurisdiction. The Skokomish had signed the Treaty of Point No Point in 1855 with the United States, but Congress would not ratify that treaty for another three years. The lands ceded in the treaty, which included all the land around the north end of Puget Sound from the Olympic Mountains to the Cascade Mountains, therefore remained Indian country. On October 6, Judge Francis Chenoweth ruled in favor of the motion, denying the territorial courts' jurisdiction.[9]

The local agent stationed at Bellingham Bay lamented the implications of the decision two years later when a Samish headman called General Pierce killed one of his slaves. "Under Judge Chenoweth's brilliant decision I can do nothing with him," the agent complained to Governor Stevens, "he [Chenoweth] having decided that they could commit murder on one another and that our courts could not interfere."[10]

On its face, *Territory v. Schotum* limited the power of American law in intra-Indian disputes only during the period before the ratification of the Stevens treaties. In fact, the Schotum case established the parameters of judicial action in the territory into the 1870s. Even after Congress ratified the treaties, the courts stayed out of intra-Indian matters, including those that occurred off the reservations. "Our courts ignore all crimes committed among the Indians, when Indians are the only parties interested," complained the superintendent of Indian affairs in 1867. The courts would deal with interracial incidents, but "where one Indian murders another Indian the courts disclaim all jurisdiction." In 1870, the officer in charge of Indian affairs at Colville, upon being informed of the murder of an "Indian doctor," doubted whether he could take any action. "Our courts I believe, have decided that an Indian murdering an Indian is not amenable to our laws."[11]

An 1871 incident suggests how entrenched the idea of judicial noninterference in intra-Indian affairs had become since the Schotum case. On February 20, the *Seattle Intelligencer* reported that a Duwamish Indian man called Jim Spoon had been found murdered on a beach outside town, his head smashed by repeated blows with a rock. The newspaper strongly suspected that the killers were other Indians of Jim Spoon's band. However, the *Intelligencer* reported, "(N)o attempts were made to obtain any clue as to the perpetrators of this murder . . . the custom here, in such cases, being to let the Indians attend to their own domestic difficulties."[12]

This "custom" grew neither out of a principled respect for Indian sovereignty in such matters nor an appreciation of Native law. Rather, it grew out of perceptions of vast cultural difference between the two races. Like the territorial legislature's desire to maintain a wall of separation between Indian and white society, the courts' noninterference suggests that Indians remained outside the institutions of white settlement.

One case in particular provides insight into the rationale behind the courts' noninterference. In February 1868, an Indian named Cisco died on the town wharf in Olympia. The superintendent of Indian affairs, suspecting that Cisco had been poisoned, wrote to County Coroner Robert Frost to request an inquest. Frost convened the inquest, and then presented his $50.60 bill for services to the county commissioners. When the commissioners disallowed the expenses, Frost appealed to the district court. The court upheld the county's position.

It is impossible to know exactly why the court threw out Frost's appeal; the county moved to dismiss the case on a number of grounds, including some technical matters of pleading. But the county's motion also put forth broader grounds for rejecting Frost's bill, which go to the heart of the perceived relationship between Indians and the law. It is also worthy of note that a former territorial court judge, Obadiah B. McFadden, argued the county's case.

The county objected to Frost's bill because it concerned an Indian. "Indians are not persons within the purview of our law," McFadden argued. "The county commissioners are not the guardians of either living or dead Indians, and the policy of the government forbids the recognition of the principle involved." This argument did not rely on jurisdictional boundaries between Indian country and the rest of the territory; such issues never arose during the appeal. Rather, McFadden stressed the racial boundaries of legal jurisdiction. The law could not concern itself with the fate of a dead Indian. "An inquest . . . can do no good. It neither advances public justice nor yet facilitates the administration of the criminal law."

The fact that Indians fell outside the purview of American law also served the interests of the county's taxpayers, and the costs of prosecution contributed to the courts' reluctance to take cognizance of intra-Indian crime. In the Frost case, McFadden argued that "the allowance of this claim would be the establishment of precedent *ruinous* to the interest of white citizens." Cost was not simply a mundane issue of county finances; it helped symbolize the exclusion of Indians from white society. Until 1869, the law exempted all Indians from the payment of property taxes; why then, the argument ran, should they enjoy the benefits of the institutions supported by that tax money?[13]

The local custom of legal noninterference in intra-Indian disputes left ample room for the continued functioning of Native law-ways. Indeed, Fisk's killing of Doctor Jackson for his use of sorcery attests to the endurance of traditional Native definitions of and responses to criminal behavior. But while the courts stood aside, the Indian agents did not. In the name of civilization and, ironically, preserving order, the agents often interfered with the very mechanisms that had traditionally worked to restore order in Native society.

When they talked about keeping order, the agents primarily meant the prevention of intra-Indian violence. In the agents' view, Native customs of dispute settlement promoted violence by legitimating private revenge. Alternately ignoring and denigrating Native law, the agents came to see themselves as the sole source of legal authority among the Indians. "It devolves entirely upon the officers of the Indian service to keep order among them," wrote one agent in 1858. In a circular sent out to all agents in Washington in 1869, the newly appointed superintendent of Indian affairs in the territory advised all personnel to "bear in mind that they are the only authorities to whom the Indians can apply for the redress of their grievances and the maintenance of their rights." Prompt and fair action by the agents would teach the Indians "to practice justice themselves."[14]

The agents decried the courts' reluctance to take cognizance of intra-Indian disputes because it dramatically increased their own administrative burdens. In the agents' eyes, the courts' noninterference made the agents themselves the principal authority over all Indians in the territory, regardless of whether they were on reservations. "All Indians violating law coming under your notice are subject to your orders whether belonging to your treaty or not," the superintendent told one agent in 1867. The large number of off-reservation Indians in Washington transformed the agents' geographically and racially limited authority to a racially specific but geographically unlimited one.[15]

To prevent violence, the agents threatened to punish Indians engaging in retaliation and urged aggrieved parties to bring their complaints to local Indian Department officials for settlement. These policies disrupted the functioning of Native law, particularly among groups in western Washington, by forbidding retaliation against those who refused to pay compensation. After a murder on the Swinomish Reservation in 1868, for example, the local agent warned the Swinomish not to strike back against the perpetrators. Similarly, in 1856, Agent Nathaniel Hill tried to dissuade a party of Snohomish from journeying across Puget Sound to a Clallam village to avenge the death of a headman's son. Failing in his

Territory v. Harry Fisk

attempt, Hill accompanied the Snohomish group and kept the two parties separated until—with the aid of a local headman—he could negotiate a compensatory settlement.[16]

As Hill's example shows, the agents' insistence on nonviolent dispute resolution led them to accept the Native mechanism of material compensation as a way to settle disputes. For example, in 1856, following the killing of a local headman, Nisqually Agent Gosnell wrote to Governor Stevens that he was encouraging the Indians to get together and talk it out. "If dolears will settle the matter well and good but I object to them fiten [sic]," Gosnell stated. In 1867, when a Klickitat man was killed in a dispute over a woman, the superintendent advised that the man could "if so disposed . . . give the father and mother of the dead man something but that it was not obligatory as the deed was done in self defense."[17]

If the Indians would not agree to pay compensation, the agents at times dispensed payment themselves to smooth over disputes. In 1862, a group of Upper Chehalis Indians came to the local agent "demanding payment for their friends that have been killed" by the Indians along the coast. The agent feared a spiral of bloodshed if the Indian Department did not take some action. The Makah agent faced a similar spiral of violence owing to a dispute between the Indians under his charge and a neighboring group of Clallams. Writing to the superintendent, the agent stated that "as this matter can be settled by a payment of blankets I request your authority."[18]

The arrival of McKenny as superintendent of Indian affairs in 1867, however, ushered in a policy of discountenancing compensation in the settlement of intra-Indian disputes. Soon after assuming office, for example, McKenny ordered the investigation of a suspicious death on the Quinault Reservation. He instructed the local agent that if it proved to be a murder, he was not to allow settlement through an exchange of goods. "The practice of cancelling murders by the payment of goods or money will not be permitted and must be broken up," McKenny wrote.[19]

Similarly, in a dispute that same year in which a Queets headman killed a Quileute man, the agent refused to allow the Queets man to make an offer of guns and blankets to the Quileutes in atonement. "I informed them that way of settling murders was stoped [sic], and could not be allowed," the agent told McKenny.[20]

In December 1868, three Nisqually Indians abducted and killed a Snohomish man called Salmon. Two months later, a group of Snohomish and Snoqualmie headmen from the Tulalip Reservation journeyed to the Puyallup Reservation, where the three culprits resided, to settle the matter. They also planned to use the opportunity to settle other disputes. "The head chief Slahat had a brother killed by the Nisqually Indians. He wishes to settle that also," the Puyallup agent informed McKenny. "Mr. Hale [the Tulalip agent] requests me to see that they settle without any difficulty of a serious nature." McKenny quickly broke up the parley, issuing instructions to the Puyallup agent not to allow negotiated settlement of murders. "I have made the Indians understand the matter distinctly," the agent reported. "I advised them to go home immediately."[21]

In place of compensation, McKenny wanted to substitute incarceration and other "civilized" forms of punishment. By the early 1860s, most reservations featured a blockhouse where malefactors could be imprisoned, and McKenny routinely urged agents to make use of the facility. Following the nonfatal stabbing of a Chehalis man by a Nisqually Indian in 1867, McKenny advised the Chehalis agent to "act promptly, arrest the offender and if necessary put irons on him, and confine him in the block house for six months or more."[22]

Under McKenny's direction, the agents often combined incarceration in the blockhouse with hard labor. After apprehending the principal culprit in an off-reservation murder on the Snohomish River, for example, Tulalip Agent Henry C. Hale reported that "I now have him confined in the jail at this place [Tulalip]. he [sic] is now ironed at night, and in the day time [kept] . . . at hard labor." When McKenny suspected another Indian on the Tulalip Reservation of inciting a murder, he ordered the agent to arrest the culprit and "make him clear farming land for three months. This is the only way for breaking up such crime." In 1872, McKenny himself sentenced an Indian called Kanaka Jack to two years' hard labor on the Nisqually Reservation for the killing of Telequoh.[23]

Agents also called on the military to apprehend and restrain prisoners. In a dispute between the Makahs and the Clallams, officials promised the Makahs that they would settle the claims arising from the murder of a Makah headman by the Clallams. After waiting in vain for several years for the officials to take action, the Makahs retaliated against the Clallams. The Indian Department requested that troops be dispatched to the Makah Reservation, where they apprehended the Makah man who had perpetrated the retaliatory killing. The soldiers hauled the perpetrator away in irons to Fort Steilacoom, the nearest military post, which assuaged the feelings of the Clallams but did little to satisfy the Makahs.[24] Such actions by the officers of the Indian Department destabilized Native law. By preventing first retaliation and then compensation for injuries, officials ate away at the sanctions that structured Native law-ways. The Native system did not stop working entirely, but the agents' interference undermined the constancy and efficacy of sanctions.

Most of the evidence about the resolution of Native disputes comes from western Washington. There is less material from the Plateau during the early territorial years, suggesting the Natives' isolation from the interference of agents. This also supports the assumption that Native dispute-resolution mechanisms, including the practices of judgment by headmen and public whipping, continued to function.

There is further support for this assumption in the observations about Native justice made by officials in eastern Washington. In 1859, the Yakima agent visited the Indians living north of the Yakima reservation, whom he had never before contacted because they never visited the agency. He praised the Okanagan headman Tonasket, "who has exercised his authority to punish wrongdoing among his people."[25]

In 1870, the agency farmer at Colville acknowledged the difficulties in trying to exercise authority among the widely dispersed groups under his jurisdiction. The sparse population and the great expanse of lands occupied by the Indians combined to make investigation of offenses and apprehension of culprits by the agent almost impossible. In intra-Indian disputes, he stated, "the chiefs must inflict the punishment." He thus conferred upon the headmen a power they already enjoyed. Nonetheless, he was able to report, "I have succeeded in awakening some of the chiefs, to a sense of their duty."[26]

White settlement did nonetheless place new demands on the Native system of controlling disputes east of the Cascades. Alcohol was especially intrusive. In February 1871, an Okanagan man called Charlie bought some whiskey, got drunk, and beat his wife to death. No doubt fearing the consequences of this action, Charlie decided to kill the head-man of the band, Sah-sah-pe-kin. "He came to the house of Sah-sah-pe-kin to put his threat into execution," wrote the Colville agent, who learned of the event some weeks later, "and as he was trying to force the door, he was shot and killed by order of Sah-sah-pe-kin."[27]

In addition to such baneful influences as whiskey dealers, those Indian groups who came under the direct influence of the Indian agents suffered the same kind of interference in dispute resolution as the groups west of the Cascades. The Colville agency, which oversaw some dozen different Native groups, exercised effective authority over only a small portion of the Indians assigned to its jurisdiction until well into the 1880s. But under the tutelage of McKenny as superintendent, the Colville agent increasingly resorted to the guardhouse and the military to wield power among the Indians in the immediate vicinity of the agency.

The agents at Colville relied heavily on the military at nearby Fort Colville to exercise authority among the Indians. "I have just released six Indians from the guard house who got drunk and quarrelsome," the physician in charge of the agency reported in January 1870. "Knives were drawn and doubtless fatal results would have occured [sic] except for the timely arrival of a party of soldiers whom I sent to arrest the ringleaders."[28]

The guardhouse in this instance was the one upon which the Indian agents typically relied—the guardhouse at the fort itself. In June 1871, however, special Agent W. P. Winans complained to McKenny that confinement in the guardhouse at the fort was not sufficient punishment for most Indian wrongdoers. "The soldiers made so much of them, and gave them so many cast off cloths when they were discharged that it was no punishment at all," Winans stated. His solution was to begin confining Indians in the county jail. "They see no one but the person attending them," Winans stated. "I think that the one or two cases I have punished that way will have a salutary influence on evil doers."[29]

Winans' monthly reports afterwards gave brief mention of those he had jailed during the previous period. In October 1871, he sentenced a man named Te-mal-le to twelve days for beating an old man and another named Casper-mene to five days for theft. In November, Winans jailed one Indian man for ten days for getting drunk and beating his wife and another for fifteen days for stealing a horse.[30]

The agents' interference led some Indian headmen on the Plateau to view them as a kind of official lasher, and they would bring offenders to the agents for punishment. Thus in June 1871, the Okanagan headman Tonasket brought to the Colville agency a man named Polotkin, "who had without provocation assaulted and beat an old Indian of his tribe,"

Agent Winans wrote. "Tonasket wanted him punished. I put Po-lot-kin in jail for fifteen days and fed him on bread and water."[31]

Intra-Indian killings proved problematic for agents on both sides of the mountains. While they often imprisoned Indians for killing other Indians, agents deemed incarceration an insufficient punishment in many cases. Even more insufficient was the Native custom of compensation paid to the victim's family. On the other hand, agents would not sanction violent retaliation by the victim's kin, and they hesitated to execute Indian prisoners under the cover of their own authority alone.

In 1870, for example, the Columbian headman Moses asked George Harvey, the officer in charge of the Colville agency, to intervene in the case of a murder perpetrated by a headman from a different tribe against a healer from Moses' band. After a curing ceremony, the other headman had poisoned the Columbian doctor and then hanged him. Moses, having been told that American officials would handle any intertribal difficulties, now expected Harvey to exercise that authority. "Moses wishes to know if I will settle the matter," Harvey wrote to the superintendent. "He says that it is a clear case of murder in the first degree and our laws have affixed the penalty of death. He therefore demands, that the murderer shall forfeit his life."

Harvey promised to investigate, but was uncertain what to do if the case should prove to be murder. "It seems to my mind that I would be exceeding my authority were I to pronounce sentence of death," he wrote. But the courts would not take cognizance of the case. "[Moses] says that if I cannot settle it, he will settle it himself," Harvey reported, "but he thinks he cannot do it without involving his people in a bloody war."[32]

Having exerted their authority in intra-Indian disputes, the agents now found themselves held to the expectations they had created among the Indians. After Superintendent McKenny sentenced one accused murderer to two years of hard labor, he reported that the Indians had not found the punishment sufficient. "The Indians say they are satisfied if a few could be hung," he stated. He added that "a large delegation of Indians, consisting principally of chiefs and head men, waited upon me urging that a law be passed affixing a death penalty to the crime of killing an Indian by an Indian."[33]

Although McKenny used the Indians' statements to support his own views that American law should be fully extended over the Indians, they really expressed less a desire for American law and more a dissatisfaction with McKenny's justice. If McKenny would not allow them to administer their own sanctions, then he should inflict an appropriate punishment. In the case at hand, if the murderer offered no compensation, they expected him to be put to death. Several Quileute men struck a similar attitude in an 1867 dispute with the Queets. They told the agent that they would forget their desires for retaliation if "the Tyee at Olympia [the superintendent] should do as he had promised them in such cases (viz) have the murderers hung."[34]

The agents initially tried to get around this problem of legitimate authority in murder cases by reshaping Native procedures to resemble more closely Anglo-American legal forms. During the first quarter of 1859, for example, a group of Lower Chehalis Indians killed an Upper Chehalis headman called Anawata. According to the Puget Sound district agent, Anawata was killed for escorting the agent down the Chehalis River in 1858 to a failed treaty conference—a motive particularly galling to the agent. He therefore offered a reward of thirty blankets for the apprehension of the killers. "Should I be fortunate enough to get them," he told the superintendent, "I will call the head men together, try, and if guilty hang them." By thus convening a jury of headmen and subjecting the defendants to a trial, the agent sought to clothe their execution with legal authority. "I only hope I may be able to make an example of the blood thirsty devils," he wrote.[35]

Although no further records exist of the agent's actions in this matter, the idea evidently served as an appealing precedent for Yakima Agent R. H. Lansdale. In July 1859, Lansdale organized the trial of an Indian man accused of murder by a court of headmen. In May, the son of Show-a-way, a Yakima headman, had disappeared on the Columbia River. Over the next two months, Lansdale learned that Toos-ka-na, a Skin Indian (one of the Sahaptin-speaking groups on the Columbia River), had killed Show-a-way's son in Wasco County, Oregon. Lansdale at first turned to Washington's territorial courts to prosecute the case, but the courts rebuffed him because the crime had occurred in Oregon. Lansdale then turned the case over to his counterpart in Oregon, but the grand jury of Wasco County "refused to take cognizance of crime committed by one Indian against another."

Undaunted, Lansdale "caused a jury of eight impartial chiefs and head men to be empanneled [sic] . . . for the trial of case according to their own usages." The eight-member jury consisted of three headmen from the Columbia River tribes, three Yakima headmen, and two Klickitat headmen. After hearing the case, this jury "unanimously pronounced Toos-ka-na guilty of murder" and sentenced him to be hanged. The jury chose "four good men" to act as executioners. Lansdale instructed the commander at Fort Dalles, where the accused was being held, to deliver Toos-ka-na to the executioners on August 2, stipulating that white witnesses be present at the hanging.[36]

By refitting Native justice with Anglo-American forms, Lansdale hoped to solve the problem of legality in the punishment of intra-Indian murders. "Toos-ka-nee [sic] has had a more formal and equitable trial than sometimes falls to the lot of Indian murderers," he explained to the superintendent of Indian affairs, "as vengeance is executed, usually by relatives of those killed." In Lansdale's eyes, Native customary law did not serve justice; only an execution following proper legal forms could do that. To Toos-ka-na, it likely made little difference.[37]

Lansdale's ploy did not satisfy the superintendent of Indian affairs. Superintendent Edward Geary requested a copy of the trial proceedings, as well as the names of the eight men who served on the jury. Geary evidently saw himself as an appellate court, responsible for certifying the fairness of the proceedings and therefore the justice of the sentence. Until he had sufficient information, he told Lansdale, he could give neither express nor tacit approval to Toos-ka-na's execution.[38]

Exasperated by what he perceived as his superior's excessive concern with due process, Lansdale explained that the headmen had kept no records of the proceedings. He repeated that Toos-ka-na's trial had adhered to "the best usages of the Indians." Nevertheless, Lansdale issued a stay of execution to the commander at Fort Dalles and told the commander that Toos-ka-na was only to be surrendered under the direct order of the superintendent. If the commander had heard nothing by August 15, he was to discharge Toos-ka-na. Lansdale "gladly" rid himself of responsibility for the case, he wrote. On August 18, the commander set Toos-ka-na free—no doubt, Lansdale said, to face lethal vengeance at the hands of Show-a-way's kin.[39]

Efforts to reorganize Native justice along lines more recognizable to Americans thus failed to solve the problem of who had authority to deliver the ultimate sanction to Native wrongdoers. According to American law, the power rested with the tribes if the crime occurred within Indian country, or with American courts if the crime occurred outside Indian country. The reluctance of Washington's territorial courts to take cognizance of intra-Indian disputes, however, effectively gave Native law an unrestricted geographic scope. But agents and superintendents increasingly opposed its unrestricted exercise. Their efforts to substitute their own authority for Native law, meanwhile, ran aground on the question of capital punishment. Their remaining choice, therefore, was to continue to lobby the courts to take cognizance of intra-Indian crimes.

In 1868, for example, Superintendent McKenny explored the sentiments of recently appointed territorial judge Charles B. Darwin. In February, a Twana headman called Tyee Charley had killed one of his female slaves, a woman known as Port Townsend Kate. By doing so, Tyee Charley openly flaunted his contempt for white authorities. "The attributed cause for the deed," the Skokomish agent told McKenny, "was that his slaves were to be taken from him and he would emancipate after his own style." The treaties had stipulated that the Indians abandon slavery, but many upper-class families continued to keep slaves in spite of the provisions. By killing Kate, Charley exercised a traditional if uncommonly practiced prerogative among slave owners and thus asserted his status as ultimate arbiter of the woman's fate.

Some of the Indians were willing to have Charley punished, the agent reported, but were fearful of giving any information against him. If the authorities failed to take some action, other Indians showed a determination to take the matter into their own hands. In late April, therefore, McKenny ordered Charley arrested by the Skokomish agent and held in the Pierce County Jail at Steilacoom. McKenny clearly wanted to use Charley as a test case for the new judge. "I was always of the opinion that the civil authorities should take cognisance of certain offences that the agents or Supt. [sic] cannot punish. I was therefore exceedingly anxious to have the question tested before you, believing . . . you to be thoroughly acquainted with the law."[40]

McKenny soon learned the disadvantages of bringing American law into the matter. Shortly after Charley's arrest, some of his followers hired a locally prominent lawyer to file a writ of habeas corpus on Charley's behalf. McKenny argued that because Charley had been arrested on the reservation by the superintendent's order, the Indian still remained subject to McKenny's jurisdiction, despite being in the custody of the Pierce County sheriff. "Can he be taken out upon Habeas Corpus?" McKenny asked the judge.[41]

Judging from the proceedings in the case, the mere threat of habeas corpus proceedings prompted the superintendent to drop the charges. However, he did request Judge Darwin's opinion on the legality of trying Indians for intra-Indian murders. "Indians have been convicted for selling liquor to Indians," McKenny noted. "Why then should not an Indian be punished for killing an Indian. If Indians can butcher each other and by paying a few blankets or an old horse make the matter all right, our chances for teaching them the ways of their more civilized brethren is rather poor."[42]

The answer must have been unsatisfactory, for several months later McKenny informed the Skokomish agent to punish a mixed-blood thief summarily. "According to the rulings of the courts an offence committed by an Indian or half breed against an Indian must be punished by the Agent as the courts will not take cognisance of the offence," McKenny stated. "The Tyee Charley case is one in point."[43]

In the same year as Tyee Charley's case, Colville Agent John G. Parker, with McKenny's encouragement, tried to get the courts to intervene in another intra-Indian murder. In November 1868, Parker heard about a killing committed by a Sanpoil man named Shew-Lack at the salmon fishery at Kettle Falls. He went to the falls, where he found Shew-Lack bound hand and foot. When asked why he was bound, Shew-Lack told him it was because he had killed an Okanagan man named Mitchell when both had been drunk. Tying up offenders is not documented as a punishment in the ethnographic literature on the Plateau, but Shew-Lack's statement indicated that the Indians had already inflicted punishment on him. Although ethnically an Okanagan, Mitchell resided with the Colville people, and the records do not show whether it was the Okanagans or the Colvilles that had administered the punishment.[44]

This exercise of Native authority notwithstanding, Parker brought Shew-Lack to Colville and confined him first in the county jail and then in the military guardhouse. Meanwhile, the Sanpoils offered two horses to the Colvilles to secure Shew-Lack's release. The Colvilles, however, refused the horses, indicating that they no longer saw themselves as having any interest in the case. McKenny approved of Parker's course of action. "Of course you will take no horses or any thing else as a compromise for the murder as it is such practices and customs as these that we are trying to break up," he wrote. He urged Parker to hire out Shew-Lack as a laborer to help defray the expenses of boarding the prisoner until the term of the district court in June. "I doubt wheather [*sic*] the Court will take cognisance of the matter," McKenny wrote, "but I belive [*sic*] they ought to."[45]

In early December, Shew-Lack finally appeared before a justice of the peace for a preliminary examination. No Indians testified, and the evidence presented by Parker did not convince the court. The justice of the peace thus ordered Shew-Lack discharged. Parker's efforts in Shew-Lack's case paralleled McKenny's efforts in Tyee Charley's case. He found the severity of Native justice insufficient, he lacked legal authority to execute Shew-lack himself, and when he tried to bring American courts into the matter, he found them unwilling to intrude.[46]

Thus by the late 1860s, nobody was sure how intra-Indian offenses, particularly capital offenses, should be punished. Agents were more likely to interfere with Native dispute resolution, but offered no substitute that was satisfactory, either to themselves or the Indians. In the agents' view, the courts stood as the only effective remedy for the deficiency of their own authority that would also curb the "law of vengeance" among the Indians. Unfortunately for the agents, the courts would not budge from their position.

Over the next few years, a broad shift in territorial legal culture came to the agents' rescue. This shift ended the courts' reluctance to intervene in intra-Indian disputes. The courts began to define their authority geographically, asserting control over all people within their jurisdictional boundaries, including Indians.

Ideological, political, and demographic factors all contributed to this development. Ideologically, the Civil War brought into question the legitimacy of a racially specific law, and many thought the war itself had been about the right of a sovereign power to enforce its laws in all parts of its domain. In Washington, changes in judicial personnel during the 1870s brought this more expansive view of the law to the territorial bench.

Defendant Fisk felt the impact of this ideological change. In his instructions to the jury, Roger Greene, a recent Republican appointee to the territorial bench and the judge in Fisk's case, clearly announced his perspective on the power of the law over the Indians. Greene sharply denied the local custom of letting the Indians settle their own domestic difficulties. "The defendant was subject to our law at the time the supposed murder is alleged to have been committed. . . . The defendant . . . must be presumed . . . to have known that law, which covers the soil on which he did what he has done."[47]

Politically, shifts in federal Indian policy during the early 1870s gave "law for the Indians" a higher priority in policy making circles. President Ulysses Grant's Peace Policy closely tied Indian policy to religious organizations. Christian reformers vowed to resolve the "Indian problem" in the only way they deemed possible—through forcible assimilation of the Indians into white society. Law stood high on the reformers' assimilationist agenda. Almost from the inception of the Peace Policy, the reformers urged that the "rule of law" be enforced among the Indians. Virtually every annual report of the Office of Indian Affairs from 1871 on urged Congress to amend the Intercourse Act to extend American law over intra-Indian crimes.[48]

While the reformers primarily targeted crimes committed on the reservations, their emphasis on law may have encouraged courts to take cognizance of the Indian-on-Indian crimes that came within their jurisdiction. Thus when the superintendent of Indian affairs asked for instructions on the Fisk case, his superiors in the nation's capital responded that "there seems to be no good reason why the criminal laws of the territory should not be inforced [sic] against the murderer who you say is now a prisoner."[49]

Demographic changes also contributed to the courts' new willingness to intervene in intra-Indian affairs. The influx of white settlers in the 1870s and 1880s increased whites' exposure to episodes of Indian-on-Indian violence, and as that exposure increased, so did the pressure on legal officials to exert control over intra-Indian conflict. The murder of Doctor Jackson, occurring so close to the territorial capital (Jackson's body was found floating in a canoe under a local bridge), simply could not be ignored.

Settlers called on both the Indian Department and legal officials to control such Indian "disorder." They continued to blast the reservation policy, which they blamed for much of the Indians' disorderly behavior, or at least the whites' exposure to it. An 1874 petition from the citizens of Pacific County, for example, asked that various nontreaty Indians be removed from the area around Oysterville and Shoalwater Bay, declaring the Indians a potentially dangerous nuisance. "But a few days since a murder was committed here by one Indian shooting another . . . the Indian is allowed to run at large, as though nothing had happened, and the white man's turn may come next," the petitioners complained. Following a fatal dispute involving a Spokane and a "Snake River Indian" in 1877, the *Walla Walla Weekly Statesman* commented that "had these Indians been kept on their reservation all this trouble might have been avoided."[50]

Concerned settlers mobilized legal authority to contain such disorder. Communities in hop-farming regions, which began to flourish in the 1870s and 1880s, organized citizens' police brigades because they feared disturbances among the mass of itinerant Indian pickers that flocked to the hops region.[51]

Individual citizens mobilized the law by calling in local law enforcement officials when they witnessed intra-Indian disputes. Despite a steady increase in personnel over the territorial period, law enforcement in the territory still depended heavily on the prosecutorial initiative of individual citizens. As in the case of interracial conflict, the law's interference in intra-Indian disputes was triggered by the day-to-day contact, the local, specific, and immediate confrontation between whites and Indians in Washington Territory.

Statistics on complaining witnesses illustrate the important role played by citizen-prosecutors in bringing Indian-on-Indian cases before the courts. Of the twenty-six cases of intra-Indian crime with identifiable complaining witnesses occurring after 1873, the local Indian agent appeared as the complaining witness in only four. In the other cases, white neighbors, white merchants, or white law enforcement officers observed the offense and filed the complaint. In the earlier years of the period, many of these cases would have gone unnoticed by whites and probably been settled through Native means of dispute resolution or by the Indian agent.[52]

The importance of citizen-prosecutors can also be seen in the difference between western and eastern Washington in the pattern of intra-Indian prosecutions. In the west, white population densities were higher, and settlers were thus more likely to be exposed to Indian disputes. East of the mountains, a significant amount of intra-Indian conflict simply fell outside the notice of the white settlers. Thus two-thirds of the forty-eight Indian-on-Indian cases heard after 1873 arose west of the Cascades.

The differences in Native legal practices in the two regions also affected prosecution patterns. West of the mountains, Indians were much more likely to be prosecuted for violent crimes against other Indians than on the Plateau. Of the thirty-two cases from west of the mountains, twenty were murders and nine were assaults. Of the sixteen cases from the eastern region, by contrast, only eight were violent crimes. Violence attracted greater attention from white observers than did other forms of "disorderly" behavior by Indians, and the more frequent practice of retaliation as a method of dispute resolution among the western Indians contributed to their higher prosecution rates. On the Plateau, the whipping complex prevented conflicts from escalating as frequently to the point of violence and thus attracting the attention of concerned whites.[53]

An 1886 case from the western side of the mountains offered a good example of the role played by citizen-prosecutors in bringing intra-Indian violence to the attention of the courts. Charles Harriman filed the initial affidavit in the case with the Snohomish County sheriff, charging an Indian called Joe Whitlouse with assault with intent to murder. Whitlouse had attacked another Indian called Doctor Sam.

Harriman deposed that while on his way to visit a neighbor, he "heard the cry of murder in the house of Indian Bill." He went to the house and found Whitlouse, knife in hand, struggling with Bill, the Indian owner of the house. Harriman ordered Whitlouse to leave and stop causing trouble. Whitlouse told Harriman to mind his own business and said, according to Harriman, "that he was going to kill somebody that night, either an Indian or a white man." Harriman then grabbed him by the hair and threw him to the floor, again ordering him to leave. Again Whitlouse refused, whereupon Harriman punched him in the face "and started him off."

Whitlouse disappeared into the brush and Harriman proceeded to his neighbor's house. "While there I heard the cry of murder and someone calling out my name to come and help them." Harriman ran back to Indian Bill's house and met Whitlouse on the way out. Whitlouse again threatened Harriman, who responded that he wanted no trouble. Harriman then entered the house and found two other Indians, Doctor Sam and his wife, alive but "both badly cut in several places and the floor covered with blood."[54]

The details of this case document the way white settlement and contact with Indians brought American law into intra-Indian disputes. Harriman initiated legal proceedings by filing his affidavit with the sheriff, who obtained a warrant for Whitlouse's arrest from the local justice of the peace. Without Harriman, the legal authorities might never have taken cognizance of the matter. Harriman's proximity to the scene of the trouble—he was close enough to render aid quickly when he heard the cries of murder from the house—allowed him to insert himself quite aggressively into the scene.

Harriman was not the only active agent in Whitlouse's prosecution, however. By crying murder and requesting help, Bill drew Harriman to the scene. Indeed, Bill or Doctor Sam may have encouraged Harriman to file charges or to render the Indians legal assistance. Bill, Doctor Sam, and Sam's wife all testified at Whitlouse's preliminary hearing and before the grand jury, as did Harriman.[55]

Nonetheless, the structure of Harriman's affidavit makes it clear that this case was oriented more toward white concerns with disorder than toward protection of Indian victims. Although the affidavit charged Whitlouse with an assault against Doctor Sam, it specified the details of that offense only in the last paragraph of the document. The bulk of the affidavit told the story of Whitlouse's confrontation with Harriman. Whitlouse's threats to kill Harriman showed that he endangered more than just other Indians; he also posed a threat to neighboring white settlers.

Interestingly, on the Plateau, white citizen-prosecutors served more frequently as complaining witnesses in instances of intra-Indian property crime than in instances of violent crime. A local citizen initiated only one of the eight post-1873 prosecutions of Indian-on-Indian violent crime on the Plateau, while local white settlers initiated three of the eight prosecutions of Indians for horse theft from other Indians.

Livestock trading was one of the most common avenues of Indian-white contact on the Plateau during the territorial period, and the white buyer of stolen Indian livestock brought at least one of these cases. In 1883, William Irwin filed a complaint against an Indian man named Howlish, charging him with stealing a horse from an Indian named Shuse-shuse-pomeen and selling it to Irwin for twenty-five dollars. The white complainants in other property cases could have been party to similar transactions, their complaints motivated by the claim of the original Indian owner on the settler's recent purchase.[56]

Cases initiated by citizen-prosecutors reflected the growing popular pressure to control Indian-on-Indian disorder. This pressure helped break down the territorial courts' reluctance to interfere in Indians' "domestic difficulties." The courts began to adjudicate intra-Indian cases where they could legitimately extend their jurisdiction, that is, in off-reservation disputes. But the courts did not always limit their activities to the jurisdictional boundaries prescribed by the Intercourse Act. In 1878 and 1879, the courts tried four separate cases in which Indian defendants were charged with crimes against other Indians on Indian reservations. The courts eventually dismissed the charges in two of these cases, but juries convicted the other two defendants, despite the fact that the courts had no jurisdiction over such matters. According to American law, these cases represented illegal usurpations of tribal authority by American courts.[57]

In sum, various popular, political, and judicial pressures propelled Fisk into an American courtroom in 1874 on a murder charge. Yet even as American authorities asserted their jurisdiction over the killing of Doctor Jackson, they did not use the Fisk case as an object lesson in the swift and sure punishments of "civilized law." Filled with hesitation and irony, the Fisk case shows the ambivalence of the white community over incorporating Indians into the arena of American law.

The Fisk case exposes the contradiction between the instrumental and the ideological ends of the law. Instrumentally, law sought to regulate Indian behavior in accordance with white notions of social order; ideologically, it sought to draw sharp lines between Indians and white society. The white participants all accepted the authority of American law over the incident, yet clashed over whether and how the law should acknowledge the differences between whites and Indians. The arguments of the defense attorney, the prosecutor, and the judge in the case illustrate the differing views within the white community.

Former territorial judge B. F Dennison volunteered to serve as Fisk's counsel during the proceedings. Dennison did not contest jurisdiction, or argue that Indian tribes had a sovereign right to rule over Indian-on-Indian crime. Instead, he pled insanity.

Dennison argued that Fisk's belief that Doctor Jackson had used witchcraft to attack his wife constituted an insane delusion. Such a delusion gave

Fisk a justification of self-defense. Laboring under the delusion that Doctor Jackson was using witchcraft to kill his wife, Fisk was justified in killing the shaman to try and save his wife. "All crime exists, primarily, in the mind," Dennison wrote. "To render an act criminal, a *criminal intent* must exist. The act itself does not make a man guilty."[58]

But the delusion itself provided another ground for acquittal, Dennison said. It showed the irrationality of the defendant. Nobody who believed in such a thing as witchcraft could be held accountable for his action. "If you believe from all the evidence," Dennison stated in the instructions he asked the court to deliver to the jury, "that the killing of Dr Jackson was the offspring of a delusion arising from a fixed and sincere belief in witchcraft and supernatural agencies, you should acquit the defendant." Dennison asked the jury to hold Fisk up to white standards of rationality. If he did not measure up, his behavior—like the behavior of any mental incompetent—could not be held against him.

The prosecuting attorney, Joseph Fletcher, on the other hand, urged the jury not to indulge the Indians' irrational beliefs. Like Dennison, Fletcher built his case around rationality, but he believed that the trial afforded the jury an opportunity to teach the Indians a lesson about superstition and about criminal responsibility. The Indians should be made to adhere to white standards of rational behavior, Fletcher stated, and when they failed, they needed to face the consequences.

Fletcher argued that "the existence of a *belief* in the mind of the defendant, or of a *delusion* arising from a defective education, will not excuse the commission of crime." He asked the judge to tell the jury that the legal definition of insanity meant the presence of a "deseased [*sic*] mind," not the mere product of cultural practice. "No belief, creed, custom, or superstition, is recognized by the law as sufficient to excuse crime," Fletcher stated. If Fisk sought acquittal because he acted to save his wife's life, then the jury could only acquit if it believed "that the defendant's wife was in *real* danger, and that the danger could be averted only by the killing of Jackson." To justify the killing, the threat needed to be reasonable. "[A] bare superstitious belief is not sufficient," Fletcher concluded.

Judge Greene rejected the versions of the law offered by both defense and prosecution. In his final charge to the jury, Greene dismissed Dennison's insanity defense. "Gentlemen," Greene told the jury outright, "I find no evidence in this case tending to show insanity or any insane delusion in the defendant." Greene also urged them to reject the prosecutor's effort to turn the law into an instrument to achieve specific social ends.

There are many extraordinary features in this trial. And one is, a strange position assumed by the prosecution. The prosecution has contended to you, that this case affords an opportunity you should not let slip, to teach the Indians by the terror of our law, that there is no such thing as *tomanowos*. But when did physical force ever convert a man or set of men? And who has sworn you as muscular evangelists? You are not sworn to bring in a verdict, which will in your view best affect the Indians. You are sworn to true deliverance make between the territory and the prisoner at the bar.

Judge Greene thus articulated a classic view of the law as an objective search for truth. Adherence to value-neutral standards of due process was, he told the jury, "the best thing you can do for all concerned, whites as well as Indians."

Greene then proceeded to instruct the jury in the legal doctrine of mistake. Mistake did not imply that the defendant had acted irrationally. Rather, the doctrine of mistake stressed that a defendant could reach an eminently reasonable conclusion, but that his reasoning could be based on a mistaken view of the facts. "The defendant is not to be by you assumed informed of all facts," Greene told the jury. To warrant acquittal, the evidence had to show that if the defendant's mistaken view of the facts had been correct, then those facts would have justified his action. Moreover, to be available for defense, the evidence had to show that the mistake was, in Greene's words, "honestly, and under all the circumstances reasonably, entertained." The jury had to determine whether the evidence in the case met those two criteria.

Regarding the first criterion, the judge told the jury, "any assault seriously threatening his wife with death . . . and which could not be otherwise repelled than by at once taking the life of the assailant, would have justified the defendant in taking life." It was upon the second criterion, therefore, that the case would be determined. Did Fisk truly believe that Doctor Jackson had been committing such an assault through the use of magic? "No pretence or affectation of belief will serve him," Greene said. "The belief must have been honestly and sincerely seated in him."

The jury's task was to gauge the honesty and sincerity of Fisk's beliefs by studying the culture to which he belonged. During the trial, Greene admitted a large amount of what might be called anthropological evidence. "A great deal of testimony has been adduced by the defence, to show a prevailing belief in the Indians of these parts in the doctrine of *musatchee tomanowas*," the judge stated. "That testimony is good, as tending to show an actual existing belief in the mind of the defendant."

Greene instructed the jury not to base their assessment of Fisk's beliefs on their own standards of what was possible or reasonable, but on Fisk's standards, given "his mental capacity, enlightenment and culture, under all the circumstances surrounding him." He told the jury not to "reject any evidence merely because in your view inconsistent with any supposed natural law, or any supposed course of nature." Knowledge of the laws of nature was imperfect, he reminded the jury, so the law could not restrict itself to facts based on the "laws of nature known and accepted among ourselves . . . at least in cases to which persons not privy to our own civilization are parties. . . . For, to do so would not be fair or just or reasonable."

In essence, Judge Greene asked the jury to determine whether or not Fisk should be counted as an Indian. If so, then his "mistake"—that is, the conclusion that Doctor Jackson was killing his wife—pardoned the killing, given the nature of Indian beliefs in the area. "The defendant presents himself before you, as a man of a different race from us, sharing with his race opinions substantially differing from some to which we give universal acceptance," Judge Greene told the jury. "He and his race claim, that a *musatchee tomanowas* man and his arts are possible, [and] that Doctor Jackson was such a man. . . . With a liberal mind, take from the defendant all evidence tending to show such a state of facts." Since the prosecution had not challenged Fisk's Indian identity, his belief in sorcery, or his stated motive for the killing, the jury had little choice but to acquit the defendant. They did so, after just eight minutes of deliberation, on March 31, 1874.[59]

It is interesting to note that Fisk's mixed-race background did not figure in the judge's instructions or in the advocates' arguments. In making his case, the prosecutor never suggested that the "sincerity" of Fisk's beliefs should be questioned because he was not a full-blood Indian. In fact, Judge Greene made it clear in his instructions that he regarded Fisk as the direct heir of all the "superstitions and customs" of the Indian race, passed down to him through "countless generations of ancestors."

Neither did Fisk's "civilized" occupation—as an interpreter for the Indian Department—or the fact that he lived off the reservation enter into Greene's instructions or, evidently, into the jury's assessment of his Indian identity. Just as Sulkanon and Heo had constructed particular identities for themselves—as "civilized" and independent individuals— so did Judge Greene construct a particular identity for Fisk, as an "uncivilized" and superstitious savage.

Judge Greene's instructions and the jury's decision placed Fisk firmly on one side of the cultural divide separating whites and Indians. Fisk appeared before the jury, Greene said, as a member of "a barbarous race." He shared with all members of his race a "dark and wild belief" in sorcery. Such beliefs were "uneradicated, perhaps ineradicable," the judge stated. For Greene, Fisk's beliefs arose from the backward state of Indian culture, its lower place upon the evolutionary scale compared to white culture. As these "wild" beliefs were "perhaps ineradicable," Greene's rhetoric made the cultural differences between Indians and whites appear virtually unbridgeable. He thus depicted a society of two races, mutually exclusive and strange to each other, with one marked as distinctly superior to the other.

Given the ongoing contact between whites and Indians that marked territorial society, Greene's effort to draw sharp and distinct lines between Indian and white cultures seems especially significant. His rhetoric implicitly denied the social reality of racial and cultural mixture taking place in the territory. At a time when racial boundaries were frustratingly indistinct, Greene's charge to the jury reaffirmed those boundaries and reemphasized the cultural gap between whites and Indians.

As an initial salvo in the law's campaign to police Indian behavior more thoroughly, the Fisk case ricocheted into indecision and ambiguity. The courts arrogated the power to pass judgment on Fisk's behavior, then depicted that behavior as being so essentially foreign that it could not be subject to the same normative standards as white behavior. Pressured by various forces to take a hand in controlling Indians' behavior, the courts feared that incorporating Indians into the American legal system would contribute to the erosion of racial boundaries.

This ambivalence had perverse effects on the place of Indians within the territorial legal system. While in the last two decades before statehood American law increasingly interfered in intra-Indian disputes, it rarely yielded satisfactory results for those who initiated the prosecutions. Of the forty-eight criminal cases heard after 1873, juries returned guilty verdicts in fifteen of them, with one additional defendant pleading guilty. In at least twelve (and probably thirteen) cases, the grand jury failed to find a true bill, and in nine others, petit juries acquitted the defendants. In at least five (and possibly seven) cases, the prosecutor dropped the charges, and in two, the judge discharged the defendants—one for lack of jurisdiction and one for an improper indictment.

Indian defendants in these cases thus faced about a one in three chance of punishment, and often for a lesser offense. Five of the fifteen guilty verdicts were for a lesser offense than that charged in the indictment. Only one Indian was hanged during the period for having killed another Indian. Of the other convictions, the longest jail sentence imposed was three years. The 31 percent conviction rate in intra-Indian cases fell significantly below the 44 percent conviction rate for white defendants charged with murdering other whites in Jefferson County. Although the Jefferson County figure is not directly comparable with the figure for Indian-on-Indian offenses, it gives a rough idea of the overall performance of the territorial justice system: Over half of all defendants charged with felonies—of either race—went free.

Much of the explanation for these apparently low conviction rates lies with the structural inadequacies of the territorial legal system, which applied to all criminal cases regardless of the racial identity of the defendants and victims. Both white and Indian witnesses often failed to show up at later proceedings after deposing at a preliminary hearing. A number of defendants escaped apprehension after the complaint was filed, fleeing to uninhabited parts of the territory or to British Columbia.[60]

In addition to these structural inadequacies, law enforcement officials made choices about where to apply their limited resources. Anecdotal evidence suggests that authorities only reluctantly devoted time and money to investigate and prosecute Indian-on-Indian offenses. Agent Eells commented on this phenomenon in 1891, after the Puyallups had received allotments and become citizens of the newly admitted state of Washington. In his annual report for that year, Eells noted that state authorities rarely prosecuted offenses in which Indians were the only parties involved. Prosecutions cost money and, as the allottees' lands were tax exempt, the state's taxpayers were "not inclined" to fund prosecutions of Indian crime.[61]

American law thus largely failed to solve the perceived problem of disorder among the Indians of Washington Territory. Arguably, it increased such disorder by disrupting Native means of dispute settlement. By asserting jurisdiction over intra-Indian conflict, the courts claimed that a uniform set of legal standards applied to all inhabitants of the territory. Yet they were also ambivalent about incorporating a racially and culturally distinct population into American law.

No uniform response characterized the reaction of Washington's Native peoples to the increasing intrusion of the legal system into intra-Indian disputes. Some Native communities strongly resisted the interference of American law into their affairs. They continued to resolve disputes according to their traditional mechanisms, and they defended the functioning of these mechanisms as legitimate exercises of authority. But other Indians came to view American law as a viable alternative to Native means of dispute resolution. The Indian-on-Indian cases that came before the territorial courts thus depict not only the ways in which white authorities imposed American law on local Indian communities, but also trace changes in Indian attitudes toward American law.

In several of the post-1873 cases, Indian victims (or their kin) mobilized American law to punish their Indian attackers. Their actions demonstrate a shift in attitudes toward white law among some Indians in Washington during the later territorial period. Indians became increasingly "law-minded"; that is, they became increasingly aware of American law as a potential tool for resolving disputes with other Indians, just as they had in their disputes with whites. To file a criminal complaint and pursue redress in an American court required an awareness and acceptance of American law as a viable mechanism for settling conflicts.[62]

Many of these cases appear as almost wholly intra-Indian affairs, with the only white participants being officers of the court. In twelve of the forty-eight intra-Indian cases occurring after 1873, Indians filed the initial complaint. Thus in an 1885 case of assault in Thurston County, an

Indian named Clilock initiated proceedings against an Indian called Dick for attacking him with a knife. An Indian woman known only as Susan filed an assault complaint against a Colville man called Baptiste in an 1888 Stevens County case. And in an 1881 murder case that went to the territorial supreme court on a point of law over evidence, Mary Smith, the mixed-blood daughter of an Indian woman called Eliza Jack, filed a complaint against Doctor Jack for stabbing her mother.[63]

Instances in which Indians mobilized white law against other Indians need to be understood in the broader legal and historical context of Indian-white relations in Washington Territory. As Indian agents and American courts meddled more in intra-Indian conflicts, the sanctions of Native law became less accessible and less reliable. As the Fisk case demonstrates, the courts sometimes infringed directly on Native law. What whites perceived as disorder, in other words, actually represented Native processes aimed at restoring order.

The intrusions of the courts added to the stresses already weakening the Native legal system. Native dispute resolution hinged on kinship connections and access to resources, and white settlement disrupted both. Disease wiped out established chains of kinship, which meant fewer people to help enforce sanctions against attackers and uncertain lines of responsibility in the event of an attack. Denied access to resources by white settlers, the Indians also had fewer means to assuage resentments and prevent violence.[64]

Integration into the white economy, moreover, often made it difficult for Native people to mobilize traditional sanctions against Native offenders. Individuals often left their villages to find employment in white settlements, and the diverse and transient nature of the Native populations that congregated in white urban centers hampered the efficient working of Native law. Indians from various groups and regions, for example, converged on Seattle, and when conflicts occurred within the Seattle Indian community, some Indians reacted by mobilizing American law.

In an 1887 case, for example, an Indian woman called Lucy Alice filed a complaint for grand larceny against a man identified in the case records only as Indian Joe. Before a Seattle justice of the peace, Lucy Alice testified that Joe stole seventy dollars that belonged to her but had been stowed in a trunk belonging to Eliza, Joe's wife. Eliza had left Joe in charge of the key to the trunk. She and Lucy Alice had gone out and when they returned, Joe had disappeared, as had Eliza's handkerchiefs and Lucy Alice's money. Eliza testified that Joe must have taken the money because the trunk was not broken open, and Joe had the only key. In his own testimony before the justice of the peace, Joe said he had been very drunk the previous evening. He admitted having the key but denied taking the money. Then he revised his story, saying that all the money in the trunk had belonged to his wife, and that he had only taken eight dollars.[65]

Living in Seattle, separated from the larger village community and thus unable or unwilling to rely on kin-group sanctions, Lucy Alice and Eliza used white law as a tool against Joe's alleged invasions of their property. In doing so, they provided additional evidence of their law-mindedness. They construed the property ownership and the personal relationships so that white law offered them the desired protection. They stipulated that the money in question belonged to Lucy Alice, not Eliza. If it had been Eliza's, white law might have conferred some legitimacy on Joe's claim to it, as Eliza's husband. Joe apparently recognized this, as he claimed that all the money in the trunk belonged to his wife. Under local Native legal practice, such distinctions were unimportant; a woman did not lose her rights to her property by entering into a marriage.[66]

While it disrupted Native means of dispute settlement, the courts' willingness to adjudicate intra-Indian disputes also gave Indians greater access to American law. When Native law offered no recourse, therefore, Indians turned to American law. In an 1877 case, Pe-Al, a Spokane Indian, killed a Northern Paiute during a quarrel. Pe-Al and the victim's son had been gambling near Waitsburg, a railroad junction north of Walla Walla. The two quarreled over ownership of a blanket, and the quarrel escalated until Pe-Al stabbed the son in the shoulder. At that point, the father intervened in the fight and Pe-Al fatally stabbed the older man. Indian Andy, a bystander to the fray, brought white law into the dispute by filing a complaint before a local justice of the peace.[67]

The intertribal nature of the dispute probably prompted Indian Andy's action. The records do not indicate Andy's tribal designation, but there is no historic evidence of an alliance between the Spokanes and the Northern Paiutes that would have structured Native punishment of the offense. Without such an established relationship, the dispute could have triggered a broader intertribal confrontation. With few Native sanctions available, Andy mobilized American law to punish Pe-Al.

Access to American law also led white neighbors and white husbands of Indian women—relationships fostered through ongoing contact—to pressure Indians to mobilize white law against other Indians. In the 1888 case involving Susan and Baptiste, for example, Baptiste had sworn an oath in 1884 before a court clerk in the town of Colville that he had "abandoned his relations" with the Colville tribe and "adopted the habits and pursuits of civilized life." Over the next three years, Susan evidently developed a relationship with a white settler named Charles Brown. In March 1887, Baptiste committed an assault against Susan, which prompted her to file a complaint before the local justice of the peace. Although the details of the relationship between Susan, Baptiste, and Charles Brown are lacking, the couple's drift away from the Colville tribe and Susan's relationship with Brown resulted in the mobilization of American law to punish Baptiste.[68]

Of course, white law did not completely replace Native law-ways. The kinship-mediated system of compensation and retaliation and the Plateau practice of punishment meted out by village headmen clearly continued to coexist with white legal institutions. A case that illustrates this coexistence occurred in 1880. On July 16, a Suquamish man called Charlie George fired from ambush at an Indian shaman known as Captain Howard at the latter's camp on Alki Point near Seattle. Captain Howard stated that he recognized Charlie's face and that the bullet had struck a rock near him.

Other Indians had warned Captain Howard that Charlie George would try and kill him. Charlie George believed that Captain Howard had used his powers to kill Charlie's son, known as Chief George. Chief George had been the leader of the Suquamish community at Old Man House, near the Port Madison Indian Reservation on the western side of Puget Sound. Captain Howard had visited the reservation in April, and greeted Chief George by shaking his hand. Chief George sickened and died the next month. Other Indians had told Captain Howard that if he did not pay a sum of money in atonement, then Charlie George would kill him. Charlie George thus invoked Native sanctions against the man he believed responsible for his son's death.[69]

Captain Howard's survival evidenced the power of his guardian spirit. According to Elmendorf's Twana informants, shamans were always killed suddenly and from ambush, which was the only way to overcome their power. Charlie George blundered by revealing himself before firing, allowing Captain Howard's power to protect him from harm.[70]

Charlie George's failure gave Captain Howard several alternatives. He could retaliate against Charlie George or another of his kin group—either overtly through physical violence or covertly through the use of magic. Persuaded by the attempt on his life, he could pay the atonement. Or he could take the dispute to a local Indian agent or superintendent.

Rather than pursuing any of these avenues, Captain Howard filed a complaint against Charlie George in a Seattle justice court on July 19. Stating that he was an "Indian citizen," Captain Howard charged Charlie George with assault with intent to kill. A Seattle city constable arrested Charlie George two days later.

At the preliminary hearing, Captain Howard testified in his own behalf, and produced two Indian witnesses who corroborated his testimony. In mounting his defense, Charlie George produced two other witnesses—one white and one Indian—who testified that he had been hunting far from Seattle on the day the alleged attack took place.[71] After hearing the testimony, the justice of the peace bound Charlie George over to district court on $200 bail. At the grand jury proceedings a month later, Captain Howard and the two prosecution witnesses again testified, but the case ended as did most intra-Indian cases; the grand jurors did not return a true bill, and Charlie George went free.[72]

It is impossible to establish the facts in this dispute, to establish whether Charlie George made the assault or whether the grand jury reached the proper conclusion. What is clear is that Captain Howard used American institutions either to go after an assailant, if Charlie George had truly committed the assault, or to harass and humble a potential antagonist, if he had not. His reasons for doing so can never be known with certainty, but his recourse to American law suggests that he did not believe that existing Native dispute-resolution mechanisms would allow him to achieve his goals or that the agent would deliver justice. Captain Howard therefore invoked citizenship to mobilize the nearest available alternative.

The fact that Captain Howard was a shaman might have led him to expect little satisfaction from Native law. Typically no sanctions befell the killer of a shaman suspected of using his power malevolently. Captain

Howard thus could not easily draw on kin-group resources to punish Charlie George. A similar explanation probably lies behind an 1888 case from King County, in which the wife of an accused shaman brought white law into a dispute to discipline her husband's alleged killers.[73]

Additional background information on the complaining witnesses in these intra-Indian cases would help answer questions of motivation with more certainty. Tribal designation, social status, and family and personal history doubtless factored into the decision to mobilize American law. Unfortunately, the written records offer little such information.

These cases nonetheless clearly suggest the existence of law-mindedness among some of the Indians in Washington, who adapted to a situation in which the Native dispute-settlement process had become less attractive. Individual Indians' close acquaintance and familiarity with white society and white institutions played an important role in this development. Unlike Indian groups more closely confined to reservations, Indians in Washington Territory observed the workings of white law, both by watching their white neighbors' court battles and by their exposure to criminal and civil prosecutions as off-reservation Indians. They had access to the legal institutions of white society and learned how to mobilize those institutions for their own ends.

In the case of Lucy Alice, the Seattle woman who prosecuted her friend's husband for theft, the records provide unusual insight into the way she mobilized the law. According to the testimony of Joseph Tebo, a mixed-blood man living in Seattle, someone awakened him on the morning of January 29, asking him to go to the Indian Camp.[74] "I wanted them to get a policeman and they said they could not get a policeman who would understand the language," Tebo testified. So Tebo went to the scene and escorted the defendant to the justice of the peace's office, where the town constable made the official arrest. Recruiting Tebo to overcome the language problem exemplifies the victims' attention to the concrete problems of bringing American law into the dispute.[75]

In other Indian-on-Indian cases, a good deal of similar Indian agency may be masked behind the standardized format of legal records. Whites filed the majority of complaints in these cases, but it is possible that some Indians requested white or mixed-blood acquaintances to initiate proceedings for them, in the same way that Lucy Alice recruited Joe Tebo. Perhaps these intermediaries knew the legal system better or, like Joe

Tebo, could surmount language barriers. Direct evidence for this conclusion is scanty, but frequently white complainants played very little role in the subsequent development of these cases. In the nineteen intra-Indian cases with identifiable white complainants, only five later appeared to testify before the grand jury.[76] Lists of witnesses compiled at the preliminary hearing level and the grand jury level for all forty-eight intra-Indian cases occurring after 1873 show that Indian witnesses outnumbered white witnesses 143 to 73.

It would be a mistake, however, to conclude that all Indians accepted the legitimacy of American law or even that certain individual Indians consistently resorted to American law to resolve their disputes with other Indians. The aftermath of the Fisk case vividly demonstrates the diversity of Native views; there was no common Indian reaction to either the killing of Doctor Jackson or Fisk's trial and acquittal.

The ethnographies of the Salish groups of southern Puget Sound indicate that Fisk acted in line with the values of Salish culture. Indeed, his acquittal rested mainly on convincing the white jury that he had behaved in consonance with that culture. Some of the Indian reactions to the case also bear out the supposition that the killing of Doctor Jackson was a legitimate response to an attack on Susie's life. The Indian witnesses at the trial testified that when Susie died some twelve hours after Doctor Jackson's death, the spirit of Doctor Jackson revealed itself as the cause of her demise. According to ethnographers, this is a common phenomenon in shaman-induced sickness, in which case it certainly must have reaffirmed Fisk's decision. One of the newspaper articles written about the case stated that the Indians present "all agreed that had Harry killed Dr. Jackson when the evil spirit was first thrown upon or into Susie, she would have recovered."[77]

It is also significant that among the numerous witnesses to the killing, none stepped in to try and mediate a settlement or prevent bloodshed. Four Indian witnesses testified at the preliminary hearing. Their testimony, transcribed by the justice of the peace, indicates that they were predominantly passive spectators of the events. "Harry took the man in the house and shot him," stated Sally, an Indian woman. Lewis testified that "five persons were present men and women but they did not help," meaning probably that they did not aid Fisk in killing Doctor Jackson. Under cross-examination, however, Lewis stated that he had actively refused to assist Doctor Jackson. Lewis had been on his way to chop wood for a white farmer and was carrying an axe. At one point, Doctor Jackson tried to get the axe from him, according to the testimony, but Lewis "would not give it up." Although sketchy, this evidence suggests that the Indians present accepted—or at least understood—Fisk's actions.[78]

Other Indians, however, had a different view. Ten days after the killing, the acting superintendent of Indian affairs reported to Washington, D.C., that "the prominent Indian chiefs in this vicinity are very anxious that the murderer should be hung. They regret the delay in having to await the action of the Court." These headmen clearly challenged the legitimacy of Fisk's action, and they now challenged the Office of Indian Affairs to live up to its policy of punishing Indian killers. After the acquittal, the superintendent feared trouble would result. "I have been using every endeavor to break up this tamanawas . . . knowing full well that it is a most superstitious delusion. The acquittal of Harry will weaken, if not utterly destroy, the influence which had been brought in some instances to bear against it."[79]

Another scrap of evidence suggests that some Indians disputed the legitimacy of Fisk's killing of Doctor Jackson, and thus the legitimacy of his acquittal by a white court. On April 1, 1874, after reporting the acquittal, the *Puget Sound Daily Courier* stated that a group of Indians had tried to kill Fisk upon his release by white authorities. These Indians were called into court and admonished, according to the *Courier*, that just because Fisk "escaped punishment because he believed he was doing right," they should not expect similar leniency. "If they, knowing better, should kill Harry or any other man, they would be punished."[80]

The motivation of the group that tried to kill Fisk cannot be known with certainty. Most likely, they were Doctor Jackson's kin, intent on retaliation. Perhaps they reacted to the fact that Susie had died after Doctor Jackson was killed. One ethnographer of the Puyallup and Nisqually says that although shaman killing was accepted as a potential remedy for power-induced sickness, it was subject to a rigorous test of effectiveness. If the sick person died after the shaman was killed, then the kin of the shaman potentially had a legitimate grievance against the killer. When Harry was released by the court, some Indians evidently decided to impose their own sanctions.[81]

Territory v. Harry Fisk

The continued enforcement of Native sanctions, despite the efforts by the courts and the Indian agents to interfere with such processes, demonstrated Native resistance to the interference of white law in other cases as well. Following the off-reservation killing of a Colville Indian by another Colville in December 1880, for example, Agent John Simms found the suspect "a prisoner in the hands of his tribe." Because the killing had been committed off the reservation, the agent expected the Stevens County District Court to assume jurisdiction over the case. He reported to the commissioner, however, that "the Indians are anxious to try him according to their tribal customs." No record of a court proceeding exists, so apparently tribal jurisdiction prevailed in this instance.[82]

In 1884, a council of Colville headmen notified Colville Agent Sidney Waters, Simms's successor, that they had apprehended an Indian suspected of murder called Grand Louis. Waters departed for the camp where the man was being held, but by the time he arrived the headmen had already exercised their authority in the case and executed Grand Louis. "I arrived on the scene just as they were holding funeral services over his remains," Waters reported. "While I do not approve of hanging yet I must say that this man's execution will constantly be brought to the memory of every one who saw it and prove a salutary lesson good in its effects."[83]

As American law became increasingly intrusive, various Indian leaders asserted their community's continuing right to settle conflicts between Indians. "Our people do not want the president to make laws for us," a Coeur d'Alene headman told Colville Agent Simms in 1872. "We have our own laws, they are good enough for us and we want to live by them."[84]

Native communities claimed authority over intra-Indian conflicts whether they occurred on or off the reservations, ignoring the jurisdictional boundaries written into federal law. In 1888, for example, the sheriff of King County arrested two Indian brothers—Roger and Dan Tecumseh—for the murder of two other Indian men near Renton, outside the boundaries of any reservation. The brothers were eventually acquitted, but after the trial, the sheriff told a local newspaper that the Indians had warned him "not to interfere with their affairs any more. They say that the Indians do not interfere with the white man, and they want us to leave them alone and let them settle their own differences." The sheriff predicted that retaliation would follow the acquittal.[85]

Besides enforcing their own sanctions, Indian communities also overtly resisted attempts by American legal officials to interfere in their affairs. Perhaps the most dramatic example of such resistance occurred when white authorities from Walla Walla County attempted to arrest an Indian named Wallela for the killing of another Indian, Stone, in 1874. When the county constable demanded the surrender of Wallela, members of the suspect's tribe informed him "that they would resist the arrest," according to the *Walla Walla Union*. When the constable and his three-man posse attempted to take Wallela by force, a gunfight broke out that left one Indian dead and sent the white authorities back without their man and seeking reinforcements. Wounded, Wallela made his escape, and the authorities made no immediate attempt to apprehend him.[86]

Some time following this incident, Wallela's supporters demanded compensation for the man killed in the gun battle, according to the Walla Walla newspaper. In their view, the death was caused by white aggression. As the aggressors, the whites should smooth over the hard feelings created. The whites, of course, refused to compensate the Indians, insisting on the primacy of American law. Wallela was eventually arrested in April, convicted, and sentenced to three years in the territorial penitentiary.[87]

Native resistance also took less dramatic forms than a shoot-out with an armed posse. In a Snohomish County case from 1885, Native leaders attempted to counter the imposition of American law through an explicit legal appeal to tribal sovereignty. On February 20, 1885, a Snohomish man named Meigs allegedly clubbed to death another Snohomish named George Toby. The killing occurred near the town of Stanwood, outside of reservation boundaries. A grand jury indicted Meigs on March 10, but his attorneys immediately moved to set aside the indictment and dismiss the case. As a member of the Snohomish tribe, counsel argued, Meigs "acknowledges allegiance only to his tribe and has never renounced his allegiance thereto nor has he addopted [*sic*] the habits and customs of the white race. . . . [N]either he nor the members of his tribe recognize the laws of the territory as having any binding force whatever in their intercourse with each other."

Two Snohomish headmen supported this motion with affidavits attesting to the existence of a tribal political and legal structure and to the subjection of both Meigs and George Toby to that structure. The attorneys also cited a recent Nevada Supreme Court decision that exempted off-reservation disputes between Indians from prosecution in state courts.[88]

In ruling on the motion, Judge Greene—the same man who presided over the prosecution of Harry Fisk—upheld the supremacy of American law, clearly expressing the shift to a geographically based conception of legal authority. Greene acknowledged that Meigs and George Toby both fell under the law of the Snohomish tribe, but dismissed the Nevada court's ruling as "not satisfactory or conclusive." Greene overruled the motion based on the absolute right of a sovereign to control the behavior of all those found within the territory under its control, including those who owed political allegiance to another sovereign. This right did not abrogate the rights of the other sovereign over its citizens, the judge argued. "To admit that to punish an Indian for a homicide committed upon another Indian of the same allegiance, upon our soil, would be an interference with the Indian law, would be to admit a great deal too much," the judge stated.

He went on to invoke the same fears of disorder that prompted white citizens to call on the law to control Indian-on-Indian violence. To follow the Nevada court's ruling, he said, would allow Indians to "go about in settled portions of the territory, and in presence of white people, in presence of our wives and children, conduct themselves in their Native savagery, without any regard for decency and to the prejudice of all morality."[89]

The judge ordered Meigs to enter a plea to the charge. The defendant pleaded not guilty, and the case proceeded to trial. At trial, inconsistencies in the testimony of the main prosecution witness—the wife of George Toby—led the jury to acquit Meigs on March 11, 1885.[90]

Harring has argued that such inconsistencies in testimony and the resulting acquittals represent another form of resistance by tribal societies to the imposition of American law. Such resistance, Harring suggests, effectively blocked efforts by white legal authorities to convict and punish Indians of wrongdoing. According to Harring, "(T)ribal society surrounded the events with secrecy, refusing to give white authorities evidence or offering only misinformation." *Territory v. Meigs* may indicate a similar type of resistance by the Snohomish community to the interference of American law.[91]

A review of all the intra-Indian prosecutions from Washington Territory, however, suggests the limits of Harring's American imperialism-

Native resistance model. As demonstrated above, Indians themselves brought American law into some intra-Indian disputes. In addition, as all forty-eight cases under consideration progressed to district court, the charges had to be judged sufficiently credible by a local magistrate during a preliminary hearing to hold the defendants for trial. Indian witnesses often provided the bulk of the evidence at these preliminary proceedings. In Fisk's case, for example, four Indian witnesses provided all the evidence at the preliminary hearing.[92]

Records from other cases are similar, providing little evidence of a consistent effort by Indian people in Washington to confound the efforts of white lawmen. The Fisk case, like the case files from other intra-Indian disputes, reveals a story vastly more complicated than that of an imperialistic American law storming the bastions of Native resistance. The increasing interference of American law in intra-Indian affairs did undermine Native customs of dispute settlement, but it also promised an avenue of redress for those victimized by others within their community. When Indians mobilized white law to cope with their drastically changed legal and social environment, however, it proved largely ineffective.

American law thus threatened Native structures for preserving and restoring order but provided no adequate substitute for them. Having been excluded from the territorial legal system for the first two decades of the period, Indians found themselves in the later period incorporated into but relegated to the margins of American legal institutions.

CONCLUSION

During the latter half of the nineteenth century, Indians in the United States suffered a loss of freedom, forced confinement on reservations, and the tyranny of corrupt Indian agents and self-interested missionaries. American law played a crucial role in this conquest throughout the country. Law legitimized the occupation of Indian lands, restricted Indians' sovereign rights, and upheld government efforts to eradicate Indian culture. On the surface, the story of Washington's Indians followed these general lines. Aided and abetted by American law, whites made war on the Indians, created small and impoverished reservations for them, and named officials with sometimes tyrannical ambitions to exercise authority over them.[1]

The stories of John Heo, Charley Julles, Robert Sulkanon, Harry Fisk, and countless other Indians, however, shred the conventional view of nineteenth-century Indian life. They lived off the reservations or left them regularly, escaping the day-to-day control of Indian agents, and made a living through a combination of traditional subsistence activities and participation in the white economy. In this context, the law played an additional and quite different role; it structured the integration of Indians into the local society.

In their continual traversal of reservation boundaries, Washington's Native peoples opened up the solid and impermeable line that policy makers had constructed between whites and Indians. The boundary between Indian country and white society—which in American ideology symbolized the line between "savagery" and "civilization"—was crossed and recrossed by both Indians and whites in Washington Territory with such ease that the meaning, even the existence, of supposedly self-evident categories like "white" and "Indian" threatened to collapse.[2]

American officials sandbagged these weakened boundaries repeatedly. They insisted that Indians move to the reservations, and Indian Department agents intruded regularly into the affairs of off-reservation Indian communities. But the federal government never deployed the resources necessary either to make the reservation policy work or to create an extended administrative authority for the Indian Department that effectively embraced off-reservation Indians. With the national state institutionally dependent on courts and political parties, the job of maintaining the boundaries between Indians and whites and managing Indian-white relations in general ebbed away from federal officials and toward the courts and other local sources of power.

Throughout the territorial period, settlers, jurists, lawmakers, and Indians went about the task of interpreting the differences between whites and Indians. Given the porousness of reservation boundaries, they did so through statutes and court cases and everyday contact and conflict. Initially, all interpretations were open to dispute, as various groups in territorial society vied for resources and power. Nonetheless, conflict by conflict and case by case, discernible answers emerged.

An initial interpretation formed during the chaotic early years of settlement and held sway into the 1870s. It posited a vast cultural gulf separating Indians and whites. Viewed as foreigners in their own land, Indians thus defined had no part to play in the construction of the new society being built in Washington. Viewed as an unwelcome and alien intrusion, American society held little allure for Native peoples.

Under the resulting regime of exclusion, territorial lawmakers banned intermarriage and denied to Indians standing in courts of law. Courts refused to take cognizance of offenses committed by one Indian against another. Local juries pardoned whites who sold whiskey to Indians, and citizens carried out private punishments of Indians rather than bringing them into court. In conflicts with settlers, Indians emphasized their own legal traditions of compensation and reciprocity and insisted on the primacy of their own law-ways for resolving intra-Indian conflicts.

Such a regime should not be construed as simple lawlessness, for the exclusion of Indians from American society was legally structured.

Statutes and court decisions provided the most visible layer of this legal regime. However, neither settlers nor Indians viewed formal legal institutions as the sole forums for the resolution of disputes; the exclusion of Indians was also sustained by the legal customs and culture of the Indians and whites who inhabited the territory.

This initial answer to the dilemma of porous reservation boundaries and to the "problem" of off-reservation Indians proved inherently unstable, thanks largely to the everyday actions of Indians and whites. Ongoing contact between them proved that Indians did have a part to play in the construction of territorial society. And unwelcome and alien as American society might be, Indian survival depended on making accommodations with its growing power.

Thus the regime of strict separation gave way in the 1870s to a new set of conclusions about the differences between Indians and whites. Perceptions of cultural difference persisted, but the import of those differences became more muted. Potential new identities opened up for Native peoples—not only Indian, but also worker, citizen, and taxpayer.

Rather than excluding Indians, courts and lawmakers in the later period sought to regulate their presence within white society. Lawmakers discarded the ban on intermarriage in favor of encouraging "squaw men" to formalize their relationships with Indian women through legal marriage. Juries grew less tolerant of whiskey sellers, and citizens were more likely to bring even minor offenses committed by Indians into court. Likewise, courts began policing intra-Indian conflicts that fell within their jurisdiction.

This change produced ambivalent feelings among both whites and Indians. Whites accepted the incorporation of Indians into the larger territorial society, but stopped well short of granting them full equality under the law, viewing them instead as particularly disorderly members of that society. Indeed, even as the courts acknowledged Indian involvement in territorial society, judges and lawyers continued to emphasize the vast and unbridgeable differences between Native savagery and white civilization.

Meanwhile, incorporation into territorial society threatened Indian authority within Indian communities. In the face of such a threat, many Indians reasserted their differences with whites in order to reassert Native authority. But others,while not welcoming American legal intrusions, at least recognized the utility of access to American law. In several cases, individual Indians mobilized American law in their disputes with white officials, white settlers, or other Indians. In doing so, they downplayed the differences between Indians and whites to invoke a commonly held set of individual legal rights.

This regime, in which Indians were incorporated into the larger society but denied full equality, looked strikingly similar to the national regime of allotment and forced assimilation embraced by Congress in the late 1880s, at about the same time as Washington gained statehood. One critical difference between this national policy and the regime that developed in territorial Washington was that the latter had emerged from the Indians' resistance to the reservation confinement mandated by Congress. Under the policy of allotment, Congress itself set out to destroy the reservations.[3]

In so doing, policy makers placed a new premium on Indian identity. Before they could carve up the reservations into individual landholdings, they had to identify just who had a legitimate claim to the lands. One of the great ironies of the turn-of-the-century federal campaign to destroy Indian culture was that it required officials to define formally the criteria of Indian identity. To make Indians vanish, in other words, the government first had to establish who the Indians were. Similarly, it required those who claimed Indian identity to prove their claims with specific evidence. As a result, the great distribution of Indian resources that occurred at the turn of the century clarified many of the lines left indistinct by the failure of the reservation policy, for it gave those who successfully fit themselves within the definition of *Indian* a specific set of group rights.[4]

During the territorial period, however, the lines remained blurry and the exact meaning of *Indian* remained unclear. As a result, those people defined as Indians claimed several different identities, depending on their particular interests. In different situations, individual Indians might identify themselves as members of a tribe that had treaty relations with the federal government, as local citizens and taxpayers, or as members of an extended kinship network. Each identity implied a different meaning for *Indian*, and other people might make contesting claims as to an individual's "true" identity. Given the limits of federal power, it fell to the courts to sort out which identity applied in any particular instance.[5]

To argue that Indians asserted different identities in order to manipulate American law is not to argue that they assimilated to the litigious standards of their white neighbors, or that they shed their own behavioral norms for those encoded in white law. Rather, Indians became increasingly aware of American law as a mechanism for redressing grievances, and they learned what was required to activate it. This "law-mindedness" allowed Indians who might not obtain satisfaction from Native law-ways, for example, to invoke an alternative set of sanctions. Individuals without local kinship connections or those viewed suspiciously by the local community (in particular, shamans and their families) could turn to American law to punish or at least harass aggressors.

This law-mindedness showed up more often and more clearly in the region west of the Cascades, where, particularly in the Puget Sound region, contact between whites and Indians was more intimate and intense. Compared to Indians on the Plateau, western Indians played a greater role in the white economy, intermarried more often with whites, and more frequently lived in or close to white settlements. As a result, they appeared more often in white courtrooms and learned how to mobilize American law more readily.

But these developments were not unique to the Puget Sound area or the region west of the mountains. Although legal activity involving Indians was less pronounced on the Plateau, given the sparseness of white settlement and the more limited economic role played by Indians, Native peoples showed the same law-mindedness and willingness to invoke American law as their western neighbors, particularly in areas marked by extensive Indian-white contact.

Neither was Indian familiarity with American law unique to Washington Territory. In many other areas of the country, reservations confined Indians less closely than intended and the federal government exercised less effective power over Indians than it claimed. Whether legal developments in other parts of the country paralleled those in Washington Territory or followed other patterns can only be determined by research that shakes the long-standing dependence on federal records and ethnographic accounts of reservation communities.. Once historians look beyond the reservations, they will find Indians in unexpected places.

In almost every historical study of the relationship between the law and minority groups in the United States, the question of fairness arises.

For many Americans, this question is paramount, for it tests the founding premise of a republic that is supposedly based on "the rule of law, and not of men." The legal treatment of minority groups becomes a measuring stick of national progress toward the universal equality proclaimed in the Declaration of Independence. Theorists who stress the hegemonic function of law also place great importance on the question of fairness. For a legal system to play its ideological role in upholding the status quo, it must present a persuasive illusion of fairness to those social groups who suffer the most injustice under the current social order.[6]

Like the jurists in Washington Territory, most Americans understand fairness as respect for the procedural safeguards built into American law. A fair trial is simply an impartial weighing of the evidence without regard to irrelevant factors such as the race of the defendant. In this most narrow sense, the territorial courts of Washington did treat Indians fairly. Respect for due process shows up not only in the procedural details of court proceedings, but also in the relatively high acquittal rates for Indian defendants. With some notable exceptions, such as the war leader Leschi, Native defendants were not railroaded by the American legal system.

Ultimately, however, due process is an inadequate measure of the law's fairness. Due process is a standard that is defined by Anglo-American law—that is, it is the product of a specific social, cultural, and ideological context. But by using due process to appraise American law we make it appear universal rather than culture-specific. Relying on standards like due process to measure legal fairness not only ignores the question of how these standards came to be established in the first place, but also gives no acknowledgment to other standards—such as Native sovereignty, Native norms, and Native law-ways.[7] Furthermore, a focus on due process masks the fundamental injustice brought about by the nation's westward expansion. Indians appeared in territorial courtrooms and faced judgment according to American law, not because they were willing participants in the American experiment, but because Americans usurped Indian lands, then legally ratified the actions through a series of fraudulent treaty negotiations supported by military force.

This fundamental abrogation of sovereignty, coupled with inconsistent adjudication in cases involving Indians—especially Indian victims of white violence—prevented law from ever achieving hegemonic stability. As critics of the hegemony thesis in the area of southern slave

Conclusion

law have suggested, the domination of slaveholders over slaves was perpetuated by force, not by the ideological justification of the rule of law. Similarly, the Indians of Washington Territory perceived that, beneath the mask of due process, their position in white society continued to be that of a subjugated people. It is true that it was partly American respect for due process that gradually brought Indians more fully into the legal system, enabling them to use the courts even to protest their subjugation. But the coercive origins of this inclusion and the reality of social inequality colored the Indians' view of the law. As Harring has noted more generally, Indians rarely recognized the decisions of American courts as final pronouncements on the justice of their cases.[8]

If it never convinced Indians of the justice of the conquest, the law played another equally important role in Washington Territory—regulating the results of conquest. In a situation where the federal government remained too weak to fulfill the mandates of its own policy, local courts and local law replaced federal policy as the mechanism for managing Indian-white relations. Indeed, if the reservation policy had worked as its architects had envisioned, few Indians would have been brought into territorial courtrooms. According to the blueprint of federal policy, the Natives would have been subject to the authority of Indian agents and missionaries, not the local laws of the settlers. When federal policy failed, some other institution had to take its place.

That law and the courts emerged as the substitution for federal policy, should not, perhaps, be a surprise, since local courts bore the primary burden for adjusting intergroup difficulties in other areas of the nation. Nonetheless, the frequent presence of Indians in territorial courtrooms comes as something of a revelation. Like the settlers and officials in Washington, present-day Americans and historians expect Indians to be on reservations, where they "belong." The Indians in Washington Territory, like their counterparts in other areas of the nation, have subverted that expectation. Out of the struggle to survive in the midst of conquest and cultural friction, they forged their own sense of belonging and their own definitions of "Indian country" within the American dominion.

APPENDIX
SOURCES AND METHODS

The following tables include most of the criminal cases in which Indians were named as either defendants or victims. They do not show "victimless crimes" charged to Indian defendants, which include twenty-one prosecutions for selling liquor to other Indians, one adultery prosecution, and three prosecutions for violations of territorial fish and game codes.

The extant territorial court cases are indexed in *Frontier Justice*, a text and microfilm guide to the case files prepared by the Washington State Archives. Indian defendants were identified either by their names as listed in the index (e.g., "Indian Joe" or "Skahr-hia-cum") or by notations of racial identity in the case file itself. The case abstracts in *Frontier Justice* generally mention the race of the defendant if the court clerks had made such a notation in the case file.

Cases with Indian victims were more difficult to identify, because the index entries do not routinely identify victims. Again, the abstracts in *Frontier Justice* indicate that a case involved an Indian victim if the court clerks prominently noted the Indian identity of the victim in the case file. Indians with English names involved in cases in which the court clerks made no mention of the defendants' or victims' race escaped notice. Thus the cases listed below represent only an approximation of the total number of cases involving Indians during the territorial period.

The case files contain warrants, indictments, motions, proceedings in preliminary hearings, and other court documents. They usually include verdicts for those cases that went to jury deliberation. They do not generally contain the judge's rulings on motions to dismiss the case, guilty pleas, or punishments meted out. This information can be researched in newspaper accounts or in the clerk's minute books, court journals, and other records detailing the day-to-day activities of the court. A full listing of the sources consulted during the process of putting together the individual histories of these cases can be found in the bibliography.

The tables below use the following headings:

1) *Year.* This indicates the date of indictment except where noted.

2) *County.* This indicates the county where the district court session was held, which may differ from the county in which the incident occurred.

3) *Code.* This is the unique code assigned to every district court case file by the Washington State Archives and indexed in *Frontier Justice.* To assist other researchers, I have supplied these codes rather than the case numbers, which often overlap. For reasons known only to long-dead court clerks, a single case sometimes generated more than one case file. One file might contain just the warrants, for example, while the other contained the indictment and other proceedings. In other cases, a single incident might generate more than one case if defendants were charged with more than one offense during the course of the incident (e.g., assault and robbery). Finally, in a handful of instances, a single case file contained information on two separate cases (e.g., Thr-656, Territory v. Charlie). Thus there were 112 separate case files involving Indians charged with committing crimes against non-Indians. These 112 case files represent 106 separate cases (as discussed in chapter 6) and 102 incidents. All the relevant case files are listed in the tables below or in the footnotes.

4) *Defendant.* These are the defendant names given in the case file (or a reasonable interpretation of the clerk's handwriting in the case file). Several cases featured more than one defendant. In cases with large groups of defendants, only the main defendant's name is given. Where individual case dispositions are known, they are noted. Otherwise, the final result applies to the entire group.

5) *Charge.* Only broad categories of offenses are listed, not the varying degrees of offense. Thus all assaults are listed simply as "assault," whether the actual charge was, say, assault with intent to kill or assault and battery.

6) *Result*. This includes punishments, where known. *Nolle* (short for *nolle prosequi*) indicates a motion by the prosecutor to drop the case. *Dismissed* indicates a court order of dismissal, usually upon a motion by the defense. In cases where the defendant was never arrested following indictment, a *nolle prosequi* was generally, but not always, requested by the prosecutor; *Not found* indicates those cases in which no record of a *nolle* has been located. *Acquitted* can refer to a judgment by either a grand jury or a petit jury.

TABLE A.1

Territorial District Court Criminal Cases
with Indian Defendants and Non-Indian Victims

Year	County	Code	Defendant(s)	Charge	Result
1854	Jefferson	Jef-2 Jef-3	Tootosh Sawinam	Murder	*Nolle*
1854	Jefferson	Jef-5	Watsissemer	Murder	Discharged on appeal
1854	Jefferson	Jef-4	Jack	Murder	Convicted, escaped
1854	Jefferson	Jef-9	Slaham	Murder	Hanged
1854	Jefferson	Jef-11	Tom Taylor	Murder	*Nolle*
1855	Jefferson	Jef-15	Eleheseu	Larceny	Unknown
1855	Jefferson	Jef-16	Sulgeanus	Murder	Acquitted
1855	Jefferson	Jef-116	Siamo	Burglary	Convicted, 1 year
1856*	Jefferson	Jef-41	Ringmaker and others	Murder	Not found
1856	Thurston	Thr-142	Leschi and others	Murder	Hanged[a]
1856	Thurston	Thr-150	Waginer	Murder	Acquitted
1856	Thurston	Thr-262	Wahoolit and others	Murder	Pardoned
1858	Jefferson	Jef-107	Skahr-hia-cum and others	Murder	*Nolle*
1858	Jefferson	Jef-121 Jef-124	Squitales and others	Murder	Hanged[b]

Year	County	Code	Defendant(s)	Charge	Result
1858	Jefferson	Jef-122 Jef-96 Jef-119 Jef-120	Niqusue John Quilaghem	Assault	Acquitted
1858	Jefferson	Jef-123	Willamakin Cherewals	Assault	Not found
1858*	Thurston	Thr-261	Mary Lawley	Murder	Acquitted
1859	Jefferson	Jef-138	Sa-hia-cum	Assault	*Nolle*
1860	Jefferson	Jef-254 Jef-255	Stopten Pike	Larceny	*Nolle*
1860	Thurston	Thr-405	Northern Indians	Piracy	Not found
1861	King	Kng-995	Peeps Harry Peeps	Murder	Convicted[c]
1861	Walla Walla	Wal-227	Thomas Roubis Muhaches Mohati	Murder	Convicted
1863[d]	Walla Walla	Wal-23	Sha-poon-mash	Murder	Discharged on appeal
1864	King	Kng-977	Indian Steve Indian Jacob	Murder	Unknown
1864	Thurston	Thr-599	Charley Wren Louis	Larceny	Pled guilty 2 years
1864	Walla Walla	Wal-122	Stanislaus Puk-el-peetsa	Murder	Hanged[e]
1865	King	Kng-976	Billy Williams	Assault	Convicted, 5 months
1865	Whitman	Whi-5	Antoine	Murder	Acquitted
1867	Jefferson	Jef-510	Yadawha Yatsaocup	Murder	Not found
1867	Thurston	Thr-656	Charlie	Larceny	*Nolle*
1867	Walla Walla	Wal-88	In-te-hi-hi	Larceny	Acquitted
1868	Thurston	Thr-656	Charlie	Larceny	Pled guilty, 3 months

TABLE A.1 *continued*

Year	County	Code	Defendant(s)	Charge	Result
1868	Walla Walla	Wal-1222	Telegetza Likekos	Larceny	Pled guilty, 6 months
1870	Jefferson	Jef-622	Jenny Lind	Larceny	Acquitted
1870*	Jefferson	Jef-653	Capt. Charley	Assault	Dismissed
1872	Thurston	Thr-1034	Peter	Assault	Dismissed
1873	Thurston	Thr-1077	Skagitan	Larceny	Acquitted
1873	Thurston	Thr-1157	Harry	Malicious injury	*Nolle*
1873	Walla Walla	Wal-1784	Three Indians	Burglary	Acquitted
1874	Walla Walla	Wal-2044	Muse-e-Muse	Murder	Hanged
1874	Walla Walla	Wal-2043	Mitchell	Obstruct. of law	Acquitted
1875	Jefferson	Jef-892	Haithlahla	Murder	Acquitted
1876	King	Kng-973	John	Burglary	Unknown
1876	Walla Walla	Wal-2393	Bill	Larceny	Unknown
1876	Walla Walla	Wal-2394	Indian Sam and others	Burglary	Acquitted
1876	Whitman	Whi-108	Alexama	Assault	Acquitted
1877	King	Kng-967 Kng-1047	Indian Andrew Cadett Smith	Larceny/ Robbery	Convicted[f], 3 years
1877	Whitman	Whi-123	Quill-quill-poe	Larceny	Pled guilty, 2 years
1877	Whitman	Whi-146	Colwas	Larceny	Convicted, 1 year
1878	King	Kng-1854	William	Attempted larceny	Convicted, 6 months
1878*	Spokane	Spo-13	Michael	Larceny	Unknown
1878	Walla Walla	Wal-2574	Stock-no-luck	Burglary	Acquitted
1879	Jefferson	Jef-1053	Mary Phillips	Murder	Convicted, 2 years
1879	Skagit	Skg-81	Kikiales Charley and others	Larceny	Pled guilty, 1 month[g]

Year	County	Code	Defendant(s)	Charge	Result
1879	Snohomish	Sno-182	Charles Snooks	Larceny	Unknown
1879*	Spokane	Spo-11	Indian Joe	Property destruction	Unknown
1879*	Spokane	Spo-5	Sam Cha	Property destruction	Unknown
1879	Walla Walla	Wal-2887	John Doe	Larceny	Acquitted
1880	Jefferson	Jef-1380	Homer	Larceny	Dismissed
1880	King	Kng-2371	Sam	Larceny	Pled guilty, 30 days
1880	Snohomish	Sno-223 Sno-230	Wilson Dick	Malicious trespass	Acquitted
1880	Walla Walla	Wal-3216	Sabot-Calona and others	Larceny	Acquitted
1881	Columbia	Col-449	Saw-yu	Assault	Convicted
1881	Whitman	Whi-364	Indian Joe	Larceny	Pled guilty, 3.5 years
1882	King	Kng-3005	John Curley	Assault	Pled guilty
1882	Pierce	Prc-1028	C. Lachlit	Assault	Unknown
1882	Skagit	Skg-218 Skg-217 Skg-26	Felix John	Assault	Convicted, 5 years
1883	Whitman	Whi-680	Indian John	Larceny	Convicted, 1 year
1883	Yakima	Yak-49	William Wanto	Larceny	Acquitted
1884	Columbia	Col-851	Indian Jim	Larceny	Unknown
1884	Jefferson	Jef-1668	Andy Johnson Pitchwood	Assault	Acquitted
1884	King	Kng-3997	Wesley Harry	Larceny	Acquitted
1884	King	Kng-4026	Bill	Larceny	Acquitted
1884	Spokane	Spo-721	Sweelock Wish-la-pooseman	Larceny	Unknown

TABLE A.1 *continued*

Year	County	Code	Defendant(s)	Charge	Result
1885	Garfield	Gar-142 Gar-191	Almota Jim Bisimuac Yatamoupah	Assault/ attempted robbery	Unknown
1885	King	Kng-4600	Curley Johnny and others	Murder	*Nolle*[h]
1885	King	Kng-4344	Alverds Bob	Assault	Acquitted
1885	King	Kng-4391	Jennie Le Muck	Manslaughter	Convicted, 2 years
1885	Snohomish	Sno-371	Jimmy Smith	Burglary	Pled guilty, 15 days
1885	Walla Walla	Wal-4696	Las Wanipum	Assault	Acquitted
1885	Whitman	Whi-949	Sam	Larceny	Acquitted
1885	Whitman	Whi-1032	Kamiakan Jim	Larceny	Convicted
1886	Columbia	Col-1429	Palouse Jim	Larceny	Acquitted
1886*	Spokane	Spo-1354	Stanislaus	Larceny	Unknown
1886	Walla Walla	Wal-5006	Wolf	Illegal branding	Acquitted
1886	Whitman	Whi-1104	Poker Jack and son	Larceny	Acquitted
1887*	Cowlitz	Cow-670	Joseph Cheholt	Murder	Dismissed
1887	Spokane	Spo-1350	Moses	Assault	Pled guilty, 6 months
1887	Yakima	Yak-164	Lucy	Larceny	Acquitted
1887	Yakima	Yak-191	Tom hy ax cee Sol-la-skit	Larceny	Acquitted
1888	Columbia	Col-1563	Kamiac	Threat of assault	Unknown
1888	Stevens	Stv-106	Jeremiah Alexander	Robbery	Convicted
1888	Stevens	Stv-115	Whistase	Larceny	Unknown
1889	Cowlitz	Cow-356	Chill Can	Murder	Convicted
1889	Grays Harbor	Grh-204	Peter Jack	Burglary	Pled guilty, $100 fine

Year	County	Code	Defendant(s)	Charge	Result
1889	King	Kng-6422	Indian John	Assault	Convicted, 1 month
1889	Klickitat	Klk-271	C. Colowasa	Assault	Convicted
1889	Klickitat	Klk-270	C. Colivos	Larceny	Acquitted
1889	Stevens	Stv-138	Indian Phillip	Assault	Acquitted
1889	Walla Walla	Wal-5429	George Mox Mox	Larceny	Acquitted
1889	Whitman	Whi-1652	Bill	Assault	Acquitted

* Indicates year of incident. Case file contains no indictment, or indictment is undated.

a Although several codefendants were named in the indictment, Leschi alone was tried and executed.

b Squitales and Sy-ya-hum were hanged; the other four defendants were not found.

c The prosecutor filed a *nolle prosequi* in the Peeps case.

d The United States district attorney prosecuted this case. As the alleged murder occurred on the Nez Perce Reservation, the case fell under federal jurisdiction.

e Puk-el-peetsa was acquitted.

f Andrew pled guilty; Cadett Smith was found guilty by a jury. Both were sentenced to three years.

g The clerk's minute book is unclear on the final result of this case. It appears that at least one of the five defendants pled guilty and was sentenced to one month in jail. (Washington State Archives, Northwest Regional Branch, Bellingham, Washington. *Skagit County Minute Book, 1878-1882*, 35.)

h This case grew out of an episode of anti-Chinese violence in King county. Several white codefendants were indicted along with Curley and Johnny. Charges against all defendants were eventually dropped.

TABLE A.2

Territorial District Court Criminal Cases
with Indian Defendants and Indian Victims

Year	County	Code	Defendant(s)	Charge	Result
1855	Jefferson	Jef-22	Schotum	Murder	Dismissed
1868*	Whitman	Whi-89	Shew-lack	Murder	Dismissed
1873	King	Kng-1018	Harry Jack	Murder	Hanged[a]
1873*	Pierce	Prc-1095	Peter Napoleon	Murder	Convicted
1873	Walla Walla	Wal-2610	John Doe	Robbery	*Nolle*
1874	Thurston	Thr-1187	Harry Fisk	Murder	Acquitted
1874	Thurston	Thr-1245	Harry	Murder	Acquitted
1874	Walla Walla	Wal-2045	Wallela	Murder	Convicted, 3 years
1875	Jefferson	Jef-937	Charley	Robbery	Convicted, 1 year
1876	Thurston	Thr-1467	Bob Lah-house	Murder	*Nolle*
1877	Pierce	Prc-113	Charley Jerry	Assault	Acquitted
1877	Thurston	Thr-1468	John Heo	Murder	Convicted, 2 years
1877	Walla Walla	Wal-2463	Pe-al	Murder	Acquitted
1878	King	Kng-1862	Tenas Jimmy	Murder	Acquitted
1878	Pierce	Prc-626	John Quicksha	Murder	Convicted
1878	Skagit	Skg-18	Tawes	Murder	Convicted
1879	King	Kng-2230	Kitsap	Murder	Acquitted
1880	King	Kng-2380	J. Schlaheuse	Murder	Dismissed
1880	King	Kng-2517	Charlie George	Assault	Acquitted
1880	Thurston	Thr-1770	W. La Plate Henry Heywood	Larceny	Convicted 1 year
1880	Walla Walla	Wal-3195	Quassas	Larceny	Acquitted
1881	Jefferson	Jef-1459	C. Bailey	Murder	Acquitted
1881	King	Kng-2699[b] Kng-2700	Doctor Jack Toby	Murder	Convicted, 3 years

Year	County	Code	Defendant(s)	Charge	Result
1881	Skagit	Skg-198	Tyah Johnny Price	Murder	*Nolle*
1881	Yakima	Yak-2	John	Larceny	Unknown
1883	King	Kng-3259	James Thompson	Murder	Acquitted
1883	King	Kng-3500	Tom Salem	Assault	Convicted, 60 days
1883	Spokane	Spo-340	Jimmie Jackson	Assault	Unknown[c]
1883	Whitman	Whi-639	Howlish	Larceny	Convicted, 1 year
1884	Columbia	Col-856	Indian Jim	Larceny	Acquitted
1884	King	Kng-4145	Tommy Paddy Johnny	Murder	Acquitted
1884	Walla Walla	Wal-4364	Columne (Joe)	Murder	Dismissed
1885	Snohomish	Sno-370	Meigs	Murder	Acquitted
1885	Thurston	Thr-2415	Dick	Assault	Convicted, 1 year
1886	Snohomish	Sno-414	Joe Whitlouse	Assault	Convicted
1887*	Asotin	Ast-45	Geo. Williams	Larceny	Unknown
1887	King	Kng-5155	Indian Joe	Larceny	Acquitted
1888	Grays Harbor	Grh-154	Hyas Man	Assault	Pled guilty, 1 year
1888	King	Kng-5877	Roger Tecumseh Dan Tecumseh	Murder	Acquitted
1888	Pierce	Prc-2827	Sam Horni	Murder	Acquitted
1888	Stevens	Stv-107	Baptiste	Assault	Acquitted
1888	Thurston	Thr-2603	J. Billyboyce	Assault	Acquitted
1888	Thurston	Thr-2670	Indian George	Assault	Acquitted
1888	Yakima	Yak-214	Dan Plano-pleopike	Murder	Convicted, 1 year
1888*	Yakima	Yak-215	Dick Wyneco	Murder	Convicted, 1 year

TABLE A.2 *continued*

Year	County	Code	Defendant(s)	Charge	Result
1888	Yakima	Yak-220	Peter Wanook	Larceny	Acquitted
1889	Jefferson	Jef-2059	Charles Thomas	Manslaughter	*Nolle*
1889	Klickitat	Klk-268	Won-Oke	Larceny	Acquitted
1889	Thurston	Thr-2721	Cultus Peter	Assault	Acquitted
1889*	Yakima	Yak-258	Penanoughtough	Manslaughter	Unknown

* Indicates year of incident. Case file contains no indictment, or indictment is undated.

a The prosecutor filed a *nolle prosequi* in Jack's case when he agreed to testify against Harry.

b Doctor Jack was initially arrested on a charge of assault with intent to kill, but when the victim died, a new charge of murder was filed. The grand jury acquitted Toby.

c Jackson evidently served some time in prison, but for how long and for what offense is uncertain. On March 19, 1885, the court clerk noted the return of a commitment signed by the warden of the territorial prison stating that Jackson's term had expired on December 24, 1884. *Spokane County Appearance Docket*, vol. A, p. 115, Spokane County Territorial District Court Records, Spokane County Courthouse, Spokane, Washington.

TABLE A.3

Territorial District Court Criminal Cases
with Non-Indian Defendants and Indian Victims

Year	County	Code	Defendant(s)	Charge	Result
1853	Thurston	Thr-35	Wm. Heebner	Murder	Acquitted
1853	Thurston	Thr-37	David Maurer	Murder	Acquitted
1853	Thurston	Thr-120	Robt. Brainard	Murder	Not found
1854	Thurston	Thr-121	John Butler	Murder	Unknown
1854	Thurston	Thr-36	James Burt	Murder	Not found
1856*	Jefferson	Jef-38	Samuel Tucker	Assault	Unknown
1856	Thurston	Thr-151	Charles Miller Herbert Jeals George Lemon	Murder	Acquitted
1856*	Thurston	Thr-141	William Mize	Assault	Unknown
1858	Jefferson	Jef-81	Thomas Ewing James Moore Jos. Sutherland	Assault	Acquitted
1858	Thurston	Thr-207	John Crawley	Murder	Acquitted
1858	Thurston	Thr-217	R. Anderson	Murder	*Nolle*
1861	Jefferson	Jef-299	John Allen	Murder	*Nolle*
1861	Thurston	Thr-433	George Wood	Murder	Unknown
1861	Walla Walla	Wal-171	William Bower Elisha Everts	Larceny	Unknown
1863	Jefferson	Jef-394	John Condra	Murder	*Nolle*
1863	Pierce	Prc-114	Nicholas Hale	Murder	Pled guilty, 15 months
1864	Jefferson	Jef-389	Eli Hathaway G. Knight John Condra	Murder	*Nolle*
1864	King	Kng-1076	J.M. Smith	Murder	Unknown
1864	King	Kng-936	James Riley	Murder	Acquitted
1875	Jefferson	Jef-921	John Keefe and others	Murder	Acquitted
1876	Whitman	Whi-124	Henry Keiting	Murder	Unknown

TABLE A.3 *continued*

Year	County	Code	Defendant(s)	Charge	Result
1877*	Snohomish	Sno-101	Joseph Roberts	Assault	Acquitted
1882	Klickitat	Klk-241	Henry Whitcom	Larceny	Not found
1883	Yakima	Yak-53	William Pyburn	Rape	Convicted, 4 years
1884	Walla Walla	Wal-4372	Fred Martin A. E. Cone	Larceny	Acquitted[a]
1885	Jefferson	Jef-1669	Ephraim Pullen	Assault	Acquitted
1885	Walla Walla	Wal-4694	Henry Roff	Murder	*Nolle*
1885	Walla Walla	Wal-4697	C. Pantacoast John Lynn	Murder	Acquitted
1885	Walla Walla	Wal-4877	James Close	Murder	Convicted, 1 year
1885	Walla Walla	Wal-4823	James Close	Murder	Convicted, 7 months
1886	Whatcom	Wtc-154	John Kilcup W. R. Moultry	Assault	Acquitted
1886	Whatcom	Wtc-155	Arthur Petit	Assault	Acquitted
1887	Jefferson	Jef-1928	John Crawford	Manslaughter	Acquitted
1887[b]	King	Kng-5518	Wm. de Shaw C. de Shaw James Thompson	Larceny	Unknown
1888*	Klickitat	Klk-261	Nathan Weldan Richard Stewart Wm. Weinshank	Assault	Weinshank convicted
1889	Pierce	Prc-2866	Peter Bargas	Murder	Acquitted

* Indicates year of incident. Case file contains no indictment, or indictment is undated.

[a] The prosecutor dropped the charges against Cone.

[b] The United States district attorney prosecuted this case. As the alleged larceny occurred on the Port Madison Indian Reservation, the case came under federal jurisdiction.

NOTES

ABBREVIATIONS

ARCIA U.S. Department of Interior. Office of Indian Affairs. *Annual Report of the Commissioner of Indian Affairs.*

LR-OIA Letters Received by the Office of Indian Affairs, 1881–1907. Records of the Bureau of Indian Affairs. National Archives. Washington, D.C.

M5 Records of the Washington Superintendency of Indian Affairs, 1853–1874. Records of the Bureau of Indian Affairs. National Archives. Washington, D.C.

M21 Letters Sent by the Office of Indian Affairs, 1824–1881. Records of the Bureau of Indian Affairs. National Archives. Washington, D.C.

M234 Letters Received by the Office of Indian Affairs, 1824–1881. Washington Superintendency, 1853–1881. Records of the Bureau of Indian Affairs. National Archives. Washington, D.C.

INTRODUCTION

1. Edwin Eells to Marshall Blinn, January 20, 1874, M5, Reel 13.

2. Throughout the book I use the terms *Native, Native American*, and *Indian* as synonyms to mean descendants of the pre-Columbian inhabitants of North America. Each of the terms has its shortcomings, yet all are commonly used by scholars and the general public, both Indian and non-Indian. Rather than enter the

semantic debate about which is least objectionable, I have chosen to use them all, without discrimination, to vary the text.

3. Indian-white contact during the colonial and early national periods, on the other hand, has been well-explored, but these works tend to stop at the boundaries of the nineteenth century and the period of United States' hegemony. See White, *The Middle Ground*; Usner, *Indians, Settlers, and Slaves in a Frontier Exchange Economy*.

4. Billington and Ridge, *Westward Expansion*, 591; Henretta, et al., *America's History*, 597; Utley, *The Indian Frontier of the American West, 1846–1890*, 198.

5. White, *"It's Your Misfortune and None of My Own,"* 91–117. Excellent recent examples of the "new" Indian history include Meyer, *The White Earth Tragedy* and Hoxie, *Parading Through History*.

6. On the contemporary importance of reservations for Indian people, see Giago, "Indian Reservations." On the civilization/savagery dichotomy, see Harring, *Crow Dog's Case*, 17; Robert Williams, Jr., *The American Indian in Western Legal Thought*, 6. See also Horsman, *Race and Manifest Destiny*; Drinnon, *Facing West*.

7. The concept of tribe is itself problematic for most of the Indian groups in Washington. Most scholars see little evidence of a distinct tribal identity prior to the coming of whites and the efforts by treaty negotiators to group people into recognizable tribes. See Miller and Boxberger, "Creating Chiefdoms"; Jay Miller, "Back to Basics"; Christopher Miller, *Prophetic Worlds*, 37–40; Hunn, *Nch'i-Wana, "The Big River,"* 23–26, 211–16.

8. Harmon, "Lines in Sand." On the importance of various markers in producing racial identities, see Holt, "Marking: Race, Race-making, and the Writing of History." On "passing" among African Americans, see Harris, "Whiteness as Property," 1710–13.

9. Hoxie, "Crow Leadership Amidst Reservation Oppression," in Castile and Bee, *State and Reservation*, 44.

10. Hurtado, *Indian Survival on the California Frontier*, 5; Phillips, "Indians in Los Angeles, 1781–1875."

11. Arkush, "The Great Basin Culture Area," 316, 326–27, 329, 335. Martha Knack's work on Utah's Indians likewise criticizes the focus on the "archetypal" treaty-generated reservation as the sole form of Indian landholding. Knack, "Utah Indians and the Homestead Laws," in Castile and Bee, *State and Reservation*, 64.

12. McClurken, "Ottawa Adaptive Strategies to Indian Removal"; Merrell, *The Indians' New World*.

13. Herring, *The Enduring Indians of Kansas*; Walter Williams, *Southeastern Indians Since The Removal Era*; Hauptman and Wherry, *The Pequots in Southern New England*.

14. The different patterns of white settlement in eastern and western Washington are explored in Ficken and LeWarne, *Washington*, chaps. 3–4. On Indian wage labor generally, see Littlefield and Knack, *Native Americans and Wage Labor*. On the Lummi experience with the labor market, see Boxberger, "In and Out of the Labor Force"; Boxberger, *To Fish in Common*. On Indian wage labor in Canada, see Knight, *Indians at Work*; Burrows, "'A Much-Needed Class of Labour.'"

15. For a list of reservations, see Prucha, *The Great Father*, 188–89. An example of the local mobilization of federal power can be seen in the political pressures by Oregon settlers to bring in the American military against Chief Joseph's band of the Nez Perces. See White, *"It's Your Misfortune"*, 107. A similar example, albeit in the very different context of the 1885 anti-Chinese riots in Wyoming, is Clayton D. Lurie, "Civil Disorder and the Military in Rock Springs, Wyoming."

16. Turner, "The Significance of the Frontier in American History." Examples of the "imperial school" of Western history include Goetzmann, *Exploration and Empire*; Prucha, *Broadax and Bayonet*.

17. Lamar, *Dakota Territory*, ix; Owens, "Pattern and Structure in Western Territorial Politics," 373–92.

18. Examples of reservation histories include Hoxie, "From Prison to Homeland," 55–75; Hoxie, "Crow Leadership Amidst Reservation Oppression," in Castile and Bee, *State and Reservation*, 38–60; Richards, "Agrarianism, United States Indian Policy, and the Muckleshoot Reservation"; Osburn, "The Navajo at the Bosque Redondo."

19. Harring, *Crow Dog's Case*, 44–45.

20. Hurtado, *Indian Survival on the California Frontier*, 2–5, 107–24.

21. On the growth of the Indian Service and the development of an Indian bureaucracy, see Stuart, *The Indian Office*.

22. Foner, *Reconstruction*, 142–70, 243–48.

23. On the relationship between cultural pluralism and American law, see Hartog, "The Constitution of Aspiration and 'The Rights that Belong to Us All'"; Cover, "Foreword: *Nomos* and Narrative."

24. On Indians' past and present struggles to preserve their own law-ways in the face of hostile American policy, see generally Harring, *Crow Dog's Case*.

25. Skowronek, *Building a New American State*, chap. 2; Karl, *The Uneasy State*; Wiebe, *The Search for Order*; Hofstadter, *The Age of Reform*.

26. The term "modality of rule" is from Christopher Tomlins (*Law, Labor and Ideology in the Early American Republic*, 19–34). See also Horwitz, *The Transformation of American Law, 1780–1860*; Forbath, "The Shaping of the American Labor Movement."

27. On the value of local court records for Indian history, see Hoxie, "Towards a 'New' North American Indian Legal History."

28. Judges were usually quite conscientious about keeping the two sides of the court's business distinct. For instance in 1889, the U.S. Supreme Court overturned the murder convictions of two Apache men because they were convicted by the territorial side of the Arizona court rather than by the federal side. See *Ex Parte Gon-Shay-ee*, 130 U.S. 348 (1889); McKanna, "Life Hangs in the Balance."

29. Washington State, Office of the Secretary of State, *Frontier Justice*, 1:7–9. See the appendix for a list of criminal cases involving Indians.

30. In the years 1857–64, Congress restricted district court sessions to one location in each district. Washington State, Office of the Secretary of State, *Frontier Justice*, 1:3.

31. Ibid.

32. Wunder, *Inferior Courts, Superior Justice*, 147; Washington State, Office of the Secretary of State, *Frontier Justice*, 1:3. For the data on Seattle justice courts, see King County Justice Court Dockets, 1877–1887, Seattle Precinct, 5 vols., Washington State Archives, Burien.

33. Individual case studies include Zanger, "Conflicting Concepts of Justice"; Harring, "Rich Men of the Country"; Foster, "Sins Against the Great Spirit"; Svingen, "The Case of Spotted Hawk and Little Whirlwind"; Kersey, "The Case of Tom Tiger's Horse."

34. Strickland, "Genocide at Law." Felix Cohen moved tribal sovereignty to the forefront of Indian legal doctrine through his pioneering effort to systematize the field. See Felix Cohen, *Handbook of Federal Indian Law*. Other recent studies of American Indian law include Wilkinson, *American Indians, Time, and the Law*; Wunder, *"Retained by the People"*; Clark, *Lone Wolf v. Hitchcock*; Harvey, "Constitutional Law"; McSloy, "American Indians and the Constitution." For the broad colonizing sweep of Western legal thought, see Robert Williams, Jr., *The American Indian in Western Legal Thought*.

35. On conflicts between the Indian Service and settlers, see Prucha, *The Great Father*, 109–15, 190–93; White, *"It's Your Misfortune"*, 91–94. On Eells's

ambiguous relationship to the Indians under his charge, see Castile, "Edwin Eells, U.S. Indian Agent, 1871–1895."

36. Hoxie, "Towards a 'New' North American Indian Legal History," 356–57.

37. On the ever-shifting lines of racial identity in western Washington, see Harmon, "Lines in Sand." Several scholars have explored the critical role law plays in upholding racial categories, though most often in the African American context. See Minow, *Making All the Difference*; Dominguez, *White By Definition*; Harris, "Whiteness as Property"; Pascoe, "Miscegenation Law, Court Cases, and Ideologies of 'Race' in Twentieth-Century America."

38. Stone, "Legal Mobilization and Legal Penetration."

39. Gordon, "New Developments in Legal Theory." Eugene Genovese used the concept of hegemony to construct an influential reading of southern slave law. See Genovese, *Roll, Jordan, Roll*, 25–49.

40. Gordon thus refers to "a larger cultural complex of shared meanings." Gordon, "New Developments in Legal Theory," 287.

41. Gramsci, *Selections from the Prison Notebooks*, 195–96, 246–47.

42. This study is thus neither an ethnohistory in Calvin Martin's sense of deciphering a distinctive Indian mind-set or an ethno-ethnohistory in Raymond Fogelson's sense of considering events deemed "historical" by Indian perceptions of significance. Martin, "An Introduction Aboard the *Fidele*," in Martin, *The American Indian and the Problem of History*, 3–26; Fogelson, "The Ethnohistory of Events and Nonevents."

43. The Smithsonian Institution's multivolume reference work on Indians also follows an organization based on culture areas. Sturtevant, *The Handbook of North American Indians*. The culture-area divisions used are those developed by Alfred L. Kroeber in *Cultural and Natural Areas of Native North America*.

44. The General Allotment Act (or Dawes Act) provided that Indians who patented their land allotments "shall have the benefit of and be subject to the laws, both civil and criminal, of the State or Territory in which they may reside." 24 Stat. 388 (1887).

45. Historians typically date the beginning of the reservation policy at 1851, with the Fort Laramie Treaty, although its intellectual antecedents date back earlier. The passage of the General Allotment Act in 1887 is generally taken to signal the demise of the reservation policy. See Billington and Ridge, *Westward Expansion*, 593, 610. Richard White provides slightly different dating. White, *"It's Your Misfortune"*, 91–92, 114–17.

CHAPTER 1

1. Elmendorf, *Twana Narratives*, 163.

2. The spelling of tribal names varies significantly from source to source. For the tribes of western Washington, this study follows the orthography of Suttles, *The Northwest Coast*. For the tribes of the Plateau, it follows Robert Ruby and John Brown, *Indians of the Pacific Northwest*.

3. Suttles, *Coast Salish Essays*; William Elmendorf, "Chemakum," in Suttles, *The Northwest Coast*, 438; Ann M. Renker and Erna Gunther, "Makah," in Suttles, *The Northwest Coast*, 422; Hunn, *Nch'i-Wana*, 58–67.

4. Hunn, *Nch'i-Wana*, 59.

5. Suttles, *Coast Salish Essays*, 3–14; Suttles, introduction to *The Northwest Coast*, 4; Colin Tweddell, "Historical and Ethnological Study of the Snohomish Indian People," in Horr, *American Indian Ethnohistory: Indians of the Northwest*, 2:561; Smith, *The Puyallup-Nisqually*, 51–52; Elmendorf, *The Structure of Twana Culture*, 3, 318–21, 337–40; Wayne Suttles and Barbara Lane, "Southern Coast Salish," in Suttles, *The Northwest Coast*, 493–94; Wayne Suttles, "Central Coast Salish," in Suttles, *The Northwest Coast*, 465.

Because the cultural characteristics of slavery, class distinctions based on wealth, and potlatching were not as elaborate in western Washington as they were further north, anthropologists have often seen these people as pale derivatives of a "true" Northwest Coast culture further to the North. Suttles criticizes this view in "The Recent Emergence of the Coast Salish—The Function of an Anthropological Myth" (in Suttles, *Coast Salish Essays*, 257).

6. Ray, *The Sanpoil and Nespelem*; Ray, *Cultural Relations in the Plateau of Northwestern America*, 35–36; Burns, *The Jesuits and the Indian Wars of the Northwest*, 8. Others have questioned Plateau pacifism, noting an increase in intervillage conflict following the advent of the horse. See Hunn, *Nch'i-Wana*, 24; Suttles, *Coast Salish Essays*, 282–86.

7. Hunn, *Nch'i-Wana*, 224–27; Burns, *The Jesuits*, 10; Suttles, introduction to *The Northwest Coast*, 14.

8. Marian Smith has noted how the placement of allotments on the Puyallup Reservation in the late nineteenth century corresponded to upriver/downriver divisions. Smith, *The Puyallup-Nisqually*, 45–47. See also Smith, "The Coast Salish of Puget Sound," 198–99; Ray, *Handbook of Cowlitz Indians*, A-7; June Collins, "Influence of White Contact on the Indians of Northern Puget Sound," in Horr, *American Indian Ethnohistory: Indians of the Northwest*, 2:142.

9. The common reliance on kin-group sanctions is clearly described in the sections on conflict for the central Coast Salish, southern Coast Salish, and southwestern Coast Salish in Suttles' volume *The Northwest Coast* (454–515). See also Castile, *The Indians of Puget Sound*, 349. For kinship-mediated dispute settlement on the Plateau, see Ray, *The Sanpoil and Nespelem*, 113–14; Ray, *Cultural Relations*, 36–37; Teit, "The Salishan Tribes of the Western Plateaus," 259–60; Walker, "Plateau: Nez Perce," 119.

10. Elmendorf, *Twana Narratives*, 163. I have converted the Twana names in this story from the phonetic spellings used by Elmendorf to reasonably approximate English equivalents.

11. On the divided loyalties that kin-group quarrels caused among the Skagit Indians, see Collins, *Valley of the Spirits*, 120–21.

12. Suttles, *Coast Salish Essays*, 210; Smith, "Coast Salish of Puget Sound," 197–98; Elmendorf, *Structure of Twana Culture*, 59, 150–52; Yvonne Hajda, "Southwestern Coast Salish," in Suttles, *The Northwest Coast*, 510–11; Wayne Suttles, "Central Coast Salish," in Suttles, *The Northwest Coast*, 457–58, 464; Hunn, *Nch'i-Wana*, 216; Teit, "The Salishan Tribes," 150, 261, 374.

13. Hunn, *Nch'i-Wana*, 219. See also Ray, *Cultural Relations*, 10; Suttles, *Coast Salish Essays*, 15–25, 219–20.

14. Hunn, *Nch'i-Wana*, 219; Suttles, *Coast Salish Essays*, 15–25.

15. Collins, *Valley of the Spirits*, 119–20; Amoss, *Coast Salish Spirit Dancing*, 25; Ray, *Cultural Relations*, 36–37; Haines, *The Nez Perces*, 16; Angelo Anastasio, "Ethnohistory of the Spokane Indians," in Horr, *American Indian Ethnohistory: Interior Salish and Eastern Washington Indians*, 156–57.

16. Ray, *The Sanpoil and Nespelem*, 113–14; Elmendorf, *Structure of Twana Culture*, 477; George Gibbs, "Tribes of Western Washington and Northwestern Oregon," 190.

17. Gunther, *Klallam Ethnography*, 267; James Elder to Thomas J. McKenny, February 16, 1869, M5, Reel 11; George Harvey to Samuel Ross, May 26, 1870, M5, Reel 20.

18. Gunther, *Klallam Ethnography*, 266; Elmendorf, *Structure of Twana Culture*, 477; Gibbs, "Tribes of Western Washington and Northwestern Oregon," 190.

19. Gunther, *Klallam Ethnography*, 266; Suttles, "Central Coast Salish," in Suttles, *The Northwest Coast*, 465; Smith, *The Puyallup-Nisqually*, 156; Collins, *Valley of the Spirits*, 120; Elmendorf, *Structure of Twana Culture*, 477–78.

20. Gibbs, "Tribes of Western Washington and Northwestern Oregon," 190; Gunther, *Klallam Ethnography*, 266; Elmendorf, *Structure of Twana Culture*, 477; Wayne Suttles and Barbara Lane, "Southern Coast Salish," in Suttles, *The Northwest Coast*, 495; Suttles, "Central Coast Salish," in Suttles, *The Northwest Coast*, 465; Collins, *Valley of the Spirits*, 120–21; Ray, *Cultural Relations*, 36–37; Teit, "The Salishan Tribes," 259–60; Rivers, "The Nez Perce Laws (1842)," 16, 18.

21. Gunther, *Klallam Ethnography*, 247; Ray, *The Sanpoil and Nespelem*, 145; Smith, *The Puyallup-Nisqually*, 161; Elmendorf, *Structure of Twana Culture*, 360–61; Mourning Dove, *Mourning Dove*, 107.

22. Smith, *The Puyallup-Nisqually*, 61; Gunther, *Klallam Ethnography*, 297–300; Elmendorf, *Structure of Twana Culture*, 509; Walker, "Plateau: Nez Perce," 121; Ray, *Sanpoil and Nespelem*, 210; Teit, "The Salishan Tribes," 196.

23. E. C. Fitzhugh to Isaac Stevens, February 7, 1857, M5, Reel 10; Smith, *The Puyallup-Nisqually*, 150.

24. Castile, *Indians of Puget Sound*, 350; Smith, *The Puyallup-Nisqually*, 52; Elmendorf, *Structure of Twana Culture*, 344–45; Donald, "Paths Out of Slavery on the Aboriginal North Pacific Coast of North America," 6–7.

25. Haines, *The Nez Perces*, 16; Elmendorf, *Structure of Twana Culture*, 477–78. See also Amoss, *Coast Salish Spirit Dancing*, 25; Collins, *Valley of the Spirits*, 119; Ray, *Cultural Relations*, 36–37.

26. Elmendorf, *Twana Narratives*, 163.

27. Smith, *The Puyallup-Nisqually*, 161; Elmendorf, *Structure of Twana Culture*, 360–61.

28. Miller and Boxberger, "Creating Chiefdoms," 267–73; Suttles, *Coast Salish Essays*, 15–25, 219–220; Smith, "The Coast Salish of Puget Sound," 197–99; Collins, "Influence of White Contact," in Horr, *American Indian Ethnohistory: Indians of the Northwest*, 2:142–44. A contrary view of native political organization has been argued by Kenneth Tollefson in "The Snoqualmie: A Puget Sound Chiefdom."

29. Christopher Miller, *Prophetic Worlds*, 37–40; Hunn, *Nch'i-Wana*, 23–26, 211–16; Burns, *The Jesuits*, 8; Stuart Chalfant, "An Ethnohistorical Report on Aboriginal Land Use and Occupancy by the Spokan Indians," in Horr, *American Indian Ethnohistory: Interior Salish and Eastern Washington Indians*, 4:89–92; Ray, *Cultural Relations*, 6–7; Ray, "The Columbia Indian Confederacy."

30. Garth, "The Plateau Whipping Complex and its Relationship to Plateau-Southwest Contacts," 142.

31. Ray, *The Sanpoil and Nespelem*, 112–13.

32. Ibid., 113.

33. Hunn, *Nch'i-Wana*, 216; Garth, "Early Nineteenth Century Tribal Relations in the Columbia Plateau," 49–50, 53, 55; Suttles, *Coast Salish Essays*, 191.

34. Ray, *Sanpoil and Nespelem*, 25–26; Hunn, *Nch'i-Wana*, 216; Suttles, *Coast Salish Essays*, 191; Garth, "The Plateau Whipping Complex," 144–64.

35. Garth, "Early Nineteenth Century Tribal Relations in the Columbia Plateau," 43–57; Burns, *The Jesuits*, 8–11, 17; Hunn, *Nch'i-Wana*, 24–26, 248–50; Miller, *Prophetic Worlds*, 37–40; Mourning Dove, *Mourning Dove*, 215 n. 13; Suttles, *Coast Salish Essays*, 189.

36. Mourning Dove, *Mourning Dove*, xiii, xvi, 107, 112, 215 nn. 13, 16.

37. Those groups west of the Cascades with the closest ties to the Plateau, such as the people dwelling on the Skagit River, appeared to develop similar authority structures under the influence of native religious leaders. See Collins, "Influence of White Contact," in Horr, *American Indian Ethnohistory: Indians of the Northwest*, 2:155–58.

38. Elmendorf, *Twana Narratives*, 163–64, 250.

39. Hunn, *Nch'i-Wana*, 228–51; Ray, *The Sanpoil and Nespelem*, 182–89; Walker, "Plateau: Nez Perce," 115–19; Elmendorf, *Structure of Twana Culture*, 481–99; Suttles, introduction to *The Northwest Coast*, 4; Wayne Suttles and Barbara Lane, "Southern Coast Salish," in Suttles, *The Northwest Coast*, 497; Yvonne Hajda, "Southwestern Coast Salish," in Suttles, *The Northwest Coast*, 512.

40. Teit, "The Salishan Tribes," 196; Wayne Suttles and Barbara Lane, "Southern Coast Salish," in Suttles, *The Northwest Coast*, 495; Elmendorf, *Structure of Twana Culture*, 474–75; Yvonne Hajda, "Southwestern Coast Salish," in Suttles, *The Northwest Coast*, 512–13.

41. Smith, *The Puyallup-Nisqually*, 61; Gunther, *Klallam Ethnography*, 297–300; Elmendorf, *Structure of Twana Culture*, 509, Walker, "Plateau: Nez Perce," 121; Ray, *Sanpoil and Nespelem*, 210; Teit, "The Salishan Tribes," 196.

42. Gunther, *Klallam Ethnography*, 397; Elmendorf, *Structure of Twana Culture*, 509; Smith, *The Puyallup-Nisqually*, 61.

43. Elmendorf, *Twana Narratives*, 164.

44. A large body of scholarship has shown that the public/private distinction is a social and historical creation of particular societies. Christopher Tomlins sees the strict boundary between public and private realms as "perhaps the most important characteristic" of the legal order in the early American republic. Tomlins, *Law, Labor, and Ideology*, xv.

45. E. A. Starling to Isaac Stevens, December 10, 1853, M5, Reel 9.

46. As several scholars have noted, the emigrants to the West brought with them predefined ideas about law and strong preferences about the way law should work. See Reid, "The Layers of Western Legal History," 39–43.

CHAPTER 2

1. Cesare Marino, "History of Western Washington Since 1846," in Suttles, *The Northwest Coast*, 171.

2. Kent Richards, *Isaac I. Stevens: Young Man in a Hurry.*

3. Marino, "History of Western Washington," in Suttles, *The Northwest Coast*, 169; Washburn, *The American Indian and the United States*, 4:2487–92; Richards, *Isaac I. Stevens*, 197–202.

4. Marino, "History of Western Washington, in Suttles, *The Northwest Coast*, 169–71; Washburn, *The American Indian and the United States*, 4:2493–98; Richards, *Isaac I. Stevens*, 202–4.

5. Marino, "History of Western Washington," in Suttles, *The Northwest Coast*, 169–71; Washburn, *The American Indian and the United States*, 4:2498–502; Richards, *Isaac I. Stevens*, 204–6.

6. Marino, "History of Western Washington," in Suttles, *The Northwest Coast*, 171; Richards, *Isaac I. Stevens*, 207–9.

7. Marino, "History of Western Washington," in Suttles, *The Northwest Coast*, 171; Richards, *Isaac I. Stevens*, 209; Yvonne Hajda, "Southwestern Coast Salish," in Suttles, *The Northwest Coast*, 514–15.

8. *ARCIA*, 1858, 10.

9. Marino, "History of Western Washington," in Suttles, *The Northwest Coast*, 169.

10. Ibid; Josephy, *The Nez Perce Indians and the Opening of the Northwest*, 307–23; Richards, *Isaac I. Stevens*, 211–26.

11. Marino, "History of Western Washington," in Suttles, *The Northwest Coast*, 171–72; Eckrom, *Remembered Drums*; Bancroft, *History of Washington, Idaho, and Montana, 1845–1889*, 118–38, 160–65; Richards, *Isaac I. Stevens*, 257–72.

12. Burns, *The Jesuits*, 126–355; Josephy, *The Nez Perces*, 335–76; Richards, *Isaac I. Stevens*, 236–56, 307–8; Bancroft, *History of Washington*, 139–50, 167–70, 176–93.

13. Josephy, *The Nez Perce Indians*, 328–33; Burns, *The Jesuits*, 67–82, 96–126; 10 Stat. 1132 (1855).

14. *ARCIA*, 1858, 218.

15. *ARCIA*, 1858, 231, 236; *Olympia Pioneer and Democrat*, October 8, 1858.

16. *Olympia Pioneer and Democrat*, November 19, 1858; *Olympia Pioneer and Democrat*, April 8, 1859 (reprinting the *Herald* article).

17. *ARCIA*, 1858, 218.

18. *ARCIA*, 1858, 214–18.

19. 4 Stat. 729 (1834). The extension of the Intercourse Act's provisions over the territory prior to treaty ratification was ruled upon by the territorial supreme court in *Patrick Fowler v. United States*, 1 Wash. Terr. 3 (1854).

20. *ARCIA*, 1858, 223, 234.

21. 12 Stat. 927–71 (1859); Marino, "History of Western Washington," in Suttles, *The Northwest Coast*, 171; *ARCIA*, 1872, 62; *ARCIA*, 1881, 158.

22. *ARCIA*, 1877, 198.

23. See, for instance, Edwin Eells to E. P. Smith, December 2, 1873, M234, Reel 912; Samuel Ross to E. S. Parker, January 18, 1870, M5, Reel 6.

24. *ARCIA*, 1876, 135. For population counts of the Medicine Creek signatory bands, see *ARCIA*, 1870, 17; *ARCIA*, 1871, 278.

25. *ARCIA*, 1869, 127.

26. *ARCIA*, 1872, 335.

27. The reservation site was the traditional home of a single Twana group, the Skokomish, but most of the Twanas eventually settled on the reserve. Elmendorf, *Structure of Twana Culture*, 273.

28. *ARCIA*, 1862, 304–5.

29. *ARCIA*, 1872, 352; *ARCIA*, 1873, 310.

30. *ARCIA*, 1874, 336; *ARCIA*, 1879, 154.

31. *ARCIA*, 1872, 339; *ARCIA*, 1874, 335; *ARCIA*, 1877, 195.

32. *ARCIA*, 1872, 357. On the troubled history of the Colville reservation and Winans's role in having its location changed, see Roy Ekland, "The 'Indian Problem': Pacific Northwest, 1879."

33. *ARCIA*, 1875, 361. As noted, some of the off-reservation groups did eventually obtain reservations in their homelands. In 1879, a reservation adjoining the Colville Reservation was created for Moses' band of Columbian Indians, although it was almost immediately reduced in size to preserve white access to mining districts. The Lower Spokanes also obtained a separate addition to the Colville Reservation in their home territory in 1881. *ARCIA*, 1882, 152; *ARCIA*, 1883, lxix–lxx; Ray, "The Columbia Indian Confederacy," 788–89.

34. *ARCIA*, 1881, 174.

35. Thomas J. McKenny to J. Huntington, October 7, 1867, M5, Reel 5. See also Robert H. Milroy to R. E. Trowbridge, March 11, 1880, M234, Reel 919; Marino, "History of Western Washington," in Suttles, *The Northwest Coast*, 172.

36. E. P. Smith to Marshall Blinn, December 22, 1873, in letterbook "Land and Civilization: Dec. 20, 1873–Apr. 7, 1874," M21, Reel 116, p. 3. This legal challenge, which involved the Menominee Indians in Wisconsin, eventually resulted in a U.S. Supreme Court decision invalidating Indian logging unless the purpose of such logging was to clear the land for farming. See *United States v. Cook*, 86 U.S. (19 Wall.) 591 (1873).

37. Petition of various chiefs on the Tulalip Reservation to the President of the United States, January 27, 1874, M234, Reel 913.

38. Columbus Delano to commissioner of Indian affairs, February 7, 1874, M234, Reel 913.

39. Edwin Eells to E. P. Smith, December 2, 1873, M234, Reel 912; Marino, "History of Western Washington," in Suttles, *The Northwest Coast*, 169; Josephy, *The Nez Perce Indians*, 307–23; Thomas J. McKenny to J. Huntington, October 7, 1867, M5, Reel 5.

40. William Miller to James Wilbur, July 31, 1865; Miller to Wilbur, May 31, 1866; Miller to Wilbur, June 30, 1866, M5, Reel 18; J. O. Clark to James Smith, July 31, 1870; James Smith to Samuel Ross, August 10, 1870, M5, Reel 19. For examples from western Washington, see Stacy Hemenway to C. S. King, May 31, 1868, M5, Reel 13; C. C. Finkboner to E. C. Chirouse, May 30, 1871, M5, Reel 12.

41. *ARCIA*, 1858, 9–10; *ARCIA*, 1863, 471; *ARCIA*, 1867, 35; Prucha, *The Great Father*, 109–10; Richards, "Agrarianism, United States Indian Policy, and the Muckleshoot Reservation." On repression of Native culture in Washington, see Marino, "History of Western Washington," in Suttles, *The Northwest Coast*, 172; Castile, "Edwin Eells, U.S. Indian Agent," 61; Castile, *The Indians of Puget Sound*, 293; Hunn, *Nch'i-Wana*, 275.

42. *ARCIA*, 1875, 85–86; Trafzer and Beach, "Smohalla, The Washani, and Religion as a Factor in Northwestern Indian History," 313–15.

43. Robert H. Milroy to R. E. Trowbridge, March 8, 1880, M234, Reel 919.

44. Wayne Suttles and Barbara Lane, "Southern Coast Salish," in Suttles, *The Northwest Coast*, 496; Elmendorf, *Structure of Twana Culture*, 358–60.

45. Robert H. Milroy to R. E. Trowbridge, March 8, 1880.

46. Robert H. Milroy to R. E. Trowbridge, March 8, 1880; *Territory v. John Heo* (1876), Case No. 1602 (THR-1468), Thurston County Territorial District Court Case Files, Washington State Archives, Olympia.

47. Robert H. Milroy to R. E. Trowbridge, March 8, 1880; *In Re John Heo* (1880), Case No. 1916 (THR-1796), Thurston County Territorial District Court Case Files, Washington State Archives, Olympia.

48. *In Re John Heo* (1880).

49. Ibid.

50. Robert H. Milroy to R. E. Trowbridge, March 8, 1880.

51. Tolmie, *The Journals of William Fraser Tolmie*, 209; Burns, *The Jesuits*, 11–13; Hunn, *Nch'i-Wana*, 32–38; Wayne Suttles and Barbara Lane, "Southern Coast Salish," in Suttles, *The Northwest Coast,* 499; Suttles, "Central Coast Salish," in Suttles, *The Northwest Coast*, 470; Yvonne Hajda, "Southwestern Coast Salish," in Suttles, *The Northwest Coast*, 514.

52. James Wilbur to Thomas J. McKenny, July 15, 1872, M234, Reel 912; Michael Simmons to J. W. Nesmith, July 27, 1858, M5, Reel 9.

53. William H. Tappan to Isaac Stevens, September 30, 1854, M5, Reel 17. On horse trading, see *ARCIA*, 1881, 174; "An Indian's View of Indian Affairs," 418.

54. Petition of citizens of Whatcom County, March 25, 1874, M5, Reel 12.

55. C. C. Finkboner to E. C. Chirouse, May 30, 1871, M5, Reel 12; Suttles, "Post-Contact Culture Change Among the Lummi Indians," 64.

56. *ARCIA*, 1870, 43. The agency farmer also reported Indian earnings of $2,500 from local farmers and others for labor and canoe services, as well as $4,700 from the sale of meat and produce. See also Boxberger, "In and Out of the Labor Force," 161–90.

57. A. Townsend to John Cain, March 1, 1857, M5, Reel 17; D. S. Maynard to Michael Simmons, September 19, 1856, M5, Reel 10.

58. *ARCIA*, 1882, 155–56; *ARCIA*, 1880, 155; Renker and Gunther, "Makah," in Suttles, *The Northwest Coast*, 428.

59. U.S. Department of Interior, Census Office, *Statistics of the Population of the United States: Tenth Census (1880)*, 3, 533; Guilmet et al., "The Legacy of Introduced Disease," 11; Robert Boyd, "Demographic History, 1774–1874," in Suttles, *The Northwest Coast*, 135.

60. The Northern Pacific announced its intention to site a railroad terminus at Tacoma on Puget Sound in 1873, but it completed its route over the Cascades

only in 1887. The Great Northern did not reach its western terminus, Seattle, until 1893. Morgan, *Puget's Sound*, 160–67; Norman Clark, *Mill Town*, 29; Ficken and LeWarne, *Washington*, 58–60.

61. Milroy to Trowbridge, March 8, 1880; *Tenth Census (1880)*, 3, 533; U.S. Department of Interior, Census Office, *Statistics of Population: Eleventh Census (1890)*, 395–97, 965; U.S. Department of Interior, Census Office, *Report on Indians Taxed and Indians Not Taxed: Eleventh Census (1890)*, 23.

62. See *Tacoma Herald*, September 8, 1877; *Yakima Herald*, September 4, 1890; *Yakima Herald*, September 11, 1890; *Yakima Herald*, August 6, 1891, in Relander Collection, File 49–22, Transcripts, Newspaper Clippings, "Hops," Yakima Valley Regional Library, Yakima, Wash. See also Castile, *The Indians of Puget Sound*, 305.

63. *ARCIA*, 1878, 133; *ARCIA*, 1867, 50; *ARCIA*, 1862, 305; *ARCIA*, 1877, 197; *ARCIA*, 1881, 171; Elkanah Gibson to Robert H. Milroy, September 30, 1872; Gibson to Milroy, October 31, 1873, M5, Reel 14.

64. *ARCIA*, 1878, 129; B. F. Yantis to J. W. Nesmith, July 20, 1857, M5, Reel 20.

65. *ARCIA*, 1867, 38–39; Robert H. Milroy to R. E. Trowbridge, March 11, 1880, M234, Reel 919.

66. *ARCIA*, 1878, 137.

67. Upon the abolition of the office of superintendent, the local agents began reporting directly to the OIA. From 1857 to 1861, Congress combined the Washington superintendency with the Oregon superintendency to save money. U.S. National Archives and Records Administration, *Guide to the Records of the Washington Superintendency of Indian Affairs*, 1–2, 9.

68. See, for example, *ARCIA*, 1867, 33; *ARCIA*, 1870, 19–20; Richards, "Agrarianism, United States Indian Policy, and the Muckleshoot Reservation," 43.

69. See Castile, "Edwin Eells, U.S. Indian Agent," 62.

70. Milroy to Trowbridge, March 8, 1880; Judson, *A Pioneer's Search for an Ideal Home*.

71. On the army's role in subduing the Indians generally, see Utley, *The Indian Frontier*; Prucha, *The Great Father*, 172–76; Billington and Ridge, *Westward Expansion*, 591–610; White, *"It's Your Misfortune"*, 92–108.

72. On the off-reservation activities of the Yakima police, see "Yakima Agency Jail Record Book, 1878–1888," Typescript, 2-3, File 56-10, Relander Collection. The order forbidding such off-reservation activities brought harsh

criticism from none other than Robert Milroy, then agent of the Yakima Reservation, who said that it would enable "bad" Indians to circumvent police authority by simply leaving the reservation. See Milroy to John Atkins, April 27, 1885, LR-OIA, Letter 10200. On the Indian police generally, see William T. Hagan, *Indian Police and Judges: Experiments in Acculturation and Control.*

73. Milroy to Trowbridge, March 8, 1880.

74. *In Re John Heo* (1880).

75. Hoxie, "Crow Leadership Amidst Reservation Oppression," in Castile and Bee, *State and Reservation*, 38.

CHAPTER 3

1. *Jack Gho v. Charley Julles* (1871), Case No. 166, Territorial Supreme Court Case Files, Washington State Archives, Olympia.

2. *Laws of Washington*, 1854–62, 152 [1854], 57 [1860]; *Laws of Washington*, 1862–63, 155; *Laws of Washington*, 1869, 103; *Laws of Washington*, 1873, 107. The territorial legislature met annually (except for a period where it met once every two years) to pass locally applicable laws. Congress could overrule such laws, but by the time Washington Territory was created, Congress rarely overturned laws passed by a territorial legislature. See the Washington Organic Act, 10 Stat. 175 (1853); Lamar, *Dakota Territory*, 14–19.

3. A. N. Merrick to E.S. Parker, March 22, 1871, M234, Reel 911.

4. E. A. Starling to Isaac Stevens, December 4, 1853, M5, Reel 9; *ARCIA*, 1867, 31; *ARCIA*, 1869, 124–25. For other examples, see George A. Paige to C. H. Hale, August 16, 1862, M5, Reel 9.

5. Thomas J. McKenny to Isaac Pincus, March 25, 1867, M5, Reel 5. Pincus responded that he had reached a settlement with John for $40, and that the Indian had told "several lies" to McKenny. Pincus to McKenny, March 27, 1867, M5, Reel 24.

6. Starling to Stevens, December 4, 1853.

7. *Puget Sound Herald* (Steilacoom), September 24, 1858; *United States v. John Crawley* (1858), Case No. 206 (THR-207), Thurston County Territorial District Court Case Files, Washington State Archives, Olympia.

8. On intermarriage and the fur trade generally, see Van Kirk, *Many Tender Ties*. During the Indian troubles of 1855–56, "squaw men," as white men who lived with Indian women were called disparagingly by incoming settlers, fell under the sharp suspicion of territorial officials and other whites for disloyalty to

the white cause. See Bancroft, *History of Washington*, 202; Eckrom, *Remembered Drums*, 143–44.

9. See "Judicial Review of the Marriage Laws," *Bellingham Bay Mail*, June 14, 1879.

10. *Laws of Washington*, 1854–62, 691.

11. Marian Smith, "The Puyallup of Washington," in Ralph Linton, *Acculturation in Seven American Indian Tribes*, 28. Reprints of the Donation Law and provisions cited here can be found in *Laws of Washington*, 1862–63, 41–42.

12. *Laws of Washington*, 1865–66, 81.

13. See Suttles, "Post-Contact Culture Change Among the Lummi Indians," 47–48. Suttles notes, however, that some Indians did actually sell female slaves to white men and that some Indian women did engage in prostitution.

14. The details of this incident are contained in *Territory v. J. M. Smith* (1864), Case No. 1074 (KNG-1076), King County Territorial District Court Case Files, Washington State Archives, Burien.

15. Stacy Hemenway to Thomas J. McKenny, April 6, 1868, M5, Reel 13.

16. Thomas J. McKenny to Stacy Hemenway, April 8, 1868, M5, Reel 5.

17. William Billings to C. H. Hale, April 5, 1863, M5, Reel 11.

18. Autobiography of Edwin Eells, 171–74, typescript, Edwin Eells Papers, Box 1, Folder 5; George Williams to Columbus Delano, December 16, 1873, M234, Reel 912. For another instance, see C. C. Finkboner to Thomas J. McKenny, July 8, 1867; Finkboner to McKenny, July 14, 1867, M5, Reel 12.

19. For total number of cases prosecuted, see Washington State, Office of the Secretary of State, *Frontier Justice*, 1:6.

20. *In Re Matthias' Estate*, 63 Fed 526 (9th Cir. 1894); *Laws of Washington*, 1854–62, 691.

21. *Laws of Washington*, 1865–66, 85.

22. *Laws of Washington*, 1865–66, 85.

23. Reprinted in *Laws of Washington*, 1863–64, 42.

24. *Laws of Washington*, 1865–66, 24; *Laws of Washington*, 1866–67, 7 (landholding requirement dropped); *Laws of Washington*, 1887–88, 93–94 (literacy requirement dropped, and women enfranchised); *Statutes and Codes of Washington* (1891), 114 (Women disfranchised).

25. *Jack Gho v. Charley Julles* (1871).

26. The published opinion can be found in 1 Wash. Terr. 325 (1871).

27. 9 Stat. 203 (1847).

28. *Jack Gho v. Charley Julles*, 1 Wash. Terr. 327–328.

29. *Laws of Washington*, 1867–68, 47–48.

30. Thomas J. McKenny to E. C. Chirouse, May 21, 1871, M5, Reel 6; Thomas J. McKenny to E. Eldridge, August 11, 1867, M5, Reel 5.

31. Keith, *The James Francis Tulloch Diary*, 1875–1910, 11–12.

32. "Judicial Review of the Marriage Laws," *Bellingham Bay Mail*, June 14, 1879.

33. *Territory v. Charles Beale* (1878), Case No. 52 (SKG-51); *Territory v. Henry Barkhousen* (1878), Case No. 51 (SKG-50); *Territory v. Alexander Hemphill* (1878), Case No. 53 (SKG-52); *Territory v. Richard Wooten* (1878), Case No. 54 (SKG-53); *Territory v. David Whitehill* (1878), Case No. 55 (SKG-54); *Territory v. Shadrick Wooten* (1878), Case No. 56 (SKG-55); *Territory v. Enoch Compton* (1878), Case No. 57 (SKG-56); *Territory v. James Taylor* (1878), Case No. 59 (SKG-58), Skagit County Territorial District Court Case Files, Washington State Archives, Olympia.

34. Records of the Bureau of the Census, 1880 Federal Census; U.S. Department of Interior, Census Office, *Tenth Census (1880)*, 413.

35. *Washington Territorial Census Rolls*, 1871 manuscript census. The bulk of these families were probably ex-Hudson's Bay men, who married Indian women and settled around Fort Colville. See Burns, *The Jesuits*, 171.

36. Van Kirk, *Many Tender Ties*, 28–33.

37. *Estate of William Butler* (1876), Case No. 22 (Old series) (SNO-577), Snohomish County Probate Case Files, Washington State Archives, Olympia. Post-statehood inheritance cases include *In Re Wilbur's Estate*, 8 Wash. 35 (1894); *Kelley v. Kitsap County*, 5 Wash. 521 (1893).

38. *Laws of Washington*, 1862–63, 305; *Laws of Washington*, 1869, 228, 249; *Laws of Washington*, 1873, 106–7, 232–33.

39. The Haidas lived on the Queen Charlotte Islands in British Columbia. Indians from various Canadian native groups frequently visited Washington Territory.

40. *Territory v. John Keefe et al.* (1875), Case No. 937 (JEF-921), Jefferson County Territorial District Court Case Files, Washington State Archives, Olympia.

41. *Puget Sound Dispatch*, June 10, 1875. The clipping is included in the case file for *Territory v. John Keefe et al.* (1875).

42. *Territory v. John Keefe et al.* (1875).

43. *Puget Sound Daily Courier* (Olympia), March 21, 1874.

44. *Jack Gho v. Charley Julles*, 1 Wash. Terr. 326 (1871).

45. These two classes do not correspond to the "blanket" and "progressive" factions often featured in agents' reports about on-reservation Indian groups. See Lewis, "Reservation Leadership and the Progressive-Traditional Dichotomy."

46. Robert H. Milroy to E. P. Smith, March 23, 1874, M234, Reel 913.

47. Robert H. Milroy to E. P. Smith, April 5, 1873; Milroy to Smith, May 10, 1873, M234, Reel 912.

48. *Laws of Washington*, 1863–64, 32; *Laws of Washington*, 1869, 177.

49. *Laws of Washington*, 1873, 205; *Laws of Washington*, 1865–66, 24. The Organic Act is reprinted in *Laws of Washingto*n, 1862–63. The suffrage provisions are on page 32.

50. *Olympia Transcript*, December 9, 1871; *Puget Sound Daily Courier* (Olympia), May 8, 1873.

51. *Puget Sound Daily Courier* (Olympia), May 8, 1873. Greene disputed this article as an incorrect rendering of his view of the law. Unfortunately, the Clark County court records have been destroyed, and I can locate no other account of this dispute or Greene's verdict. See *Puget Sound Daily Courier*, May 10, 1873. Greene's interpretation was given the imprimatur of the U.S. Supreme Court in *Elk v. Wilkins*, 112 U.S. 94 (1884).

52. Robert H. Milroy to E. P. Smith, May 10, 1873, M234, Reel 912; Smith to Milroy, May 6, 1873, in letterbook "Land and Civilization: Mar. 21–July 26, 1873," M21, Reel 112, p. 218.

53. Robert H. Milroy to E. P. Smith, March 23, 1874, M234, Reel 913.

54. Robert H. Milroy to E. P. Smith, March 23, 1874; E. M. Marble to Robert H. Milroy, November 8, 1880, in letterbook "Land: April 6, 1880–May 6, 1881," M21, Reel 158, p. 407. The Indian Homestead Act is 18 Stat. 402 (1875).

55. *Code of Washington*, 1881, 173, 182. *Kanaka* is a Chinook Jargon term for native Hawaiian. As crew members of trading vessels, Hawaiians frequently visited the North American coast, and some stayed on after the ships left.

56. 4 Stat. 732 (1834); Clark, *The Dry Years*, 24. There were significant differences between federal law and local law. The territorial statute covered a broader range of alcoholic beverages than did the federal law. More significantly, the territory declared the offense a misdemeanor, subject to fines of no more than $500, later lowered to $100. The federal law held out the prospect of up to two years imprisonment and a maximum fine of $300. Finally, while the federal law had allowed Indian testimony in liquor-law prosecutions since 1847, the territory did not allow Indian witnesses until 1869. See 9 Stat. 203 9 (1847);

12 Stat. 339 (1862); *Laws of Washington*, 1866–67, 96; *Laws of Washington*, 1869, 228.

57. The assumptions behind the liquor laws are more fully developed in the following chapter.

CHAPTER 4

1. *United States v. Charles Vogelsong* (1889), Case No. 6248 (KNG-6248), King County Territorial District Court Case Files, Washington State Archives, Burien.

2. 4 Stat. 732 (1834).

3. The Muckleshoot Reservation was created after the Indian wars as a residence for several hostile bands. It sometimes fell under the jurisdiction of the agent to the Medicine Creek treaty groups and at other times under that of the agent to the Point Elliott treaty groups. On the amendment of the Intercourse Act, see 12 Stat. 339 (1862). The 1862 law also lowered the maximum fine to $300, from $500, but established a uniform maximum prison term of two years. Deady, a federal judge in Oregon, reviewed the statute in *United States v. Winslow*, 28 Fed. Cas. 739 (1875).

4. See *ARCIA*, 1860, 17.

5. *ARCIA*, 1859, 404. See also *ARCIA*, 1863, 404, regarding the liquor traffic on the Makah Reservation; *ARCIA*, 1869, 140, regarding the Skokomish Reservation.

6. Congress temporarily backed off from this concurrent jurisdiction in 1873, with the compilation of the Revised Statutes. The revisers, apparently striving for consistency, exempted Indians in Indian country from the law prohibiting liquor sales to Indians. In other words, an Indian could sell or trade whiskey to another Indian within Indian country without calling down the penalties of federal law. See 1 Rev. Stat. (18 Stat.) 373 (1878). The exemption did not last long. White liquor sellers seized the opportunity to use Indians as middlemen to channel liquor onto the reservations. In 1877, in legislation aimed at correcting flaws in the revision, the offending exemption was stricken out. 19 Stat. 244 (1877).

7. King County Justice Court Dockets, 1877–87, Seattle Precinct, vols. 1–4 (Scott, 1877–1880; Scott/Cann, 1880–1883; Cann, 1883–1884; Cann/Hill, 1884–1887); King County Justice Court Dockets, 1877–1887, Seattle Precinct, vol. 5

(Lyon/Jones, 1885–1887), Washington State Archives, Burien; Wunder, *Inferior Courts, Superior Justice.*

8. Washington State, Office of the Secretary of State, *Frontier Justice*, 1:6–7. If the assault and larceny/fraud categories are broken into their respective components, selling liquor to Indians may have been the single most common felony prosecution. The compilers of *Frontier Justice* counted 709 liquor cases, but examination of the case records turned up a handful of these that did not actually involve liquor sales to Indians. Additional research also uncovered some violations that were not included in the index. It is probable that neither my estimate nor theirs is absolutely accurate.

9. For this study, 573 (81 percent) of the 708 cases were traced to their final disposition.

10. *ARCIA*, 1862, 407–8. On conflicts between settlers and officials, see Prucha, *The Great Father*, 107; White, *The Roots of Dependency*, 120–22.

11. *United States v. Fogerty* (1862), Case No. 35 (WAL-35), Walla Walla County Territorial District Court Case Files, Washington State Archives, Olympia.

12. James Kavanaugh to C. H. Hale, October 16, 1862, M5, Reel 24.

13. C. C. Finkboner to W. H. Waterman, September 16, 1865, M5, Reel 12.

14. James Kavanaugh to C. H. Hale, October 16, 1862, M5, Reel 24; Nathaniel Hill to Isaac Stevens, October 31, 1856, M5, Reel 10.

15. *ARCIA*, 1862, 407–8.

16. James Kavanaugh to C. H. Hale, October 16, 1862, M5, Reel 24; S. D. Howe to C. H. Hale, October 13, 1862, M5, Reel 12.

17. These figures are based on the 708 case files for liquor prosecutions.

18. James Kavanaugh to C. H. Hale, October 16, 1862, M5, Reel 24; Thomas J. McKenny to Nathaniel Taylor, November 9, 1867, M5, Reel 5.

19. Major P. Lugenbeel to E. R. Geary, February 12, 1861, M5, Reel 20; Clark, *The Dry Years*, 24–25.

20. Thomas J. McKenny to Nathaniel Taylor, November 9, 1867, M5, Reel 5; Thomas Hanna to Michael Simmons, June 27, 1857, M5, Reel 10.

21. Clark, *The Dry Years*, 23–24; E. C. Chirouse to Samuel Ross, February 4, 1870, M5, Reel 12; John Knox to C. A. Huntington, November 6, 1866, M5, Reel 13; George Paige and Giles Ford to C. H. Hale, September 19, 1863, M5, Reel 15.

22. Major P. Lugenbeel to E. R. Geary, January 5, 1861, M5, Reel 20; George Paige to Thomas J. McKenny, February 8, 1868, M5, Reel 20; William Barnhart to B. F. Kendall, December 3, 1861, M5, Reel 21.

23. Henry Webster to C. H. Hale, July 19, 1862, M5, Reel 14.

24. *ARCIA*, 1862, 400.

25. Ibid.

26. Michael Simmons to Isaac Stevens, July 1, 1854, M5, Reel 9; C. C. Finkboner to W. H. Waterman, September 16, 1865, M5, Reel 12.

27. Michael Simmons to J. W. Nesmith, March 31, 1858, M5, Reel 9.

28. *ARCIA*, 1858, 239.

29. Thomas J. McKenny to Messrs. Renton, Smith & Co, May 17, 1867, M5, Reel 5; *ARCIA*, 1867, 31.

30. Thomas J. McKenny to Renton, Smith & Co, May 17, 1867, M5, Reel 5. For an overview of the economic development of Washington during the territorial period, see Ficken and LeWarne, *Washington*, 21–68.

31. *United States v. Abraham Gervais* (1874), Case No. OS-890 (WAL-2031), Walla Walla County Territorial District Court Case Files, Washington State Archives, Olympia; see also *United States v. James Dixon* (1876), Case No. 1166 (KNG-1168), King County Territorial District Court Case Files, Washington State Archives, Burien.

32. *Territory v. Richard Roe* (1876), Case No. 1122 (KNG-1124), King County District Court Case Files, Washington State Archives, Burien; *United States v. Charles Lovett* (1875), Case No. 965 (JEF-949), Jefferson County District Court Case Files, Washington State Archives, Olympia.

33. *United States v. William Parsons* (1868), Case No. 561 (JEF-549), Jefferson County Territorial District Court Case Files, Washington State Archives, Olympia.

34. "Implicit plea bargaining" is the term used by Milton Heumann to describe the hope entertained by defendants that they will be rewarded for pleading guilty, as distinguished from the explicit plea bargains struck between prosecutors and defendants in the current criminal justice system. Milton Heumann, cited in Friedman and Percival, *The Roots of Justice*, 179–81.

35. The average jail sentence for those who pleaded guilty during the 1870s, 135 days, was also significantly lower than for those who were convicted by jury, but there were only fifteen cases that ended in guilty pleas during that decade.

36. Friedman, *Crime and Punishment in American History*, 9–11.

37. Leland, *Firewater Myths*, 1–2. On the development of these attitudes during the colonial period, see Mancall, *Deadly Medicine*.

38. *ARCIA*, 1860, 17.

39. Prucha, *The Great Father*, 40; Norman Clark, *The Dry Years*, 6. For a review of the literature with an extensive bibliography, see Hill, "Ethnohistory and Alcohol Studies." For drinking on the Northwest Coast, see Lemert, *Alcohol and the Northwest Coast Indians*. For Indian drinking among the tribes of the eastern woodlands, see Mancall, *Deadly Medicine*.

40. MacAndrew and Edgerton, *Drunken Comportment*, 100–73.

41. The scholarly literature on Indians and alcohol has, for the most part, tried to explain why Indians drink. See Hill, "Ethnohistory and Alcohol Studies." It has not, therefore, paid much attention to the liquor laws. By conveying certain messages about race, the Intercourse Act contributed to the meaning Indians attached to drinking. Several years ago, Nancy Lurie suggested that heavy drinking and aggressive behavior became vehicles for expressing "Indianness" in the absence of other acceptable forms of expressing that identity. Efforts to deny liquor to Indians helped transform drinking into that vehicle of expression. Nancy Lurie, "The World's Oldest On-Going Protest Demonstration."

42. E. C. Chirouse to Robert H. Milroy, July 1, 1874, M5, Reel 12; *ARCIA*, 1867, 38. For the Skokomish Reservation, see Castile, *The Indians of Puget Sound*, 349.

43. *ARCIA*, 1858, 218. The data on defendants in the 708 cases bear out the perception that most sellers were white men. Out of 708 cases, 651 defendants (92 percent) were white. Fifteen defendants were Chinese, nine were identified as having mixed Indian/white parentage, and twenty-one were identified as Indians. There were only nineteen female defendants, six Indians and thirteen whites.

44. E. C. Fitzhugh to Isaac Stevens, September 18, 1856, M5, Reel 10; Michael Simmons to Isaac Stevens, July 1, 1854, M5, Reel 9.

45. Michael Simmons to Isaac Stevens, July 1, 1854; Michael Simmons to J. W. Nesmith, July 27, 1858, M5, Reel 9.

46. John Knox to C. H. Hale, May 24, 1864, M5, Reel 13.

47. C. C. Finkboner to W. H. Waterman, September 16, 1865, M5, Reel 12; *ARCIA*, 1858, 234; Absalom Armstrong to Edward R. Geary, November 5, 1860, M5, Reel 16; Edwin Eells to Marshall Blinn, January 20, 1874, M5, Reel 13.

48. MacAndrew and Edgerton, Drunken Comportment, 123–35.

49. *ARCIA*, 1872, 344.

50. E. A. Starling to Isaac Stevens, December 4, 1853, M5, Reel 9. In 1859, the Nez Perce agent was told not to interfere with the liquor trade between whites so long as the vendors were licensed by the territory, despite the fact that the liquor inevitably found its way into Indian hands. Samuel Smith to A. J. Cain, February

19, 1859, enclosed in Cain to J. W. Nesmith, February 28, 1859, M5, Reel 21. For early efforts at temperance reform in Washington, see Clark, *The Dry Years*, 21–27.

51. *United States v. Charles Vogelsong* (1889).

52. *United States v. Holliday*, 70 U.S. 407 (1865).

53. *United States v. John McBride* (1872), Case No. OS-488 (WAL-1729), Walla Walla County Territorial District Court Case Files, Washington State Archives, Olympia.

54. See, for example, *United States v. William Goellert* (1877), Case No. 1034 (JEF-1017), Jefferson County Territorial District Court Case Files, Washington State Archives, Olympia; *United States v. Richard Roe* (1876), Case No. 1122 (KNG-1124), King County Territorial District Court Case Files, Washington State Archives, Burien.

55. *United States v. Richard Fryer* (1880), Case No. 2417 (KNG-2418), King County Territorial District Court Case Files, Washington State Archives, Burien.

56. *United States v. Charles Wilcox* (1885), Case No. 4637 (KNG-4637), King County Territorial District Court Case Files, Washington State Archives, Burien.

57. *United States v. Charles Fisher* (1880), Case No. 1904 (THR-1784). See also *United States v. Stephen Barker* (1880), Case No. 1908 (THR-1788), Thurston County Territorial District Court Case Files, Washington State Archives, Olympia.

58. *United States v. Frank Joe* (1888), Case No. 2751 (THR-2627), Thurston County Territorial District Court Case Files, Washington State Archives, Olympia.

59. *United States v. Richard Fryer* (1880).

60. *United States v. Isaac Jones* (1876), (COW-607), Cowlitz County Territorial District Court Case Files, Washington State Archives, Olympia.

61. *United States v. W. J. Wilson* (1874), Case No. 994 (WAL-2129), Walla Walla County Territorial District Court Case Files, Washington State Archives, Olympia.

62. *United States v. Charles Vogelsong* (1889).

63. See Castile, *The Indians of Puget Sound*, xvii.

CHAPTER 5

1. *Territory v. James Close* (1885), Case No. 4496, 2d series (WAL-4823), Walla Walla County Territorial District Court Case Files, Washington State Archives, Olympia.

2. Richard Maxwell Brown found a similar attitude toward summary proceedings among vigilante groups. See Brown, *Strain of Violence*, 96.

3. Robert Johannsen, "The Sectional Controversy and the Frontier," 5–7; U.S. Department of Interior, Census Office, *Population of the United States in 1860*, 584.

4. McGilvra, *Reminiscences of the Early Days of the Washington Bar*, 24; Johannsen, "The Sectional Controversy and the Frontier," 1–7. See also Bancroft, *History of Washington*, 207.

5. On southern legal culture, see Ayers, *Vengeance and Justice*; Hindus, *Prison and Plantation*.

6. Whipping was practiced within native societies on the Plateau, but was an innovation among the societies along Puget Sound. James Swan also reported some whippings of white men—"a miserable loafer" and "a thief"—during the early years of settlement at Shoalwater Bay. Swan, *The Northwest Coast*, 281–82.

7. E. C. Fitzhugh to Isaac Stevens, February 16, 1857, M5, Reel 10.

8. *Olympia Pioneer and Democrat*, April 17, 1857; *Puget Sound Herald* (Steilacoom), October 15, 1858.

9. *Olympia Pioneer and Democrat*, April 17, 1857.

10. E. A. Starling to Isaac Stevens, December 4, 1853, M5, Reel 9.

11. *Territory v. James Close* (1885), Case No. 4496 (WAL-4823).

12. *Territory v. George Wood* (1861), Case No. 428 (THR-433), Thurston County Territorial District Court Case Files, Washington State Archives, Olympia.

13. "Charges and Specifications against James Lake," Washington Territorial Volunteers Papers, Box 14, Washington State Archives, Olympia.

14. *Olympia Pioneer and Democrat*, November 28, 1856; *The Oregonian*, November 29, 1856; Eckrom, *Remembered Drums*, 153.

15. See, for example, *Olympia Pioneer and Democrat*, September 12, 1856; October 10, 1856; February 27, 1857. See also Major General John Wool to Lt. Col. L. Thomas, April 2, 1856, in U.S. Senate, *Report of the Secretary of War*, 54–61; Meeker, *Pioneer Reminiscences of Puget Sound and the Tragedy of Leschi*, 232–62.

16. *Olympia Pioneer and Democrat*, September 12, 1856; *Olympia Pioneer and Democrat*, November 7, 1856.

17. Sidney S. Ford to Isaac Stevens, November 27, 1856, M5, Reel 16; *Olympia Pioneer and Democrat*, November 28, 1856.

18. *Olympia Pioneer and Democrat*, February 27, 1857.

19. Ibid.

20. Isaac Stevens to Captain Samuel Swartout, June 2, 1856, Washington Territorial Volunteers Papers, Box 7.

21. Of the thirteen additional prosecutions against non-Indians, eight were for assault, one was for rape, and four were for property crimes. See the appendix for details.

22. *Puget Sound Herald* (Steilacoom), September 24, 1858; September 26, 1861.

23. *Territory v. James Close* (1885), Case No. 4496 (WAL-4823).

24. *Walla Walla Union*, March 26, 1885.

25. Ibid. The case against Me-ats's companion is *Territory v. Las Wanipum* (1885), Case No. 4341, 2d series (WAL-4696), Walla Walla County Territorial District Court Case Files, Washington State Archives, Olympia. The grand jury did not indict Las Wanipum.

26. U.S. Department of Interior, Census Office, *Population of the United States in 1860*, 582; U.S. Department of Interior, Census Office, *Statistics of the Population: Tenth Census (1880)*, 3.

27. Johannsen, "The Sectional Controversy," 345–46, 358–59; Bancroft, *History of Washington*, 285.

28. See Duncan Kennedy's article, "Toward an Historical Understanding of Legal Consciousness," for an analysis of the post–Civil War rise of the legal theory of absolute sovereign authority of society's governing institutions.

29. *Territory v. Alverds Bob* (1885), Case No. 4344 (KNG-4344), King County Territorial District Court Case Files, Washington State Archives, Burien.

30. *ARCIA*, 1879, xv; Ray, "The Columbia Indian Confederacy," 786–87.

31. *ARCIA*, 1879, xv–xvi. I have been unable to locate the case file containing the proceedings against Moses or the case against the accused killers of the Perkins family. According to the annual report of the commissioner, three Indians were convicted and sentenced to hang for the Perkins murder in October 1879. The January 17, 1882 issue of the *Seattle Daily Chronicle* contains an account of the execution of Tommy Hop-Tweowne for participation in the Perkins affair.

32. *Tacoma Herald*, September 6, 1878 and September 27, 1878, in File 49-8, "Crime and Criminals," Relander Collection. See Brown, *Strain of Violence*, 144–67 for a general analysis of vigilante attitudes toward the law.

33. *Seattle Daily Chronicle*, January 18, 1882; Clerk's Minute Book, vol. 9, 100, King County Territorial District Court Records, Washington State Archives, Burien; *Dalles Times-Mountaineer*, May 7, 1887, and *Yakima Herald*, August 15, 1889, in File 49-8, "Crime and Criminals," Relander Collection.

34. The prosecutor added that because there was no statute of limitations on murder, Roff could always be reindicted if he was ever retaken. *Territory v. Henry Roff* (1885), Case No. 4339, 2d series (WAL-4694), Walla Walla County Territorial District Court Case Files, Washington State Archives, Olympia.

35. The second case is *Territory v. James Close* (1885), Case No. 4565, 2d series (WAL-4877), Walla Walla County Territorial District Court Case Files, Washington State Archives, Olympia.

36. *Territory v. James Close* (1885), Case No. 4496, 2d series (WAL-4823).

37. *Walla Walla Union*, December 6, 1885.

38. *Territory v. James Close* (1885), Case No. 4565, 2d series (WAL-4877); *Walla Walla Union*, July 10, 1886.

CHAPTER 6

1. *Robert Sulkanon v. David Lewis and John Doe* (1885), Case No. 149 (WTC-146), Whatcom County Territorial District Court Case Files, Washington State Archives, Olympia.

2. On criminal jurisdiction in Indian country, see Robert Clinton, "Development of Criminal Jurisdiction over Indian Lands."

3. Robert Williams, Jr., *The American Indian in Western Legal Thought*, 229–323; Wilkinson, *American Indians, Time, and the Law*, 55.

4. See Kawashima, *Puritan Justice and the Indian*, 28; Wilkinson, *American Indians, Time, and the Law*, 109.

5. *ARCIA*, 1858, 220–21.

6. White, *The Middle Ground*, x–xv.

7. Harmon, "A Different Kind of Indians," 71.

8. Reid, "Principles of Vengeance," 21. Richard White accords similar importance to homicide settlement in the development of the "middle ground" in the Great Lakes area, where he finds a similar hybrid system at work. White, *The Middle Ground*, 75–82.

9. The young man had killed Black after Black fell under suspicion for the death of the man's uncle, a Shuswap headman. See Reid, "Principles of Vengeance," 21–23; Tolmie, *The Journals of William Fraser Tolmie*, 239.

10. John McLoughlin to unidentified correspondent, November 15, 1843, *McLoughlin's Fort Vancouver Letters*, 3d series, 1844–46, Hudson's Bay Company Series, vol. 7, 118; Reid, "Principles of Vengeance," 40–41.

11. See, for instance, Josiah Spalding's report on Company atrocities in U.S. House of Representatives, *Military Posts: Council Bluffs to the Pacific Ocean*, 27th Cong, 2d sess., 1842, H. Rept. 830 to accompany H.R. 465, 59.

12. Eckrom, *Remembered Drums*, 16; Ruby and Brown, *Indians of the Pacific Northwest*, 123.

13. The June 7, 1888 issue of the *Seattle Post-Intelligencer* contains an account of the incident and Judge Bryant's report to the Governor. The only official record I could locate was *Journal, 1849–1853*, 3–5, Lewis County (Oregon Territory) District Court Records, Washington State Archives, Olympia.

14. *Seattle Post-Intelligencer*, June 7, 1888.

15. Ibid.; Ruby and Brown, *Indians of the Pacific Northwest*, 123.

16. Michael Simmons to Isaac Stevens, March 26, 1855, M5, Reel 9.

17. Washington State, Office of the Secretary of State, *A Guide to the Records of Washington Territorial Supreme Court*, 3–4.

18. *Elick, an Indian, v. Washington Territory*, 1 Wash. Terr. 140 (1861).

19. Isaac Stevens to Major General John Wool, March 20, 1856, in U.S. Senate, *Report of the Secretary of War*, 42.

20. *Olympia Pioneer and Democrat*, September 12, 1856.

21. Robert Burns uses the phrase "policy of hanging" in his discussion of negotiations with the Spokanes and Coeur d'Alenes (*The Jesuits*, 299–313). Also see *Olympia Pioneer and Democrat*, October 8, 1858.

22. *Olympia Pioneer and Democrat*, October 22, 1858; Josephy, *The Nez Perce Indians*, 374; Burns, *The Jesuits*, 298–314.

23. Josephy, *The Nez Perce Indians*, 374–75; Burns, *The Jesuits*, 314–19; *Olympia Pioneer and Democrat*, October 29, 1858.

24. Records of Military Commissions, Washington Territorial Volunteers Papers, Box 14.

25. Eckrom, *Remembered Drums*, 153–68; *Territory v. Leschi* (1856), Case No. 140 (THR-142); *Territory v. Waginer* [Winyea] (1856), Case No. 149 (THR-150); *Territory v. Wahoolit* (1856), Case No. 262 (THR-262), Thurston County Territorial District Court Case Files, Washington State Archives, Olympia. I could not locate any case file for proceedings against Kitsap. According to Eckrom in *Remembered Drums*, Kitsap was discharged before trial. According to Agent

Simmons, Kitsap was tried but discharged for lack of evidence. Michael Simmons to J. W. Nesmith, March 31, 1859, M5, Reel 9.

26. *Leschi v. Washington Territory*, 1 Wash. Terr. 14 (1857); *Leschi v. Washington Territory* (1856), Case No. 3, Territorial Supreme Court Case Files, Washington State Archives, Olympia.

27. *Leschi v. Washington Territory* (1856), Case No. 3, Territorial Supreme Court Case Files; *Olympia Pioneer and Democrat*, February 5, 1858, February 26, 1858; Eckrom, *Remembered Drums*, 157.

28. Leschi's quote is from Eckrom, *Remembered Drums*, 156. For criticisms of the trial, see *Olympia Pioneer and Democrat*, March 12, 1858; Meeker, *Pioneer Reminiscences of Puget Sound*, 205–12, 452–53; Norman Clark, *Washington*, 44–45.

29. The charge of "unlawful war" rested on the fact that the Indians had signed treaties with the United States immediately prior to the war. See "Charges and Specifications Against Certain Indians of the Dwamish and Sawamish tribes, by order of the Gov and Cmdr in Chief W.T. Vols, May 10, 1856," Washington Territorial Volunteers Papers, Box 14; *Yelm Jim [a.k.a. Wahoolit] v. Washington Territory*, 1 Wash. Terr. 67–68 (1859). Wahoolit was eventually pardoned for his "crimes."

30. For a discussion of the underlying legality of Indian wars, see Harring, *Crow Dog's Case*, 251–62; on differing cultural perceptions of what constitutes an historical event, see Fogelson, "The Ethnohistory of Events and Nonevents."

31. Wesley Gosnell to J. W. Nesmith, September 30, 1857, M5, Reel 11.

32. *Olympia Pioneer and Democrat*, November 5, 1858; *Territory v. Indians* (1858), Case No. 130 (JEF-121), Jefferson County Territorial District Court Case Files, Washington State Archives, Olympia.

33. *Territory v. Skahr-hia-cum et al.* (1858), Case No. 116 (JEF-107), Jefferson County Territorial District Court Case Files, Washington State Archives, Olympia; *Olympia Pioneer and Democrat*, September 25, 1857; Thomas Hanna to Michael Simmons, September 18, 1857; Hanna to Simmons, September 21, 1857, M5, Reel 10.

34. *Territory v. Three Indians* (1858), Case No. 131 (JEF-122); *Territory v. Nequisault et al.* (1858), Case No. 105 (JEF-96); *Territory v. John Niqusue and Quilaghem* (1858), Case No. 129 (JEF-120); *Territory v. Three Indians* (1858), Case No. 128 (JEF-119), Jefferson County Territorial District Court Case Files, Washington State Archives, Olympia; *Olympia Pioneer and Democrat*, September 10, 1858; September 17, 1858; November 5, 1858.

35. Prucha, *Broadax and Bayonet*, 85.

36. Sidney S. Ford to Isaac Stevens, December 31, 1856, M5, Reel 10.

37. B. F. Shaw to William Miller, September 21, 1861, M5, Reel 12.

38. *Territory v. Peeps and Harry Peeps* (1861), Case No. 994 (KNG-995), King County Territorial District Court Case Files, Washington State Archives, Burien; *Elick, an Indian, v. Washington Territory*, 1 Wash. Terr. 140–41 (1861). The supreme court reversed the conviction on the ground that no interpreter had been provided for Elick. Legally, therefore, he had never entered a plea.

39. *Territory v. Peeps and Harry Peeps* (1861).

40. Nathaniel Hill to Isaac Stevens, June 16, 1856, M5, Reel 10.

41. B. F. Shaw to William Miller, September 21, 1861, M5, Reel 12.

42. Giles Ford and George Paige to C. H. Hale, September 19, 1863, M5, Reel 15.

43. George Paige to C. H. Hale, July 20, 1864, M5, Reel 15; Nathaniel Hill to Isaac Stevens, June 18, 1856, M5, Reel 10; R. C. Fay to Isaac Stevens, November 15, 1856, M5, Reel 10.

44. R. H. Lansdale to J. W. Nesmith, September 20, 1858, M5, Reel 17.

45. E. A. Starling to Isaac Stevens, December 16, 1853, M5, Reel 9. A substitute culprit did not satisfy the authorities, who persisted until they arrested two Clallam men, Watsissemer and Jack. The two were convicted and sentenced to death on October 5, 1854. Jack died after escaping from custody; Watsissemer's case was appealed to the territorial supreme court, which sent it back to the lower court for retrial. At Watsissemer's second trial, the charges were dismissed. See *Territory v. Watsissemer* (1854), Case No. 5 (JEF-5); *Territory v. Jack* (1854), Case No. 4 (JEF-4), Jefferson County District Court Case Files, Washington State Archives, Olympia. Also see *Olympia Pioneer and Democrat*, December 2, 1854; *Puget Sound Herald* (Steilacoom), April 21, 1855.

46. James G. Swan to Henry Webster, March 31, 1863, M5, Reel 14; F. C. Chirouse to Samuel Ross, February 4, 1870, M5, Reel 12.

47. *Territory v. Ephraim Pullen* (1885), Case No. 749, 2d series (JEF-1669), Jefferson County Territorial District Court Case Files, Washington State Archives, Olympia.

48. *Territory v. Andy Johnson and Pitchwood* (1885), Case No. 748, 2d series (JEF-1668), Jefferson County Territorial District Court Case Files, Washington State Archives, Olympia.

49. The record is not clear as to the final disposition of the gun. The justice of the peace obviously intended to return it to Johnson, for Pullen objected to the

move on the ground that he feared for his life. The justice of the peace agreed to consult with the district attorney on the issue, but with the acquittal of Johnson, there is no reason to suppose the gun was not returned.

50. *Territory v. John Kilcup and W. R. Moultry* (1885), Case No. 157 (WTC-154), Whatcom County Territorial District Court Case Files, Washington State Archives, Olympia.

51. *Whatcom Reveille*, October 30, 1885.

52. *Territory v. John Kilcup and W.R. Moultry* (1885); *Territory v. Arthur Petit* (1885), Case No. 158 (WTC-155), Whatcom County Territorial District Court Case Files, Washington State Archives, Olympia; *Whatcom Reveille*, November 13, 1885. "Siwash" is a Chinook Jargon term for Indian, largely used in a derogatory fashion by whites. Siwash derived from the French term "sauvage," or savage.

53. *Henry Dewey et. al. v. William B. Moore* (1879), Case No. 1991 (KNG-1992), King County Territorial District Court Case Files, Washington State Archives, Burien.

54. *Henry Jackson, an Indian v. Steamer Capital* (1880), Case No. 1884 (THR-1765), Thurston County Territorial District Court Case Files, Washington State Archives, Olympia; "A Mad Chief," *Seattle Post-Intelligencer*, June 21, 1888.

55. On Nooksack history, see Amoss, *Coast Salish Spirit Dancing*, 21–27; Suttles, "Central Coast Salish," in Suttles, *The Northwest Coast*, 471; Suttles, "Post-Contact Culture Change," 97–102.

56. *Whatcom Reveille*, May 22, 1885; *Robert Sulkanon v. David Lewis and John Doe* (1885) Case No. 149 (WTC-146), Whatcom County Territorial District Court Case Files, Washington State Archives, Olympia.

57. *Robert Sulkanon v. David Lewis and John Doe* (1885).

58. "Yakima Agency Jail Record Book, 1878–1888," 4.

59. Declarations of intention filed by Te-at-a-mus (William), Case No. 1391 (WAL-6387); We-ut-que-e-secan (Charley), Case No. 1392 (WAL-6388); Wa-woo-nu-seatmu (Lyman), Case No. 1393 (WAL-6389); Pow-wow-kee (John), Case No. 1394 (WAL-6390); Sue-e-kat-schet (Jacob), Case No. 1395 (WAL-6391); Ta-mut-sa (Timothy), Case No. 1385 (WAL-6394); Stem-millic (Moses), Case No. 1386 (WAL-6395); Herman Stoop-stoop-min (John Levi), Case No. 1387 (WAL-6396); Tipes (Daniel), Case No. 1388 (WAL-6397), Walla Walla County Territorial District Court, Naturalizations, Washington State Archives, Cheney; *Walla Walla Weekly Statesman*, June 2, 1877.

60. *ARCIA*, 1884, 173.

61. Barnett, *Indian Shakers*, 59.

62. David Charley to D. W. Smith, April 1885, included with D. W. Smith to commissioner of Indian affairs, April 24, 1885, LR-OIA, Letter 9832; Affidavit of William Pasper to commissioner of Indian affairs, April 21, 1885, LR-OIA, Letter 9869. David Charley had an earlier run-in with Eells during the initial disturbances caused by the visions of John Slocum. See Barnett, *Indian Shakers*, 49–55.

63. Affidavit of George Henry (Indian) to commissioner of Indian affairs, April 11, 1885, LR-OIA, Letter 10049.

64. Affidavit of William Pasper to commissioner of Indian affairs, April 21, 1885, LR-OIA, Letter 9869.

65. Affidavit of George Henry (Indian) to commissioner of Indian affairs, April 11, 1885, LR-OIA, Letter 10049.

66. Affidavit of George Henry (Indian) to commissioner of Indian affairs, April 11, 1885, LR-OIA, Letter 10049; D. W. Smith to commissioner of Indian affairs, May 14, 1885, LR-OIA, Letter 11778.

67. See generally Hagan, *Indian Police and Judges*.

68. Hunn, *Nch'i-Wana*, 284–85. See also Fay Cohen, *Treaties on Trial*.

69. Robert H. Milroy to H. Price, August 22, 1884, LR-OIA, Letter 16704.

70. Hunn, *Nch'i-Wana*, 93–94.

71. *United States v. Winans*, 198 U.S. 371 (1905). In the initial proceeding on the injunction, the district court found in favor of Taylor, but the result was reversed by the territorial supreme court, which remanded the case back to the district court for rehearing. In 1887, the district court issued a decree upholding the Indians' access to the fishery. See *United States v. Taylor*, 3 Wash. Terr. 88 (1887). Continued violations by white landowners resulted in *United States v. Winans*.

72. Milroy to Price, August 22, 1884, LR-OIA, Letter 16704

73. *William Spedis v. Thomas Simpson, et al.* (1884), Case No. 126 (KLK-126), Klickitat County Territorial District Court Case Files, Washington State Archives, Olympia.

CHAPTER 7

1. *Tamanawas* (there are various spellings) is a Chinook Jargon term for power, or guardian spirit. *Masatchie tamanawas* refers to sorcery or black magic, the use of power for harmful ends.

2. The newspaper article (n.p., n.d.), which was based on interviews with Indian informants, is included in Robert Milroy to E. P. Smith, April 14, 1874, M234, Reel 913. In a slightly different version of events presented in the *Puget Sound Daily Courier* (Olympia) on December 15, 1873, Fisk called on Doctor Jackson to cure Susie. When Susie died despite the shaman's efforts, Fisk—acting "according to Indian custom"—took Doctor Jackson's life. While there is ethnographic support for the practice of killing a shaman for failed professional services, the lack of corroborating evidence leads me to discount this version of events. It certainly is not the version heard by the jury during Fisk's trial.

3. *Territory v. Henry Fisk* (1874), Case No. 1249 (THR-1187), Thurston County Territorial District Court Case Files, Washington State Archives, Olympia; *Puget Sound Daily Courier* (Olympia), December 15, 1873; *The Olympia Transcript*, December 20, 1873.

4. Harring, *Crow Dog's Case*, 1–24, 57–99; Stevens and Fiddler, *Killing the Shamen*; Zanger, "Conflicting Concepts of Justice." Studies of Native law in specific tribes include Strickland, *Fire and the Spirits*; Reid, *A Law of Blood*; Llewellyn and Hoebel, *The Cheyenne Way*.

5. Clinton, "Development of Criminal Jurisdiction," 962–64; Prucha, *The Great Father*, 42–44; 4 Stat. 732 (1834); 23 Stat. 385 (1885); *Ex Parte Crow Dog*, 109 U.S. 556 (1883).

6. Prucha, *The Great Father*, 229–30; Harring, *Crow Dog's Case*, 142.

7. The Major Crimes Act vested jurisdiction over intra-Indian crimes in the federal side of the territorial courts.

8. Harring, *Crow Dog's Case*, 269–70; *Territory v. Dan Planopleopike* (1888), Case No. 211 (YAK-214); *Territory v. Dick Wyneco* (1888), Case No. 212 (YAK-215), Yakima County Territorial District Court Case Files, Washington State Archives, Ellensburg.

9. *Territory v. Schotum* (1855), Case No. 22 (JEF-22), Jefferson County Territorial District Court Case Files, Washington State Archives, Olympia.

10. E. C. Fitzhugh to Isaac Stevens, February 7, 1857, M5, Reel 10.

11. Thomas J. McKenny to Nathaniel Taylor, November 26, 1867, M5, Reel 5; George Harvey to Samuel Ross, May 26, 1870, M5, Reel 20. See also *ARCIA*, 1858, 235.

12. *Seattle Intelligencer*, February 20, 1871.

13. *Robert Frost v. County Commissioners of the County of Thurston* (1868), Case No. 727 (THR-711), Thurston County Territorial District Court Case Files,

Washington State Archives, Olympia; *Record Book*, 4:67, Thurston County Territorial District Court Records, Thurston County Courthouse, Olympia.

14. *ARCIA*, 1858, 235; Circular issued by Samuel Ross, August 4, 1869, M5, Reel 6.

15. Thomas J. McKenny to Joseph Hill, December 24, 1867, M5, Reel 5; Edwin Eells to Edward P. Smith, December 2, 1873, M234, Reel 912.

16. Henry C. Hale to Thomas J. McKenny, February 23, 1868, M5, Reel 12; Nathaniel Hill to Isaac Stevens, February 10, 1856, M5, Reel 10.

17. Wesley B. Gosnell to Isaac Stevens, April 22, 1856, M5, Reel 10; Thomas J. McKenny to James Wilbur, July 25, 1867, M5, Reel 5.

18. John Anderson to B. F. Kendall, March 26, 1862, M5, Reel 15; Henry Webster to B. F. Kendall, September 24, 1861, M5, Reel 14.

19. Thomas J. McKenny to Joseph Hill, May 2, 1867, M5, Reel 5.

20. Joseph Hill to Thomas J. McKenny, August 12, 1867, M5, Reel 15.

21. James Elder to Thomas J. McKenny, November 9, 1868; Elder to McKenny, February 16, 1869; Elder to McKenny, February 25, 1869, M5, Reel 11.

22. Thomas J. McKenny to Joseph Hill, December 24, 1867, M5, Reel 5; Hill to McKenny, November 23, 1867, M5, Reel 15.

23. Henry C. Hale to Thomas J. McKenny, August 10, 1868, M5, Reel 12; McKenny to Hale, April 24, 1869, M5, Reel 5; McKenny to Francis Walker, May 10, 1872, M234, Reel 912; McKenny to Walker, April 30, 1872, M234, Reel 912; Robert H. Milroy to commissioner of Indian affairs, December 26, 1873, M234, Reel 913. Superintendent McKenny treated Kanaka Jack throughout this incident as an Indian, but his name suggests that he may have been of mixed Hawaiian-Indian parentage.

24. *ARCIA*, 1866, 69.

25. R. H. Lansdale to Edward Geary, September 30, 1859, M5, Reel 17.

26. George Harvey to Samuel Ross, May 5, 1870, M5, Reel 20.

27. William P. Winans to Thomas J. McKenny, February 28, 1871, M5, Reel 20.

28. E. Chase to Samuel Ross, January 29, 1870, M5, Reel 20.

29. William P. Winans to Thomas J. McKenny, June 30, 1871, M5, Reel 20.

30. William P. Winans to Thomas J. McKenny, October 31, 1871; Winans to McKenny, November 30, 1871, M5, Reel 20.

31. William P. Winans to Thomas J. McKenny, June 30, 1871, M5, Reel 20.

32. George Harvey to Samuel Ross, May 26, 1870, M5, Reel 20.

33. Thomas J. McKenny to Francis Walker, May 10, 1872, M234, Reel 912; McKenny to Walker, April 30, 1872, M234, Reel 912; Robert H. Milroy to commissioner of Indian affairs, December 26, 1873, M234, Reel 913.

34. Joseph Hill to Thomas J. McKenny, August 12, 1867, M5, Reel 15.

35. Michael Simmons to J. W. Nesmith, March 31, 1859, M5, Reel 9.

36. R. H. Lansdale to Edward Geary, July 5, 1859, M5, Reel 17.

37. R. H. Lansdale to Edward Geary, July 27, 1859, M5, Reel 17.

38. Edward Geary to R. H. Lansdale, July 18, 1859, M5, Reel 17.

39. R. H. Lansdale to Edward Geary, July 27, 1859; R. H. Lansdale to Edward Geary, September 1, 1859, M5, Reel 17.

40. Stacy Hemenway to Thomas J. McKenny, April 29, 1868, M5, Reel 13; Addeus Mason to Thomas J. McKenny, February 24, 1868, M5, Reel 13; Thomas J. McKenny to Charles B. Darwin, June 3, 1868, M5, Reel 5.

41. C. A. Huntington to Charles B. Darwin, May 15, 1868, M5, Reel 5.

42. Thomas J. McKenny to Charles B. Darwin, June 3, 1868, M5, Reel 5; Charles B. Darwin to Thomas J. McKenny, June 6, 1868, M5, Reel 24. Darwin's letter includes a copy of the proceedings in the case from Pierce County District Court Journal, May term, 1868, 280.

43. Thomas J. McKenny to C. S. King, September 2, 1868, M5, Reel 5.

44. *Territory v. Shew-Lack* (1868), Case No. 96 (WHI-89), Whitman County Territorial District Court Case Files, Washington State Archives, Olympia.

45. John G. Parker to Thomas J. McKenny, November, 12, 1868, M5, Reel 20; Thomas J. McKenny to John G. Parker, December 3, 1868, M5, Reel 5.

46. *Territory v. Shew-Lack* (1868); John G. Parker to Thomas J. McKenny, December 23, 1868, M5, Reel 20.

47. *Territory v. Henry Fisk* (1874). Judge Joseph R. Lewis, another Republican appointee, frequently instructed jurors along similar lines. See, for example, *Territory v. Wallela* (1874), Case No. 904, 2d series (WAL-2045), Walla Walla County Territorial District Court Case Files, Washington State Archives, Olympia.

48. On "law for the Indians," see Harring, *Crow Dog's Case*, 115–18, 134–40; *ARCIA*, 1871, 16–17. On the peace policy generally, see Priest, *Uncle Sam's Stepchildren*, 28–41; Prucha, *The Great Father*, 152–66.

49. E. P. Smith to Marshall Blinn, January 27, 1874, in letterbook "Land and Civilization: Dec. 20, 1873–Apr. 7, 1874," M21, Reel 116, p. 191.

50. Petition of G. Hansen and other citizens of Pacific County, n.d., M234, Reel 913; *Walla Walla Weekly Statesman*, May 5, 1877.

51. Tomlan, *Tinged with Gold*, 131; *Seattle Daily Post-Intelligencer*, September 8, 1885.

52. Skokomish Agent Eells was designated in the witness list as the private prosecutor in *Territory v. James Thompson* (1883), Case No. 3259 (KNG-3259), King County Territorial District Court Case Files, Washington State Archives, Burien; Tulalip Agent John O'Keane was the complaining witness in *Territory v. Charlotte Bailey* (1882), Case No. 437, 2d series, (JEF-1459), Jefferson County Territorial District Court Case Files, Washington State Archives, Olympia; Puyallup Agent Robert H. Milroy filed the initial complaint in *Territory v. Bob Lah-house* (1876), Case No. 1601 (THR-1467), Thurston County Territorial District Court Case Files, Washington State Archives, Olympia; and in *Territory v. John Boyce Quicksha* (1878), Case No. 611 (PRC-626), Pierce County Territorial District Court Case Files, Washington State Archives, Burien.

53. Garth, "The Plateau Whipping Complex," 142.

54. *Territory v. Joe Whitlouse* (1886), Case No. OS-443 (SNO-414), Snohomish County Territorial District Court Case Files, Washington State Archives, Olympia.

55. Whitlouse was eventually found guilty of assault with a deadly weapon; the case file does not show what punishment he received.

56. *Territory v. Howlish* (1883), Case No. 930 (WHI-639), Whitman County Territorial District Court Case Files, Washington State Archives, Olympia. Howlish was convicted and sentenced to one year in the territorial penitentiary.

57. *Territory v. John Boyce Quicksha* (1878); *Territory v. Johnny Schlaheuse* (1879), Case No. 2379 (KNG-2380); *Territory v. Kitsap* (1879), Case No. 2229 (KNG-2230), King County Territorial District Court Case Files, Washington State Archives, Burien; *Territory v. Willie and Henry Heywood* (1879), Case No. 1890 (THR-1770), Thurston County Territorial District Court Case Files, Washington State Archives, Olympia.

58. *Territory v. Henry Fisk* (1874). All the quotations from the white participants in the case, unless otherwise noted, come from the case file.

59. *Puget Sound Daily Courier* (Olympia), April 1, 1874.

60. See *Territory v. Tawes* (1878), Case No. 18 (SKG-18), Skagit County Territorial District Court Case Files, Washington State Archives, Olympia. After killing another Indian, called William, Tawes went to British Columbia. He eventually came back, only to be arrested and stand trial nearly a year after the crime was committed.

61. *ARCIA*, 1891, 1:451.

62. This does not mean that Indians moved from a "pre-legal" to a "legal" state of mind, nor does it mean that Indians adopted a white legal consciousness. For an alternative interpretation in a different setting, see Matsuda, "Law and Culture in the District Court of Honolulu." On the question of legal consciousness and its place in critical legal studies, see Gordon, "Critical Legal Histories," 109-13, 120–21.

63. *Territory v. Dick, an Indian* (1885), Case No. 2537 (THR-2415), Thurston County Territorial District Court Case Files, Washington State Archives, Olympia; *Territory v. Baptiste* (1888), Case No. 96 (STV-107), Stevens County Territorial District Court Case Files, Washington State Archives, Olympia; *Territory v. Dr. Jack* (1881), Case No. 2699 (KNG-2699) and Case No. 2700 (KNG-2700), King County Territorial District Court Case Files, Washington State Archives, Burien; *Dr. Jack v. Territory* (1882), Case No. 340, Territorial Supreme Court Case Files, Washington State Archives, Olympia.

64. Pamela Amoss, for example, notes an increase in interpersonal violence among the Nooksacks following white colonization, suggesting that peaceful settlement of disputes through compensation became more difficult to arrange. Amoss, *Coast Salish Spirit Dancing*, 25. On the impact of disease, see Guilmet et al., "The Legacy of Introduced Disease," 1–32; Hunn, *Nch'i-Wana*, 27–32.

65. *Territory v. Indian Joe* (1887), Case No. 5155 (KNG-5155), King County Territorial District Court Case Files, Washington State Archives, Burien.

66. Smith, *The Puyallup-Nisqually*, 142–43; Castile, *The Indians of Puget Sound*, 350. Frederick Hoxie has pointed out similar uses of Anglo-American law by Lakota women. See Hoxie, "Towards a 'New' North American Indian Legal History," 356.

67. *Territory v. Pe-Al* (1877), Case No. 1371, 2d series (WAL-2463), Walla Walla County Territorial District Court Case Files, Washington State Archives, Olympia.

68. *Territory v. Baptiste* (1888).

69. *The Olympia Transcript*, May 22, 1880; *Puget Sound Dispatch* (Seattle), July 26, 1880.

70. Elmendorf, *Structure of Twana Culture*, 509.

71. The linguistic situation in the courtroom was clearly quite complex. The justice of the peace swore in two interpreters—one to translate Chinook Jargon into English, the other to translate directly from "the Indian language."

72. *Territory v. Charlie George* (1880), Case No. 2517 (KNG-2517), King County Territorial District Court Case Files, Washington State Archives, Burien.

73. *Territory v. Dan and Roger Tecumseh* (1888), Case No. 5877 (KNG-5877), King County Territorial District Court Case Files, Washington State Archives, Burien. This case attracted a good deal of newspaper coverage, giving some insight into the background of the case. See *Seattle Post-Intelligencer*, March 8, 1888–March 10, 1888. On the killing of shamans, see Smith, *The Puyallup-Nisqually*, 61; Gunther, *Klallam Ethnography*, 297–300; Elmendorf, *Structure of Twana Culture*, 509.

74. Many towns in Washington had an area of Indian residence referred to as the Indian Camp. In Seattle, this probably referred to the mud flats near Elliott Bay southwest of the city. This area was also called "the sawdust" because the lumber mills dumped their residue there.

75. *Territory v. Indian Joe* (1887).

76. When presenting a bill of indictment, the district attorney routinely noted the witnesses who were sworn and testified before the grand jury.

77. Newspaper article included in Robert Milroy to E. P. Smith, April 14, 1874, M234, Reel 913. On the shaman's spirit revealing itself, see Smith, *The Puyallup-Nisqually*, 61.

78. *Territory v. Henry Fisk* (1874), Case No. 1249 (THR-1187).

79. Marshall Blinn to E. P. Smith, December 25, 1873, M234, Reel 913; Robert Milroy to E. P. Smith, April 14, 1874, M234, Reel 913.

80. *Puget Sound Daily Courier* (Olympia), April 1, 1874.

81. Smith, *The Puyallup-Nisqually*, 62.

82. John Simms to R. E. Trowbridge, January 6, 1881, LR-OIA, Letter 1419.

83. Sidney Waters to H. Price, April 3, 1884, LR-OIA, Letter 7054.

84. "Speeches by Indian Chiefs at a Council with Agent John Simms," November 6, 1872, M234, Reel 912.

85. *Seattle Post-Intelligencer*, June 23, 1888.

86. *Walla Walla Union*, February 14, 1874.

87. *Walla Walla Union*, April 18, 1874; May 30, 1874; *Territory v. Wallela* (1874).

88. *Territory v. Meigs* (1885), Case No. OS-394 (SNO-370), Snohomish County Territorial District Court Case Files, Washington State Archives, Olympia; *Snohomish Eye*, March 7, 1885; March 21, 1885.

89. *Snohomish Eye*, March 21, 1885.

90. *Territory v. Meigs* (1885); *Snohomish Eye*, March 14, 1885.

91. Harring, *Crow Dog's Case*, 170–71.

92. *Territory v. Henry Fisk* (1874).

CONCLUSION

1. See Robert Williams, Jr., *The American Indian in Western Legal Thought*, 6–7; Harring, *Crow Dog's Case*, 8–9.

2. Harmon, "Lines in Sand," 429–53.

3. Hoxie, *A Final Promise*.

4. The allotment of the Puyallup Reservation, for example, touched off a sharp debate over what determined "true" Puyallup identity. See Tillicum, "Monograph on the Puyallup Indians of the State of Washington"; Harmon, "Lines in Sand," 450–51.

5. On the shifting bases of Indian identity in western Washington, see Harmon, "A Different Kind of Indians."

6. The question of fairness has preoccupied most of the scholars who have examined Indian legal materials from the colonial era. See Kawashima, *Puritan Justice and the Indian*, especially 149–79; Koehler, "Red-White Power Relations and Justice in the Courts of Seventeenth-Century New England." For the importance of fairness in establishing legal hegemony, see Gordon, "New Developments in Legal Theory," 285–86.

7. Robert Williams, Jr., *The American Indian in Western Legal Thought*, 312–17; Harring, *Crow Dog's Case*, 15–17.

8. Harring, *Crow Dog's Case*, 287. For critiques of the hegemonic function of slave law, see Hindus, "Black Justice Under White Law: Criminal Prosecutions of Blacks in Antebellum South Carolina"; McLaurin, *Celia, A Slave*, 140–41.

BIBLIOGRAPHY

ARCHIVES AND RECORDS

Edwin Eells Papers. Washington State Historical Society. Tacoma, Washington.

McGilvra, John J. *Reminiscences of the Early Days of the Washington Bar.* Undated pamphlet. Pacific Northwest Collection. Suzzallo Library. University of Washington. Seattle.

Records of the Bureau of the Census. 1880 Federal Census. Washington Territory. Manuscript Population Schedules. National Archives Microfilm Publication T9. RG 29. National Archives, Washington, D.C.

Records of the Bureau of Indian Affairs. RG 75. National Archives, Washington, D.C.

    Letters Received by the Office of Indian Affairs, 1824–1881. Washington Superintendency, 1853–1881. National Archives Microfilm Publication 234.

    Letters Received by the Office of Indian Affairs, 1881–1907.

    Letters Sent by the Office of Indian Affairs, 1824–1881. National Archives Microfilm Publication 21.

    Records of the Washington Superintendency of Indian Affairs, 1853–1874. National Archives Microfilm Publication 5.

Records of the Bureau of Prisons. McNeil Island Federal Prison. Register of Prisoners, 1875–1892. RG 129. National Archives, Regional Branch, Seattle, Washington.

Relander Collection. Yakima Valley Regional Library. Yakima, Washington.

Spokane County Courthouse. Spokane, Washington. Spokane County. Territorial District Court. Appearance Docket, vols. A–C, 1880–1889.

Thurston County Courthouse. Olympia, Washington.

Thurston County. Territorial District Court. Execution Docket, vol. 2, 1861–1876.

Thurston County. Territorial District Court. Record, vols. 2–6, 1859–1878.

Washington State Archives. Olympia, Washington.

Asotin County. Territorial District Court Case Files, 1886–1889.

Columbia County. Territorial District Court Case Files, 1878–1889.

Cowlitz County. Territorial District Court Case Files, 1872–1889.

Garfield County. Territorial District Court Case Files, 1883–1889.

Grays Harbor County. Territorial District Court Case Files, 1884–1889.

Jefferson County. Territorial District Court Case Files, 1854–1888.

Klickitat County. Territorial District Court Case Files, 1880–1889.

Lewis County (Oregon Territory). Territorial District Court. Journal, 1849–1853.

Lincoln County. Territorial District Court Case Files, 1886–1889.

Records of the Territorial Supreme Court. Record Group 27. Territorial Supreme Court Case Files, 1853–1889.

Skagit County. Territorial District Court Case Files, 1878–1889.

Snohomish County. Territorial District Court Case Files, 1876–1889.

Snohomish County. Territorial Probate Case Files, 1866–1889.

Spokane County. Territorial District Court Case Files, 1879–1887.

Stevens County. Territorial District Court Case Files, 1882–1889.

Thurston County. Territorial District Court. Execution Docket, vol. 3, 1876–1886.

Thurston County. Territorial District Court. Judgment Docket, vol. 3, 1876–1882.

Thurston County. Territorial District Court Case Files, 1852–1889.

Walla Walla County. Territorial District Court Case Files, 1860–1889.

Washington Territorial Volunteers Papers. Correspondence and Reports, 1854–57.

Whatcom County. Territorial District Court Case Files, 1883–1889.

Whitman County. Territorial District Court Case Files, 1862–1886.

Washington State Archives. Central Regional Branch. Ellensburg, Washington.

Yakima County. Territorial District Court. Clerk's Minute Book, Criminal, 1887–1902.

Yakima County. Territorial District Court. Criminal Docket, 1882–1886.

Yakima County. Territorial District Court Case Files, 1881–1889.

Washington State Archives. Eastern Regional Branch. Cheney, Washington.

Walla Walla County. Territorial District Court. Naturalization Files, 1860–1889.

Washington State Archives. Northwest Regional Branch. Bellingham, Washington.

Jefferson County. Territorial District Court. Final Record, vol. A, 1877–1889.

Jefferson County. Territorial District Court. Journal, vols. A–H, 1853–1889.

Jefferson County. Territorial District Court Case Files, 1888–1889.

Skagit County. Territorial District Court. Docket, 1878–1879.

Skagit County. Territorial District Court. Minute Book, 1878–1882.

Washington State Archives. Puget Sound Regional Branch. Burien, Washington.

King County. Justice Court Dockets, 1877–1890. Seattle Precinct. 11 vols.

King County. Territorial District Court. Clerk's Minute Books, 1877–1886. 19 vols.

King County. Territorial District Court Case Files, 1864–1889.

Pierce County. Territorial District Court Case Files, 1855–1889.

Washington Territorial Census Rolls. Microfilm copy. Suzzallo Library. University of Washington. Seattle.

Whitman County Courthouse. Colfax, Washington.

Territorial District Court Calendar, vol. A, 1880–1885.

Territorial District Court Final Record, vol. A, 1878–1884.

Territorial District Court Journal, vol. A (1878–1882) and vol. D (1887–1889).

Territorial District Court Record, vol. B, 1874–1877.

Territorial District Court Case Files, 1886–1889.

GOVERNMENT PUBLICATIONS

U.S. Congress. House. *Military Posts: Council Bluffs to the Pacific Ocean.* 27th Cong., 2d sess., 1842. H. Rept. 830 to accompany H.R. 465.

U.S. Congress. Senate. *Report of the Secretary of War, in Compliance with a Resolution of the Senate of the 21st ultimo, Calling for Copies of All Letters of the Governor of Washington Territory, Addressed to Him During the Present Year; And All Correspondence Relative to the Indian Disturbances in the Territories of Washington and Oregon.* 34th Cong., 1st sess., 1856. Senate Ex. Doc. 66.

U.S. Department of Interior. Census Office.

The Seventh Census of the United States, 1850.

Population of the United States in 1860.

The Statistics of the Population of the United States: Ninth Census (1870).

Statistics of the Population of the United States: Tenth Census (1880).

Statistics of the Population of the United States: Eleventh Census (1890).

Report on Indians Taxed and Indians Not Taxed: Eleventh Census (1890).

U.S. Department of Interior. Office of Indian Affairs. *Annual Report of the Commissioner of Indian Affairs*, 1858–1863, 1866–1884, 1891.

U. S. National Archives and Records Administration. *Guide to the Records of the Washington Superintendency of Indian Affairs.* Washington, D.C.: Government Printing Office, n.d.

United States Statutes at Large. Vols. 4, 9, 10, 12, 18, 19, 23, 24.

Washington State. Office of the Secretary of State. Division of Archives and Records Management. *Frontier Justice: Guide to the Court Records of Washington Territory, 1853–1889.* 2 vols. Olympia, Wash., 1987.

————. *A Guide to the Records of Washington Territorial Supreme Court.* Olympia, Wash., 1983

Washington State. *Code of Washington.* Olympia: C.B. Bagley, public printer, 1881.

Washington State. *Laws of Washington, 1854–1889.* Seattle: Tribune Printing Co., 1895–96.

Washington State. *Statutes and Codes of Washington.* San Francisco: Bancroft and Whitney, 1891.

COURT CASES

United States v. Holliday. 70 U.S. 407 (1865).

United States v. Cook. 86 U.S. (19 Wall.) 591 (1873).

Ex Parte Crow Dog. 109 U.S. 556 (1883).

Elk v. Wilkins. 112 U.S. 94 (1884).

Ex Parte Gon-Shay-ee. 130 U.S. 348 (1889).

In Re Matthias' Estate. 63 Fed. 526 (9th Cir., 1894).

United States v. Winans. 198 U.S. 371 (1905).

Patrick Fowler v. United States. 1 Wash. Terr. 3 (1854).

Leschi v. Washington Territory. 1 Wash. Terr. 14 (1857).

Yelm Jim v. Washington Territory. 1 Wash. Terr. 68 (1859).

Elick, an Indian, v. Washington Territory. 1 Wash. Terr. 140 (1861).

Jack Gho v. Charley Julles. 1 Wash. Terr. 325 (1871).

United States v. Taylor. 3 Wash. Terr. 88 (1887).

Kelley v. Kitsap County. 5 Wash. 521 (1893).

In Re Wilbur's Estate. 8 Wash. 35 (1894).

NEWSPAPERS

"Judicial Review of the Marriage Laws." *Bellingham Bay Mail*, June 14, 1879.
Olympia Pioneer and Democrat, 1854–1860.
The Olympia Transcript, 1871–1880.
The Oregonian (Portland), 1856.
Puget Sound Daily Courier (Olympia), 1873–1874.
Puget Sound Dispatch (Seattle), 1880.
Puget Sound Herald (Steilacoom), 1855–1861.
Seattle Daily Chronicle, 1882.
Seattle Post-Intelligencer, 1871–1888.
Snohomish Eye, 1885.
Walla Walla Union, 1874–1886.
Walla Walla Weekly Statesman, 1877.
Whatcom Reveille, 1885.

BOOKS AND ARTICLES

Amoss, Pamela. *Coast Salish Spirit Dancing: The Survival of an Ancestral Religion.* Seattle: University of Washington Press, 1978.
Arkush, Brooke. "The Great Basin Culture Area." In *Native North Americans: An Ethnohistorical Approach,* edited by Daniel Boxberger. 301–59. Dubuque, Iowa: Kendall/Hunt Publishing Co., 1990.
Ayers, Edward. *Vengeance and Justice: Crime and Punishment in the 19th-Century American South.* New York: Oxford University Press, 1984.
Bancroft, Hubert Howe. *History of Washington, Idaho, and Montana, 1845–1889.* Vol. 31 of *The Works of Hubert Howe Bancroft.* San Francisco: The History Company, 1890.
Barnett, Homer. *Indian Shakers: A Messianic Cult of the Pacific Northwest.* Carbondale: Southern Illinois University Press, 1957.
Billington, Ray Allen, and Martin Ridge. *Westward Expansion: A History of the American Frontier.* 5th ed. New York: Macmillan Publishing Co., 1982.
Boxberger, Daniel. "In and Out of the Labor Force: The Lummi Indians and the Development of the Commercial Salmon Fishery of North Puget Sound, 1800–1900." *Ethnohistory* 35 (1988): 161–90.
———. *To Fish in Common: The Ethnohistory of Lummi Indian Salmon Fishing.* Lincoln: University of Nebraska Press, 1989.

Brown, Richard Maxwell. *Strain of Violence: Historical Studies of American Violence and Vigilantism.* New York: Oxford University Press, 1975.

Burns, Robert Ignatius. *The Jesuits and the Indian Wars of the Northwest.* Moscow: University of Idaho Press, 1966.

Burrows, James K. "'A Much-Needed Class of Labour': The Economy and Income of the Southern Interior Plateau Indians, 1897–1910." *BC Studies* 71 (1986): 27–46.

Castile, George. "Edwin Eells, U.S. Indian Agent, 1871–1895." *Pacific Northwest Quarterly* 72 (1981): 61–68.

Castile, George, ed. *The Indians of Puget Sound: The Notebooks of Myron Eells.* Seattle: University of Washington Press, 1985.

Castile, George, and Robert Bee, eds. *State and Reservation: New Perspectives on Federal Indian Policy.* Tucson: University of Arizona Press, 1992.

Clark, Blue. *Lone Wolf v. Hitchcock: Treaty Rights and Indian Law at the End of the Nineteenth Century.* Lincoln: University of Nebraska Press, 1994.

Clark, Norman. *The Dry Years: Prohibition and Social Change in Washington.* Rev. ed. Seattle: University of Washington Press, 1988.

―――. *Mill Town: A Social History of Everett, Washington, from Its Earliest Beginnings on the Shores of Puget Sound to the Tragic and Infamous Event Known as the Everett Massacre.* Seattle: University of Washington Press, 1970.

―――. *Washington: A Bicentennial History.* New York: W. W. Norton, 1976.

Clinton, Robert. "Development of Criminal Jurisdiction over Indian Lands: The Historical Perspective." *Arizona Law Review* 17 (1975): 951–91.

Cohen, Fay. *Treaties on Trial: The Continuing Controversy over Northwest Indian Fishing Rights.* Seattle: University of Washington Press, 1986.

Cohen, Felix. *Handbook of Federal Indian Law.* Washington, D.C.: Government Printing Office, 1942.

Collins, June. *Valley of the Spirits: The Upper Skagit Indians of Western Washington.* Seattle: University of Washington Press, 1974.

Cover, Robert. "Foreword: Nomos and Narrative," *Harvard Law Review* 97 (1983): 4–68.

Dominguez, Virginia. *White by Definition: Social Classification in Creole Louisiana.* New Brunswick, N.J.: Rutgers University Press, 1986.

Donald, Leland. "Paths Out of Slavery on the Aboriginal North Pacific Coast of North America." *Slavery and Abolition* 10 (1989): 1–22.

Drinnon, Richard. *Facing West: The Metaphysics of Indian Hating and Empire Building.* Minneapolis: University of Minnesota Press, 1980.

Eckrom, J. *Remembered Drums: A History of the Puget Sound Indian War.* Walla Walla, Wash.: Pioneer Press Books, 1989.

Ekland, Roy. "The 'Indian Problem': Pacific Northwest, 1879." *Oregon Historical Quarterly* 70 (1969): 115–18.

Elmendorf, William. *The Structure of Twana Culture.* Washington State University Research Studies, vol. 28, Monographic Supplement No. 2. Pullman: Washington State University Press, 1960.

———. *Twana Narratives: Native Historical Accounts of a Coast Salish Culture.* Seattle: University of Washington Press, 1993.

Ficken, Robert, and Charles LeWarne. *Washington: A Centennial History.* Seattle: University of Washington Press, 1988.

Fogelson, Raymond. "The Ethnohistory of Events and Nonevents." *Ethnohistory* 36 (1989): 133–47.

Foner, Eric. *Reconstruction: America's Unfinished Revolution, 1863–1877.* New York: Harper and Row, 1988.

Forbath, William. "The Shaping of the American Labor Movement." *Harvard Law Review* 102 (1989): 1109–256.

Foster, Hamar. "Sins Against the Great Spirit: The Law, the Hudson's Bay Company, and the Mackenzie River Murders, 1835–1839." *Criminal Justice History: An International Annual* 10 (1989): 23–76.

Friedman, Lawrence. *Crime and Punishment in American History.* New York: Basic Books, 1993.

Friedman, Lawrence, and Robert Percival. *The Roots of Justice: Crime and Punishment in Alameda County, California, 1870–1910.* Chapel Hill: University of North Carolina Press, 1981.

Garth, Thomas. "Early Nineteenth Century Tribal Relations in the Columbia Plateau." *Southwestern Journal of Anthropology* 20 (1964): 43–57.

———. "The Plateau Whipping Complex and its Relationship to Plateau-Southwest Contacts," *Ethnohistory* 12 (1965): 141–70.

Genovese, Eugene. *Roll, Jordan, Roll: The World the Slaves Made.* New York: Random House, 1974.

Giago, Tim. "Indian Reservations: The Only Land We Know." In *Major Problems in American Indian History*, edited by Albert Hurtado and Peter Iverson, 536–37. Lexington, Mass.: D.C. Heath and Co., 1994.

Gibbs, George. "Tribes of Western Washington and Northwestern Oregon." *Contributions to North American Ethnology* 1 (1877): 157–361.

Goetzmann, William. *Exploration and Empire: The Explorer and the Scientist in the Winning of the American West*. New York: W. W. Norton, 1966.

Gordon, Robert. "Critical Legal Histories." *Stanford Law Review* 36 (1984): 57–125.

———. "New Developments in Legal Theory." In *The Politics of Law: A Progressive Critique*, edited by David Kairys, 281–93. New York: Pantheon Books, 1982.

Gramsci, Antonio. *Selections from the Prison Notebooks*. Edited and translated by Quinton Hoare and Geoffrey Nowell-Smith. New York: International Publishers, 1971.

Guilmet, George, Robert Boyd, David L. Whited, and Nile Thompson. "The Legacy of Introduced Disease: The Southern Coast Salish." *American Indian Culture and Research Journal* 15 (1991): 1–32.

Gunther, Erna. *Klallam Ethnography*. University of Washington Publications in Anthropology, vol. 1. Seattle: University of Washington Press, 1927.

Hagan, William T. *Indian Police and Judges: Experiments in Acculturation and Control*. New Haven: Yale University Press, 1966.

Haines, Francis. *The Nez Perces: Tribesmen of the Columbia Plateau*. Norman: University of Oklahoma Press, 1955.

Harmon, Alexandra. "A Different Kind of Indians: Negotiating the Meanings of 'Indian' and 'Tribe' in the Puget Sound Region, 1820s–1970s." Ph.D. diss., University of Washington, 1995.

———. "Lines in Sand: Shifting Boundaries Between Indians and Non-Indians in the Puget Sound Region." *Western Historical Quarterly* 26 (1995): 429–53.

Harring, Sidney. *Crow Dog's Case: American Indian Sovereignty, Tribal Law, and United States Law in the Nineteenth Century*. Cambridge: Cambridge University Press, 1994.

———. "Rich Men of the Country: Canadian Law in the Land of the Copper Inuit." *Ottawa Law Review* 21 (1989): 1–64.

Harris, Cheryl. "Whiteness as Property." *Harvard Law Review* 106 (1993): 1707–91.

Hartog, Hendrik. "The Constitution of Aspiration and 'The Rights that Belong to Us All.'" *The Journal of American History* 74 (1987): 1013–34.

Harvey, Irene. "Constitutional Law: Congressional Plenary Power over Indian Affairs—A Doctrine Rooted in Prejudice." *American Indian Law Review* 10 (1982): 117–50.

Hauptman, Laurence M., and James D. Wherry, eds. *The Pequots in Southern New England: The Fall and Rise of an American Indian Nation.* Norman: University of Oklahoma Press, 1990.

Henretta, James; W. Elliot Brownlee, David Brody, Susan Ware. *America's History.* Chicago: The Dorsey Press, 1987.

Herring, Joseph. *The Enduring Indians of Kansas: A Century and a Half of Acculturation.* Lawrence: University Press of Kansas, 1990.

Hill, Thomas W. "Ethnohistory and Alcohol Studies." *Recent Developments in Alcoholism* 2 (1984): 313–37.

Hindus, Michael. "Black Justice Under White Law: Criminal Prosecutions of Blacks in Antebellum South Carolina." *The Journal of American History* 63 (1976): 575–99.

———. *Prison and Plantation: Crime, Justice, and Authority in Massachusetts and South Carolina, 1767–1878.* Chapel Hill: University of North Carolina Press, 1980.

Hofstadter, Richard. *The Age of Reform: From Bryan to F.D.R.* New York: Knopf, 1955.

Holt, Thomas. "Marking: Race, Race-making, and the Writing of History." *American Historical Review* 100 (1995): 1–20.

Horr, David, ed. *American Indian Ethnohistory: Indians of the Northwest. Coast Salish and Western Washington Indians.* 2 vols. New York: Garland Publishing, 1974.

———, ed. *American Indian Ethnohistory: Interior Salish and Eastern Washington Indians.* Vol. 4. New York: Garland Publishing, 1974.

Horsman, Reginald. *Race and Manifest Destiny: The Origins of American Racial Anglo-Saxonism.* Cambridge: Harvard University Press, 1981.

Horwitz, Morton. *The Transformation of American Law, 1780–1860.* Cambridge: Harvard University Press, 1977.

Hoxie, Frederick. *A Final Promise: The Campaign to Assimilate the Indians, 1880–1920.* Lincoln: University of Nebraska Press, 1984.

———. "From Prison to Homeland: The Cheyenne River Indian Reservation Before World War I." In *The Plains Indians of the 20th Century*, edited by Peter Iverson, 55–75. Norman: University of Oklahoma Press, 1985.

———. *Parading Through History: The Making of the Crow Nation in America, 1805–1935.* Cambridge: Cambridge University Press, 1995.

———. "Towards a 'New' North American Indian Legal History." *The American Journal of Legal History* 30 (1986): 351–57.

Hunn, Eugene. *Nch'i-Wana, "The Big River:" Mid-Columbia Indians and Their Land.* Seattle: University of Washington Press, 1990.

Hurtado, Albert. *Indian Survival on the California Frontier.* New Haven: Yale University Press, 1988.

"An Indian's View of Indian Affairs," *North American Review* 128 (1879): 415–33.

Johannsen, Robert. "The Sectional Controversy and the Frontier: Pacific Northwest Politics on the Eve of the Civil War." Ph.D. diss., University of Washington, 1953.

Josephy, Alvin M., Jr. *The Nez Perce Indians and the Opening of the Northwest.* Abridged ed. Lincoln: University of Nebraska Press, 1979.

Judson, Phoebe Goodell. *A Pioneer's Search for an Ideal Home: A Book of Personal Memoirs.* Tacoma: Washington State Historical Society, 1966.

Karl, Barry. *The Uneasy State: The United States from 1915 to 1945.* Chicago: University of Chicago Press, 1983.

Kawashima, Yasuhide. *Puritan Justice and the Indian: White Man's Law in Massachusetts, 1630–1763.* Middletown, Conn.: Wesleyan University Press, 1986.

Keith, Gordon, ed. *The James Francis Tulloch Diary, 1875–1910.* Portland, Oreg.: Binford and Mort, 1978.

Kennedy, Duncan. "Toward an Historical Understanding of Legal Consciousness: The Case of Classical Legal Thought in America, 1850–1940." *Research in Law and Sociology* 3 (1980): 3–24.

Kersey, Harry A., Jr. "The Case of Tom Tiger's Horse: An Early Foray into Indian Rights." *Florida Historical Quarterly* 53 (1975): 306–18.

Knight, Rolf. *Indians at Work: An Informal History of Native Indian Labour in British Columbia, 1858–1930.* Vancouver, B.C.: New Star Books, 1978.

Koehler, Lyle. "Red-White Power Relations and Justice in the Courts of Seventeenth-Century New England." *American Indian Culture and Research Journal* 3 (1979): 1–31.

Kroeber, Alfred L. *Cultural and Natural Areas of Native North America.* University of California Publications in American Archaeology and Ethnology, 38:1–242. Berkeley: University of California Press, 1939.

Lamar, Howard. *Dakota Territory, 1861–1889: A Study in Frontier Politics.* New Haven: Yale University Press, 1956.

Leland, Joy. *Firewater Myths: North American Indian Drinking and Alcohol Addiction.* New Brunswick, N.J.: Publication Division, Rutgers Center of Alcohol Studies, 1976.

Lemert, Edwin. *Alcohol and the Northwest Coast Indians*. University of California Publications in Culture and Society, vol. 2: 303–406. Berkeley: University of California Press, 1955.

Lewis, David Rich. "Reservation Leadership and the Progressive-Traditional Dichotomy: William Wash and the Northern Utes, 1865–1928." *Ethnohistory* 38 (1991): 124–42.

Littlefield, Alice, and Martha Knack, eds. *Native Americans and Wage Labor: Ethnohistorical Perspectives*. Norman: University of Oklahoma Press, 1996.

Llewellyn, Karl N., and E. Adamson Hoebel. *The Cheyenne Way: Conflict and Case Law in Primitive Jurisprudence*. Norman: University of Oklahoma Press, 1941.

Lurie, Clayton D. "Civil Disorder and the Military in Rock Springs, Wyoming: The Army's Role in the 1885 Chinese Massacre." *Montana: The Magazine of Western History* 40 (1990): 44–59.

Lurie, Nancy. "The World's Oldest On-Going Protest Demonstration: North American Indian Drinking Patterns." In *The American Indian: Essays from the Pacific Historical Review*, edited by Norris Hundley, Jr., 55–76. Santa Barbara, Calif.: Clio Books, 1974.

MacAndrew, Craig, and Robert Edgerton. *Drunken Comportment: The Natural History of Society*. Chicago: Aldine Publishing Co., 1969.

Mancall, Peter. *Deadly Medicine: Indians and Alcohol in Early America*. Ithaca, N.Y.: Cornell University Press, 1995.

Martin, Calvin, ed. *The American Indian and the Problem of History*. New York: Oxford University Press, 1987.

Matsuda, Mari J. "Law and Culture in the District Court of Honolulu, 1844–1845: A Case Study of the Rise of Legal Consciousness." *The American Journal of Legal History* 32 (1988): 16–41

McClurken, James. "Ottawa Adaptive Strategies to Indian Removal." *Michigan Historical Review* 12 (1986): 29–55.

McKanna, Clare V., Jr. "Life Hangs in the Balance: The U.S. Supreme Court's Review of *Ex Parte* Gon-Shay-Ee." *Western Legal History* 3 (1990): 197–211.

McLaurin, Melton. *Celia, A Slave: A True Story*. New York: Avon Books, 1993.
McLoughlin's Fort Vancouver Letters. 3d series, 1844–1846.

Hudson's Bay Company Series, vol. 7. Toronto: The Champlain Society, 1944.

McSloy, Steven. "American Indians and the Constitution: An Argument for Nationhood." *American Indian Law Review* 14 (1986): 139–91.

Meeker, Ezra. *Pioneer Reminiscences of Puget Sound and the Tragedy of Leschi.* Seattle: Lowman and Hanford, 1905.

Merrell, James. *The Indians' New World: Catawbas and Their Neighbors from European Contact through the Era of Removal.* Chapel Hill: University of North Carolina Press for the Institute of Early American History and Culture, Williamsburg, Va., 1989.

Meyer, Melissa. *The White Earth Tragedy: Ethnicity and Dispossession at a Minnesota Anishinaabe Reservation, 1889–1920.* Lincoln: University of Nebraska Press, 1994.

Miller, Bruce, and Daniel Boxberger. "Creating Chiefdoms: The Puget Sound Case." *Ethnohistory* 41 (1994): 267–93.

Miller, Christopher. *Prophetic Worlds: Indians and Whites on the Columbia Plateau.* New Brunswick, N.J.: Rutgers University Press, 1985.

Miller, Jay. "Back to Basics: Chiefdoms in Puget Sound," *Ethnohistory* 44 (1997): 375–87.

Minow, Martha. *Making All the Difference: Inclusion, Exclusion and American Law.* Ithaca, N.Y.: Cornell University Press, 1990.

Morgan, Murray. *Puget's Sound: A Narrative of Early Tacoma and the Southern Sound.* Seattle: University of Washington Press, 1979.

Mourning Dove. *Mourning Dove: A Salishan Autobiography.* Edited by Jay Miller. Lincoln: University of Nebraska Press, 1990.

Osburn, Katherine. "The Navajo at the Bosque Redondo: Cooperation, Resistance and Initiative, 1864–1868." *New Mexico Historical Review* 60 (1985): 399–415.

Owens, Kenneth. "Pattern and Structure in Western Territorial Politics." *Western Historical Quarterly* 1 (1970): 373–92.

Pascoe, Peggy. "Miscegenation Law, Court Cases, and Ideologies of 'Race' in Twentieth-Century America." *The Journal of American History* 83 (1996): 44–69.

Phillips, George Harwood. "Indians in Los Angeles, 1781–1875: Economic Integration, Social Disintegration." *Pacific Historical Review* 49 (1980): 427–51.

Priest, Loring B. *Uncle Sam's Stepchildren: The Reformation of United States Indian Policy, 1865–1887.* New Brunswick, N.J.: Rutgers University Press, 1942.

Prucha, Francis Paul. *Broadax and Bayonet: The Role of the United States Army in the Development of the Northwest, 1815–1860.* Madison: The State Historical Society of Wisconsin, 1953.

―――. *The Great Father: The United States Government and the Indians.* Abridged ed. Lincoln: University of Nebraska Press, 1986.

Ray, Verne. "The Columbia Indian Confederacy: A League of Central Plateau Tribes." In *Culture in History: Essays in Honor of Paul Radin,* edited by S. Diamond, 771–89. New York: Columbia University Press, 1960.

―――. *Cultural Relations in the Plateau of Northwestern America.* Publications of the Frederick Webb Hodge Anniversary Publication Fund, vol. 3. Los Angeles: The Southwest Museum, 1939.

―――. *Handbook of Cowlitz Indians.* Seattle: Northwest Copy Company, 1966.

―――. *The Sanpoil and Nespelem: Salishan Peoples of Northeastern Washington.* University of Washington Publications in Anthropology, vol. 5. Seattle: University of Washington Press, 1932.

Reid, John Phillip. "The Layers of Western Legal History." In *Law for the Elephant, Law for the Beaver: Essays in the Legal History of the North American West,* edited by John McLaren, Hamar Foster, and Chet Orloff, 23–73. Pasadena, Calif.: Ninth Judicial Circuit Historical Society, 1992.

―――. *A Law of Blood: The Primitive Law of the Cherokee Nation.* New York: New York University Press, 1970.

―――. "Principles of Vengeance: Fur Trappers, Indians, and Retaliation for Homicide in the Transboundary North American West." *Western Historical Quarterly* 24 (1993): 21–43.

Richards, Kent D. "Agrarianism, United States Indian Policy, and the Muckleshoot Reservation." In *Centennial West: Essays on the Northern Tier States,* edited by William L. Lang, 39–58. Seattle: University of Washington Press, 1991.

―――. *Isaac I. Stevens: Young Man in a Hurry.* Provo, Utah: Brigham Young University Press.

Rivers, Theodore John. "The Nez Perce Laws (1842): The Introduction of Laws Foreign to an Independent People." *The Indian Historian* 11 (1978): 15–24.

Ruby, Robert, and John Brown. *Indians of the Pacific Northwest.* Norman: University of Oklahoma Press, 1981.

Skowronek, Stephen. *Building a New American State: The Expansion of National Administrative Capacities, 1877–1920.* Cambridge: Cambridge University Press, 1982.

Smith, Marian. "The Coast Salish of Puget Sound." *American Anthropologist* 43 (1941): 197–211.

————. *The Puyallup-Nisqually*. Columbia University Contributions to Anthropology, vol. 32. New York: Columbia University Press, 1940.

————. "The Puyallup of Washington." In *Acculturation in Seven American Indian Tribes*, edited by Ralph Linton, 3–36. New York: D. Appleton-Century Co., 1940.

Stevens, James, and Chief Thomas Fiddler. *Killing the Shamen.* Moonbeam, Ontario: Penumbra Press, 1985.

Stone, Thomas. "Legal Mobilization and Legal Penetration: The Department of Indian Affairs and the Canadian Party at St. Regis, 1876–1918." *Ethnohistory* 22 (1975): 375–408.

Strickland, Rennard. *Fire and the Spirits: Cherokee Law from Clan to Court.* Norman: University of Oklahoma Press, 1975.

————. "Genocide at Law: An Historic and Contemporary View of the Native American Experience." *Kansas Law Review* 34 (1986): 713–55.

Stuart, Paul. *The Indian Office: Growth and Development of an American Institution, 1865–1900.* Ann Arbor, Mich.: UMI Research Press, 1979.

Sturtevant, William, ed. *The Handbook of North American Indians.* 20 vols. Washington, D.C.: The Smithsonian Institution, 1978–.

Suttles, Wayne. *Coast Salish Essays.* Seattle: University of Washington Press, 1987.

————. "Post-Contact Culture Change Among the Lummi Indians." *British Columbia Historical Quarterly* 18 (1954): 29–102.

————, ed. *The Northwest Coast.* Vol. 7 of *The Handbook of North American Indians*, edited by William Sturtevant. Washington, D.C.: The Smithsonian Institution, 1991.

Svingen, Orlan. "The Case of Spotted Hawk and Little Whirlwind: An American Indian Dreyfus Affair." *Western Historical Quarterly* 15 (1984): 281–98.

Swan, James G. *The Northwest Coast, Or, Three Years' Residence in Washington Territory.* Seattle: University of Washington Press, 1972.

Teit, James A. "The Salishan Tribes of the Western Plateaus." *45th Annual Report of the Bureau of Ethnology* (1927–28): 23–396.

Tillicum, A Boston (pseud.) [Wickersham, James]. "Monograph on the Puyallup Indians of the State of Washington." Tacoma: Daily News Printing, 1892. Newberry Library. Chicago, Ill.

Tollefson, Kenneth. "The Snoqualmie: A Puget Sound Chiefdom," *Ethnology* 26 (1987): 121–36.

Tolmie, William Fraser. *The Journals of William Fraser Tolmie, Physician and Fur Trader*. Vancouver, B.C.: Mitchell Press, 1963.

Tomlan, Michael. *Tinged with Gold: Hop Culture in the United States*. Athens: University of Georgia Press, 1992.

Tomlins, Christopher. *Law, Labor and Ideology in the Early American Republic*. Cambridge: Cambridge University Press, 1993.

Trafzer, Clifford E., and Margery Ann Beach. "Smohalla, The Washani, and Religion as a Factor in Northwestern Indian History." *American Indian Quarterly* 9 (1985): 309–24.

Turner, Frederick Jackson. "The Significance of the Frontier in American History." In *Frontier and Section: Selected Essays of Frederick Jackson Turner*, 37–62. Englewood Cliffs, N.J.: Prentice-Hall, 1961.

Usner, Daniel. *Indians, Settlers, and Slaves in a Frontier Exchange Economy: The Lower Mississippi Valley before 1783*. Chapel Hill: University of North Carolina Press for the Institute of Early American History and Culture, Williamsburg, Va., 1992.

Utley, Robert. *The Indian Frontier of the American West, 1846–1890*. Albuquerque: The University of New Mexico Press, 1982.

Van Kirk, Sylvia. *Many Tender Ties: Women in Fur-Trade Society, 1670–1870*. Norman: University of Oklahoma Press, 1980.

Walker, Deward, Jr. "Plateau: Nez Perce." In *Witchcraft and Sorcery of the American Native Peoples*, edited by Deward Walker, Jr., 113–32. Moscow: University of Idaho Press, 1989.

Washburn, Wilcomb, ed. *The American Indian and the United States: A Documentary History*. 4 vols. New York: Random House, 1973.

White, Richard. *"It's Your Misfortune and None of My Own": A New History of the American West*. Norman: University of Oklahoma Press, 1991.

———. *The Middle Ground: Indians, Empires, and Republics in the Great Lakes Region, 1650–1815*. Cambridge: Cambridge University Press, 1991.

———. *The Roots of Dependency: Subsistence, Environment, and Social Change Among the Choctaws, Pawnees, and Navajos*. Lincoln: University of Nebraska Press, 1983.

Wiebe, Robert. *The Search for Order, 1877–1920*. New York: Hill and Wang, 1967.

Wilkinson, Charles F. *American Indians, Time, and the Law: Native Societies in a Modern Constitutional Democracy*. New Haven: Yale University Press, 1987.

Williams, Robert A., Jr. *The American Indian in Western Legal Thought: The Discourses of Conquest.* New York: Oxford University Press, 1990.

Williams, Walter L., ed. *Southeastern Indians Since The Removal Era.* Athens, Ga.: University of Georgia Press, 1979.

Wunder, John. *Inferior Courts, Superior Justice: Justices of the Peace on the Northwest Frontier, 1853–1889.* Westport, Conn.: Greenwood Press, 1979.

———. *"Retained by the People:" A History of American Indians and the Bill of Rights.* New York: Oxford University Press, 1994.

Zanger, Martin. "Conflicting Concepts of Justice: A Winnebago Murder Trial on the Illinois Frontier." *Journal of the Illinois State Historical Society* 73 (1980): 263–76.

INDEX

Peeps, 138
Peish, Ann, 73
Pend Oreille Indians, 55
Pettingall, Albert, 140
Phillips, George, 6
Pierce County, 83, 87, 168
Pincus, Isaac, 61–62
Planopleopike, Dan, 157
Plateau whipping complex. *See* Native law, and whipping
Polotkin, 164–65
Poole, Jimmie, 143–44
Port Madison Reservation, 35, 184
Port Townsend Kate, 168
Port Townsend, Washington Territory, 74, 86, 88, 93, 97, 148–49
Powers, Annie, 102
Prucha, Francis Paul, 94, 136, 156
Pullen, Ephraim, 142–43
Puyallup Indians, 26, 28, 32, 42, 180–81, 188
Puyallup Reservation, 35, 55, 58, 65–66, 82–83, 162

Qualchin, 132
Quallahwowt, 129–30
Queets Indians, 36, 161, 166
Quiemuth, 112, 114, 137
Quilcene, 24
Quileute Indians, 20, 36, 45, 161, 166
Quinault Indians, 36, 45
Quinault Reservation, 36, 45, 161

Race, 5, 15, 64, 70, 80–81, 98–101, 103–106, 155, 158–59, 170, 175, 178–79, 194–95, 198
Ray, Verne, 23, 29
Reid, John Phillip, 128
Reservations, 4, 5, 34, 36, 38–40, 43–48, 51, 56–57, 65, 81–82, 95– 96, 145, 150, 155–56, 171–72, 193, 195, 197, 199, 225, 233; allotment of, 18, 105–107, 181, 196, 220; populations of, 42. *See also names of specific reservations*
Ridderbjilke, Adolph, 124–25, 146
Roberts, Francis, 65
Roberts, John, 135, 138
Roff, Henry, 116, 120–21

Sah-sah-pe-kin, 163
Salmon, 161
Samish Indians, 40, 158
Sanpoil Indians, 27, 29, 45–46, 169
Sbithla, 24, 27, 30–32
Schotum, 157
Seattle, Washington Territory, 53, 81, 83–84, 102, 110, 112, 130, 182–85
Sentencing, 93, 137, 235
Shamanism, 19, 26, 29, 31–32, 154, 157, 159, 175–77, 184–88, 245–46
Shelton, 138
Shew-Lack, 169–70
Shoalwater Bay, 53, 172
Shoalwater Bay Reservation, 40
Shoshone Indians, 6
Show-a-way, 166
Shuse-shuse-pomeen, 174
Shuswap Indians, 128
Simmons, Michael, 36, 38, 40, 89–90, 96–97, 130, 135–36
Simms, John, 46, 189
Skagit Indians, 25, 26, 52
Skin Indians, 166
Skokomish Indians, 148–49, 157
Skokomish Reservation, 3, 35, 44, 46–47, 65, 148–49
Skowronek, Stephen, 11
Slahat, 162
Slavery, 22, 27, 48, 110, 141, 158, 168, 230
Slocum, John, 148
Smith, D. W., 150
Smith, J. M., 64–65
Smith, Marian, 63
Smith, Mary, 182
Smohalla, 48
Snohomish County, 64, 71, 73, 144, 173, 190
Snohomish Indians, 25, 52, 60, 76, 135, 160–61, 190–91
Snoqualmie Indians, 25, 46, 52, 129, 135–36, 139, 162
Sorcery. *See* Shamanism
Sovereignty: and Indian tribes, 9, 14, 16, 134–35, 155–57, 189–90, 193, 198; and United States, 126, 131, 136, 170, 191
Spedis, William, 150–52
Spencer, Kitty, 101–102

Index   273

Spokane Indians, 29, 37, 45, 132, 172, 183
Spokane Reservation, 40
Spoon, Jim, 158
Squaxin Indians, 30, 34–35, 42, 154
Squaxin Island Reservation, 35, 55
Starling, E. A., 33, 61, 111
Steilacoom, Washington Territory, 61, 111, 168
Steptoe, Col. Edward, 38
Stevens, Isaac Ingalls, 35–38, 52, 56, 96, 112–14, 131, 133, 137–39, 158, 161
Stevens County, 72, 182, 189
Stone, 190
Suffrage, 68–69, 77–78
Sulkanon, Robert, 124–25, 137, 141, 145–46, 179, 193
Suquamish Indians, 184
Susan, 182, 184
Susie (Fisk), 154, 187–88
Swan, James, 141
Swinomish Indians, 135, 160
Swinomish Reservation, 35, 160

Taylor, Frank, 151–52
Tebo, Joseph, 186–87
Tecumseh, Dan, 189
Tecumseh, Roger, 189
Telequoh, 162
Te-mal-le, 164
Territory v. Meigs, 191
Territory v. Schotum, 158
Theft. *See* Larceny
Thurston County, 83, 89, 102, 181
Toby, George, 190–91
Tolmie, William F., 128–29
Tonasket, 163–65
Toos-ka-na, 166–67
Treaties, 35, 157, 159, 168, 198; and fishing rights, 47, 150–51; and ratification, 38, 40. *See also names of specific treaties*
Treaty of Medicine Creek, 35, 38, 42, 135
Treaty of Neah Bay, 36
Treaty of Olympia, 36, 45
Treaty of Point Elliott, 35, 40, 145
Treaty of Point No Point, 35, 44, 157
Tulalip Reservation, 25, 35, 46–47, 60–61, 96, 141, 162

Turner, Frederick Jackson, 8
Twana Indians, 19–20, 24, 26–28, 30, 32, 35, 44–45, 54, 140, 168, 184
Tyee Charley, 168

Umatilla Indians, 37
Umatilla Reservation, 37
United States Army, 38, 57, 162, 164
United States commissioner, 13, 89
United States Government, 8, 11, 56–57, 156, 197, 199
United States v. Holliday, 99–100
United States v. Charles Vogelsong, 95
United States v. W. J. Wilson, 104
United States v. Winans, 151

Vader, Charles, 118–19
Vogelsong, Charles, 81–84, 95, 98–99, 105

Wage labor, 53–56, 61–62, 144
Wahoolit, 133–34
Wallace, Leander, 129
Walla Walla County, 104, 107, 116, 190
Wallawalla Indians, 29, 37, 132
Wallela, 190
Wal-sut-ut, 107–109, 111, 121–22
War, 37, 53, 132, 229–30; and crime, 134–36; and war trials, 112, 131, 133–34
Warren, A. C., 101
Washington Territory: boundaries, 17; district courts, 12, 81, 84, 131, 201; Organic Act, 12, 77, 229; population, 53–54, 83, 109–10, 116–17; supreme court, 13, 60, 69–70, 130–31, 133–34
Waters, Sidney, 189
Webster, Henry, 84, 86, 88–89
Whatcom County, 52, 71, 85, 143–44
Whipping, 110–11. *See also* Native law, and whipping
Whiskey. *See* Liquor
White, Richard, 4, 126
Whitlouse, Joe, 173–74
Wilbur, James, 46, 52
Wilson, Jack, 66
Winans, William P., 45, 164–65